BATTLE OVER THE REICH

BATTLE OVER THE REICH

THE STRATEGIC AIR OFFENSIVE OVER GERMANY

VOLUME TWO

1943 - 1945

Dr. Alfred Price

CLASSIC

An imprint of
Ian Allan Publishing

First published 2005

ISBN 1 903223 48 2

Produced by Chevron Publishing Limited

Project Editor: Chevron Publishing Limited

© Colour Illustrations: Colour profiles by Tim Brown, TomTullis, and Jim Laurier (2005).

With thanks to Mark Postlethwaite at ww2images.com

The artwork of Jim Laurier can be seen at www.jimlaurier.com

Published by Classic Publications an imprint of Ian Allan Publishing Ltd, Hersham, Surrey KT12 4RG

Printed in England by Ian Allan Printing Ltd, Hersham, Surrey KT12 4RG

Visit the Ian Allan Publishing website at www.ianallanpublishing.com

CONTENTS

PROLOGUE AND ACKNOWLEDGEMENTS

This is the second of two Volumes on the air battles fought over Germany during the Second World War, as seen through the eyes of the British, American and German combatants. In writing this book, it has been my purpose to present a broad picture of actions that took place between November 1943 and May 1945. I made no attempt to describe every single action, for to do so would have required a book many times the length of this one. Instead, I have chosen as examples those actions which in my view illustrated the general pattern – although, of course, every action contained unique features of its own.

'Battle Over the Reich' would not have been possible without the co-operation of many members of the 'original cast' most of whom, sadly, are no longer with us. Men like General Adolf Galland, General Roderick Cescotti, Colonel Hans-Ulrich Flade, Hans Seyringer, Willi Herget, Hans Kogler, and Hanfried Schliephake of the *Luftwaffe*; Air Marshal Sir Robert Saundby, Group Captain Hamish Mahaddie, Group Captain Bob Braham and Flight Lieutenant Bob Brydon of the RAF; and August Briding, Bernard Dopko, General Tom Marchbanks, William Murphy, Harold Stearns, Lowell Watts, Colonel Hubert Zemke and Colonel Ross Miller of the USAAF.

My good friends Werner Girbig, Horst Götz Bergander, Franz Selinger, Roger Freeman, Hans Ring, Danny Morris, Norbert Krüger, Hans Redemann, Richard Smith, Eddie Creek, Arno Arbendroth, Günter Heise and the late Hans Obert helped to amass the necessary material and photographs. Finally I should like to thank my dear wife Jane, for support that went far beyond that laid down in the small print of our marriage contract.

ALFRED PRICE
Uppingham Rutland

Other books by Dr Alfred Price:

Instruments of Darkness
Aircraft versus Submarine
Battle of Britain Day, 15 September 1940
The Hardest Day, 18 August 1940
Blitz on Britain
The Spitfire Story
Spitfire at War
The Last Year of the Luftwaffe
Luftwaffe Data Book
War in the Fourth Dimension
Targeting the Reich
Sky Battles
Sky Warriors
Skies of Fire

Written in Co-operation with the late Jeff Ethell:
Target Berlin, 6 March 1944
One Day in a Long War, 10 May 1972
Air War South Atlantic
World War II Combat Jets

Editor's note: The weights, measurements and distances used in the text correspond to the national equivalent - e.g. German usage = metric, British usage = imperial and American usage = US standard

From English fields
Not theirs the sudden glow
Of triumph that their fighter-brothers know;
Only to fly through cloud, through storm, through night
Unerring, and to keep their purpose bright,
Nor turn until, their dreadful duty done,
Westward they climb to race the awakened sun.

Anon

BATTLE OF ATTRITION BY NIGHT

November 1943 - March 1944

"Every attack, once undertaken, must be fought to a finish; every

defence, once begun, must be carried on with the utmost energy."

Field Marshal Foch

The spring, summer and autumn of 1943 had seen an unremitting series of disasters for German arms at each of the far-flung battlefronts. In May the remaining Axis units in North Africa surrendered. In July Allied troops landed in Sicily, and in September Italy changed sides and declared war on her one-time ally. In the Soviet Union, Adolf Hitler's attempt to secure a decisive victory resulted in the gigantic set-piece clash between armoured forces at Kursk. It failed in its purpose, and left the Soviet Army holding the initiative on the Eastern Front for the remainder of the war. In the North Atlantic the U-boats had suffered a crushing defeat at the hands of the Allied convoy escorts and patrol aircraft, and would never regain their previous stranglehold on the shipping routes.

As described in Volume One, over Germany itself the RAF and the US strategic air forces had delivered a series of telling blows against the nation's cities and industries. Yet this had been achieved at no small cost to the raiders. For its part, the *Luftwaffe* was now seriously over-extended at every crisis point. Only by pulling fighter units away from the battlefronts, and concentrating its main effort in the defence of the homeland, was the *Luftwaffe* able to mount a credible air defence over Germany.

At the end of 1943, RAF Bomber Command was still by far the larger of the two forces raiding the Reich. Following the hard-fought night actions in the summer of 1943, *Luftwaffe* commanders had every reason to believe they had overcome the problems caused by the use of 'Window', the metal strips dropped to jam their precision radars.

During the summer and autumn of 1943 the *Luftwaffe* night fighter force made a major transformation in its tactics. Previously, its twin-engined fighters had operated singly, engaging enemy bombers one-on-one under close control from the *Himmelbett* ground radar stations. Since the 'Window' debacle that method had largely to be abandoned in favour of the new *Zahme Sau* (Tame Boar) freelance operating tactic. Under this method, the twin-engined night fighters took off en mass soon after the incoming raiding force was detected running in over the North Sea. As the raiders' route became clear, the night fighters were directed to one or more radio beacons thought to be in the bombers' path. Night fighters hopped from beacon to beacon until they were near enough to the bomber stream to be vectored into it. In that way the *Luftwaffe* ground controllers sought to create long-running battles, perhaps extending over 200 kilometres, that would inflict heavy losses on the raiders.

Complementing the *Zahme Sau* fighters were *Wilde Sau* (Wild Boar) *Gruppen* equipped with fast and manoeuvrable Messerschmitt Bf 109 and Focke-Wulf Fw 190 single-seaters. These fighters were to be directed towards the raiders' presumed target. There, the massed searchlights, the Pathfinders' markers, and explosions and fires on the ground would illuminate individual bombers which could then be picked off relatively easily. While the *Wilde Sau* fighters were operating over a target, the local *Flak* defences were ordered to restrict themselves to engaging only targets below a certain level, typically 5,000 metres.

◄ ◄ A Pathfinder Lancaster of 156 Squadron is caught by the camera of another aircraft as it drops marker flares over the German city of Hanau. Although this photograph was taken on 18 March 1945, the city had been targeted by the RAF as early as July 1940.

► A Ju 88 G-6 night
fighter fitted with SN-2 radar
which was flown to England
after the war for technical
evaluation. The bulge on top
of the cockpit canopy housed
the Naxos device for homing
on the H2S radar emissions
from RAF bombers. The
aircraft also has a twin 20
mm cannon weapons pack
fitted to its belly.

► A Ju 88 G-7 bearing the
code of NJG 102 and fitted
with two 20 mm MG 151
cannon in a Schräge Musik
upward-firing installation.
NJG 102 had been formed in
December 1943 as a night
fighter training unit whose
cadre was made up of
experienced former Zerstörer
and bomber pilots as well as
flying instructors. The unit
was later based in East
Prussia.

With the new tactics came new electronic systems to assist *Luftwaffe* twin-engined fighters to find their quarry. Since July 1943 the *Lichtenstein* radar fitted initially to night fighters had been seriously jammed by 'Window' metal foil strips. To defeat that countermeasure the *Luftwaffe* introduced a new type of radar for its night fighters, the SN-2. The latter operated on a frequency of 90 MHz and, initially, was not affected by 'Window'. By November 1943 the SN-2 radar equipped a small but growing proportion of the twin-engined night fighter force.

As mentioned in Volume One, during 1943 the RAF had fitted the H2S ground mapping equipment and the 'Monica' tail warning radar in its bombers. Once it learned of these systems, the *Luftwaffe* lost no time in devising ways to exploit their radiations. *Naxos* and *Korfu* equipments, installed at ground direction-finding stations, were able to track the movements of H2S-fitted aircraft. Also, an airborne version of *Naxos*, *Naxos-Z*, was produced for installation in night fighters. Other night fighters carried the *Flensburg* homing receiver which enabled them to home on signals from the bombers'

"We can wreck Berlin from end to end if the USAAF will come in on it. It may cost us 400-500 aircraft. It will cost Germany the war."

'Monica' radars. These electronic systems would all play a major part in the large-scale nightly battles to follow. Although it had been attacked several times, Berlin remained a remote and heavily defended target. By the late autumn the nights were darker than in the summer, allowing Air Chief Marshal Sir Arthur Harris to launch a series of heavy attacks on the enemy capital. On 3 November 1943 he minuted Mr Churchill: *"We can wreck Berlin from end to end if the USAAF will come in on it. It may cost us 400-500 aircraft. It will cost Germany the war."*

◄ A 105 mm Flak 38 gun in action on a Flak tower. Firing 14.5 kg shells at a muzzle velocity of 880 metres per second, this weapon was introduced just before the Second World War to provide greater hitting power and a higher engagement ceiling than was possible with the earlier 88 mm guns. The gun incorporated electrical ramming and power-assisted laying, and had a practical rate of fire of 10-15 rounds per minute, operated usually by a crew of nine.

▶ Route flown by RAF Bomber Command during the attack on Magdeburg, on 21 January 1944. Note the reduced length of the bomber stream compared with that of seven months earlier. The total length of the bomber stream was 88 miles (compared with 150 miles during the Wuppertal raid the previous May), a concentration made possible by the general improvement in navigation. The shorter the bomber stream, the smaller the target it presented to enemy fighters.

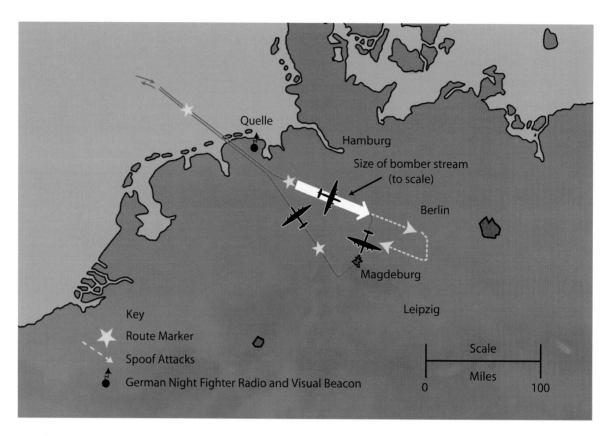

Quelle

Hamburg

Size of bomber stream (to scale)

Berlin

Magdeburg

Leipzig

Key

★ Route Marker

╌╌▶ Spoof Attacks

● German Night Fighter Radio and Visual Beacon

Scale

Miles

0   100

That was the sort of promise the Prime Minister could not resist, and he gave permission to launch the all-out attack on the German capital. The US bomber force was still licking its wounds after its costly long-range penetrations into enemy territory a few weeks earlier, and could not yet 'come in on it'. The RAF night bombers were to attempt to destroy the city alone.

At first, the RAF raids on the enemy capital took place with relatively low loss rates. During four heavy attacks in November 1943 and a further four in December, 180 bombers were lost in the course of nearly 4,100 sorties – an acceptable 4.4 per cent of the force involved.

Early in the New Year, the defenders started to hit back, however. The night fighter crews were fighting to defend their homes and loved ones, and they did so with bravery, skill and determination. The two heavy attacks on Berlin on the first two days of January 1944, by 421 and 383 aircraft respectively, cost a total of 55 bombers or nearly 7 per cent of those taking part. Moreover, in each case the attackers encountered poor weather over the target, and as a result their bombs were scattered over a wide area.

Later in the month Bomber Command visited Stettin and Braunschweig. Then it returned to Berlin on the 20th, and suffered a relatively low 4.5 per cent loss. That did not indicate any weakening of the defences, however. The following night, the 21st, saw the hardest-fought night action for several months. Since it will serve

to illustrate the tactics employed by both the defenders and the attackers, we shall look at this action in some detail.

The target was Magdeburg, an important manufacturing centre situated 112 km south-west of Berlin, and 648 Lancasters and Halifaxes took off to attack the city. Since the target lay deep inside enemy territory, the bombers had to rely on their H2S ground mapping radars to find the city. No longer was that radar the sole prerogative of the Pathfinder Force, and on this night 242 of the aircraft involved carried the device. The new radar was now recognised as a useful aid to navigation, along the route and during the approach to the target, as well as over the target itself.

The raiders were drawn up in five waves, with a stream having a length of 88 miles (compared with the 150 miles during the raid on Wuppertal in May 1943). The greater degree of concentration was made possible by a general improvement in navigation since the previous spring which meant the bomber stream presented a smaller target for pursuing enemy night fighters. Yet even that degree of concentration left plenty of empty sky around the individual aircraft: 648 bombers spread across 88 miles meant an average of only seven aircraft per mile.

Luftwaffe early warning radars observed the bombers when they climbed above the radar horizon as they ran in over the North Sea. That was the cue for night fighters based in eastern France and southern Germany to scramble, soon followed by those from airfields in Holland, Belgium and northern Germany It was important for the *Luftwaffe* controllers to get their night fighters airborne early. Burdened by radar and other electronic systems, these aircraft cruised little faster than the bombers they were to hunt. Moreover, the night fighters from outlying bases had nearly as far to go as the bombers, to reach potential targets in northern Germany. As they were becoming airborne, crews tuned to the *Reichsjägerwelle* (fighter broadcast channel) for their instructions after take-off. The ground controller ordered them to head for radio beacon *Quelle*, between Hamburg and Cuxhaven, and orbit until the air situation clarified. In all, 169 *Luftwaffe* night fighters took off to meet this attack.

Unknown to the bomber crews in the vanguard of the force, as they neared the German coast they were on a collision course for a disaster: radio beacon *Quelle*, over which the *Luftwaffe* night fighters were assembling, lay almost under the bombers' flight path. The defenders would have scored a major victory, had not the *Luftwaffe* controller misjudged the direction in which the swarm of bombers was heading. At 21.30 hrs, seven minutes before the first raiders crossed the coast and 14 minutes before they reached *Quelle*, he gave the probable target as Hamburg and ordered all night fighters to re-position

in front of that city. As a result, *Quelle* was clear of fighters when the bomber stream thundered past it between 22.44 hrs and 23.02 hrs. Hundreds of RAF crewmen had been sentenced to death, then reprieved, without ever suspecting it.

Then, as the bombers skirted their way past the concentration of *Luftwaffe* fighters, a Pathfinder crew unwittingly gave the game away. The plan had called for one of these aircraft to drop a salvo of red target

▲ The RAF discovered the secret of the German 'Schräge Musik' upward-firing cannon after examining bombers that had survived attacks with this weapon. This Lancaster, belonging to No 100 Squadron, was fortunate to escape without taking a hit on the fuel tank situated between the engines. Steel rods show the angle of penetration and subsequent paths of the cannon shells, fired at the aircraft from below. Grand-Dalton via Garbett/Goulding

◄ Night fighter ace Major Wilhelm Herget (right) commanded II./NJG 4 from October 1942 until December 1944. He ended the war credited with 63 victories. On the left is his radar operator, Oberfeldwebel Hans Liebherr, and in the centre Oberfeldwebel Emil Groess, his radio operator and rear gunner.

► Generaloberst Hans-Jürgen Stumpff had commanded Luftflotte 5 during the Battle of Britain in 1940. From early in 1944 until the end of the war he commanded Luftflotte Reich, during which he had to fight the Battle of Britain in reverse, to try to defend his country against the Allied raiding formations.

▼ In following the shifting pattern of Allied air attacks, Flak weapons mounted on railway flats were moved rapidly with their crews, ammunition and stocks of essential supplies, to protect threatened areas. In this photograph, 105 mm guns are seen during a night engagement.

indicators at a point some twenty miles south of Hamburg, to serve as a route marker for the rest of the force. On time, just before 23.00 hrs, in position and as briefed, the markers went down.

On seeing the red target indicators, the bolder spirits in the night fighter force disregarded the order to remain over Hamburg, and headed south. By then the *Luftwaffe* radio channels carried their usual cacophony of interference. Some channels carried bell sounds, others an undulating howl similar to bagpipes, on yet others there were recordings of Hitler's speeches with the odd false order thrown in for good measure. If there were questions afterwards, night fighter crews could safely argue that they thought they had heard the order to fly south.

Near the route marker the first few night fighters made contact with the bomber stream. The bombers' route took them past Hamburg, heading towards Berlin as if for yet another attack on the capital. Then, some 40 miles short of the capital, the attackers wheeled sharply to starboard and headed for Magdeburg. To camouflage that all-important final turn, a spoofing force of 13 Mosquitoes and 20

MAJOR WITTGENSTEIN'S LAST VICTORIES

▲ Major Prince Heinrich zu Sayn Wittgenstein was killed in action on the night of 21 January 1944 during the attack on Magdeburg. At the time of his death, he was the top-scoring Luftwaffe night fighter pilot with 83 night victories.

One of the pilots engaging the bombers near Magdeburg on 21 January 1944 was Major *Prinz* Heinrich zu Sayn Wittgenstein, commander of *Nachtjagdgeschwader* 2 and holder of the Knight's Cross with Oakleaves. With 79 victories, he was the current top-scoring night fighter pilot in the *Luftwaffe*. Wittgenstein had taken off in his Junkers 88 from Stendal near Berlin shortly before 21.00 hrs. The combat report written afterwards by his radar operator, *Feldwebel* Ostheimer, illustrates the mayhem that followed when an *Experte* of Wittgenstein's calibre got inside the bomber stream:

"At about 22.00 hrs I picked up the first contact on my [SN-2] search equipment. I passed the pilot directions and a little later the target was sighted: it was a Lancaster. We moved into position and opened fire, and the aircraft immediately caught fire in the left wing. It went down at a steep angle and started to spin. Between 22.00 and 22.05 hrs the bomber crashed and went off with a violent explosion; I watched the crash.

"Again we searched. At times I could see as many as six aircraft on my radar. After some further directions the next target was sighted: again a Lancaster. Following the first burst from us there was a small fire, and the machine dropped its left wing and went down in a vertical dive. Shortly afterwards I saw it crash. It was some time between 22.10 and 22.15 hrs. When it crashed there were heavy detonations, most probably it was the bomb load.

"After a short interval we again sighted a Lancaster. There was a long burst of fire and the bomber ignited and went down. I saw it crash some time between 22.25 and 22.30 hrs; the exact time is not known.

"Immediately afterwards, we saw yet another four-engined bomber; we were in the middle of the so-called 'bomber-stream'. After one firing pass this bomber went down in flames; at about 22.40 hrs I saw the crash.

"Yet again I had a target on my search equipment. After a few directions we again sighted a Lancaster and after one attack it caught fire in the fuselage. The fire then died down, and we moved into position for a new attack. We were again in position and Major Wittgenstein was ready to shoot when, in our own machine, there were terrible explosions and sparks. It immediately caught fire in the left wing and began to go down. As I heard this, the canopy above my head flew away and I heard on the intercom a shout of "Raus!" [Get out!]. I tore off my oxygen mask and helmet and was then thrown out of the machine. After a short time I opened my parachute, and landed east of the Hohengöhrener Dam, near Schönhausen."

On the following day Wittgenstein's body was found in the wreckage of his aircraft. Two returning bombers reported having shot down Ju 88s in the area of the target, and it is possible that one of these belonged to the fighter ace. Ironically he had been surprised by an attack from below, the form of attack he himself had most favoured.

◀ The tail unit of the Ju 88 C-6, coded C9+AE, with 29-victory bars which belonged to Hptm. Heinrich Prinz zu Sayn-Wittgenstein while he was Kommandeur of IV./NJG 5, probably then based in the Insterburg area of East Prussia in May or June 1943.

JUNKERS Ju 88 G-1

Junkers Ju 88 G-1, 3C+FK of 2./NJG 4, Mainz-Finthen, winter 1944/45.

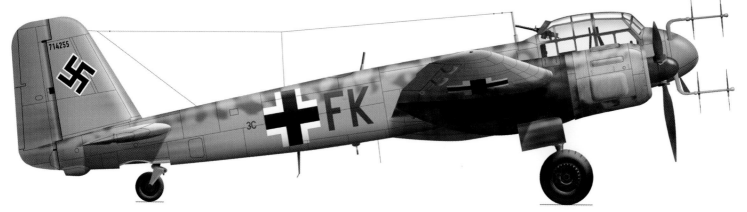

► A Ju 88 G-1 of 2./NJG 4 in the winter of 1944/45 based at Mainz-Finthen. This variant, first introduced in the late spring of 1944, was equipped with FuG 220 SN-2 AI radar and a FuG 227 Flensburg passive homer. Ground crew are seen here using a mobile heating generator fitted with flexible hoses for pre-heating the engines. This method of warming the engines was used in order to conserve aviation fuel which was becoming short in supply.

Lancasters continued on to Berlin and marked the city as if for an attack. Zero hour for both the main attack, and the spoof attack on the capital, was 23.00 hrs.

By now the main body of night fighters was heading south-east in hot pursuit of the bombers. The spoof attack on Berlin failed in its purpose, for operators at the German ground monitoring posts recognised the turn to starboard by the mass of heavy bombers running their H2S radars. Yet again, however, the *Luftwaffe* fighter controller misjudged the sharpness of the turn. He ordered the night fighters to head for what he thought was the most likely target: Leipzig. Sometimes two wrongs make a right during an air battle, and that happened now.

Magdeburg lay almost exactly on the line running from Hamburg to Leipzig. The fighters, struggling to overhaul the mass of bombers cruising almost as fast as they were, shifted their course a few degrees and headed for Leipzig. In doing so they cut the corner intended to deceive them, and began to catch up with their prey.

Near Magdeburg the two masses of aircraft met, and

a running battle developed which extended up to the target and continued along the initial part of the bombers' homeward track. Some crews found the stream using their SN-2 radar, others used their *Naxos-Z* or *Flensburg* homing receivers, while some first made contact with the stream when their aircraft juddered as it passed through the turbulent slipstream that trailed up to 600 yards behind each four-engined bomber. The battle was on.

Fifty-five of the bombers sent to attack Magdeburg, and one of those engaged in the spoof on Berlin, failed to return. Bomber crews reported seeing 13 aircraft fall to *Flak* and 14 to fighters. The remaining losses could not be accounted for, but as the official Bomber Command report on the action stated, "*most were probably due to fighters*". Many night fighters carried upward-firing *Schräge Musik* cannon which fired non-tracer ammunition and, since use of the latter often led to bombers falling out of the sky without the cause being readily apparent to crews flying nearby, this assumption has the ring of truth. Certainly there was a measure of agreement between the *Luftwaffe* claims for the night and RAF losses, for the German night fighter force was credited with 37 confirmed kills and four probables.

Three returning bombers were wrecked in landing accidents after the raid. Fifty more landed with battle damage, in 30 cases due to *Flak* and the rest due to night fighters. Five bombers returned with scars that bore testimony to the hazards of night operations in a tight bomber stream, for two of these had survived a mid-air collision, and three more had been hit by incendiary bombs dropped from aircraft above (but which did not ignite).

The general shuttling-about of the *Luftwaffe* night fighter force during the battle left the short-range *Wilde Sau* aircraft orbiting over targets which were never attacked, and it is doubtful whether any of them went into action. Four *Luftwaffe* fighters were lost that night, and these corroborate the three aircraft claimed by the bombers' gunners, i.e two Ju 88s – one being Major Wittgenstein's aircraft, as described on page 175 – and a Messerschmitt Bf 110. The loss of Hauptmann Manfred Meurer, the third-highest night scorer credited with 65 victories, did not appear in any RAF victory claim. He fired a lethal burst into a Lancaster from below, whereupon his victim dropped a wing sharply and plunged into his He 219 fighter. Locked together, the two aircraft spun out of the sky carrying their crews to their deaths. With two of its highest scorers killed in a single night, the *Luftwaffe* night fighter force also had good reason to grieve after the Magdeburg action.

The next four heavy raids on Berlin, at the close of

THE FATE OF THE LONE BOMBER

Bombers' routes were carefully planned to take the force around the heavier concentrations of *Flak*. Provided their navigation was accurate, therefore, crews usually did not have to face this hazard until they reached the target area. There, the combination of a large number of aircraft and huge quantities of falling 'Window' meant that the majority of bombers passed through the area unscathed.

For those crews that deviated from the set route and left the anonymity of the bomber stream, however, the path could be treacherous indeed. These automatically became the centre of attention for all gun batteries within range, and the relatively small quantity of 'Window' dropped from a single aircraft provided little protection. An example of the fate meted out to a lone bomber can be seen in the action report submitted by the commander of *Flakgruppe Frankfurt am Main*, following an engagement on 24 February 1944. On its way home from an attack on Schweinfurt, a lone RAF bomber strayed across the city:

"The enemy aircraft was located at 5,300 metres altitude; between 23.21 and 23.22 tracking was electrical [i.e. by radar], and between 23.22 and 23.25 hrs it was optical [i.e. the aircraft was coned by searchlights and was observed visually]. It was engaged by six batteries, which fired 129 rounds of 105 mm and 281 rounds of 88 mm ammunition. The machine, which was recognised as a Halifax when it was illuminated by the searchlights, flew well within the engagement range of the batteries. During the four-minute engagement it lost 3,800 metres altitude... A fire broke out in the aircraft, and the searchlights illuminated a thick trail of smoke behind it... The bomber crashed at about 23.35 hrs near Kirschofen."

◄ The crew of Lancaster ED831 from 9 Squadron preparing to board their aircraft for another raid over Germany.

▲ Mosquito bombers taxi out for a raid over Germany. The versatile and fast Mosquito proved to be a major aggravation to the German defences throughout the campaign. Such aircraft also carried out spoof attacks against Berlin, Cologne and Kassel in the spring of 1944.

▶▶ An RAF Bomb aimer peers down from the flat perspex viewing panel in the front panel of a Lancaster. The flat panel was designed to give a distortion-free view of the target area below.

January and early in February, cost the RAF 158 bombers. The attack on Leipzig on the night of 19 February resulted in the heaviest loss to date – 78 bombers failed to return out of 823 despatched.

Now the protracted slugging-match in the night skies over Germany was nearing its climax. During these hard-fought battles, the defending fighters did not escape scot-free although their main hazards were running short of fuel and trying to land at their bases in poor weather, rather than the bombers' return fire. After the action on the night of 15 March, for example, when 863 bombers attacked Stuttgart, the war diary of *Nachtjagdgeschwader 6* carried the entry:

> "Own take-off was too early, and as a result fuel began to run low. Twenty-six Bf 110s and three Ju 88s took off. Three four-engined bombers shot down for certain, and two probables. Five Bf 110s crashed because they ran out of fuel, one more made a belly landing, and one force-landed at Zurich/Dübendorf [airfield in Switzerland]."

That night, 36 RAF bombers failed to return, a 4.1 per cent loss rate. During these battles the *Flak* batteries played a subsidiary role, as *Generalfeldmarschall* Milch pointed out at a conference held in Berlin on 23 February:

> "The English have worked out exactly how many attacks they need to make on Berlin – probably twenty-five. Now they have done fifteen, that leaves ten. Furthermore, we

know that when Berlin has been dealt with they will go on to the central German industrial region: Halle, Leipzig, Dessau and so on. These are all involved in the production of armaments and equipment. There is only one way to overcome this threat, and that is with fighters . . . There is no need for us to kid ourselves about the effectiveness of Flak. We know it is necessary, that it harasses the enemy, that it forces him to operate at altitudes where accurate aiming is no longer easy. But the enemy bombers seem to have got over the problem of aiming from great heights. Even by night a city such as Hamburg or Essen can't be missed [sic] . . ."

Although Milch had calculated that the RAF would need about 25 attacks on Berlin to raze large parts of the city, in fact the German capital proved a very difficult nut to crack. By the beginning of March 1944 it had taken several nasty knocks, but there was none of the concentrated devastation visited on Hamburg in the previous July. Moreover, time was running out for Sir Arthur Harris since on 1 April, as part of the preparations for the forthcoming invasion of France, operational control of his command would pass to the Supreme Allied Commander, General Eisenhower.

The sixteenth and final RAF attack on Berlin in this series took place on the night of 24 March and would prove to be the costliest so far. The Battle of Berlin had been characterised by difficult weather during many of the attacks, but never before was the weather so disruptive as it was during that final raid in the series.

Nowadays, flight above 30,000 feet is commonplace

"....the inevitable happened: there was an extremely loud bang and a lot of crunching, and the Lancaster seemed to rear up."

and a great deal is known about the phenomenon of the jet stream. This is the narrow cylinder of air at high-altitude where wind speeds often exceed 100 mph in the central core (and where, exceptionally, speeds in excess of 300 mph have been measured). In 1944, however, relatively little was known of this occurrence. So it came as a surprise to RAF bomber crews that night when they ran into a jet stream over northern Germany. The powerful wind from the north-west greatly assisted the raiders on their way to the target. The penetration was accomplished with relatively little interference from the defences, though the navigators found themselves checking and re-checking ground speeds that seemed

unbelievably high. A feature of the jet stream is that there is a rapid rise in wind speed as an aircraft nears the narrow central core, and an equally rapid fall in the wind speed as it passes out the other side. The effect of that was to spread out the raiding force to such an extent that the term 'bomber stream' bore no tactical meaning.

The attack on Berlin that night was diffuse, and added little to the damage already inflicted. Then, when the bombers turned west for home, they found that they were heading into the teeth of the hurricane-force winds. The result was that while some bombers were making their way home in numerous small clusters, others were flying singly, and this, together with the almost clear skies, provided a rare opportunity for the *Flak* crews to prove their worth. Sergeant Bob Brydon, navigator aboard a Lancaster of No 630 Squadron, later recalled:

"With that jet stream wind almost on our nose, our ground speed was little over 100 mph, which meant that we must have presented a pretty easy target for the German gunners below. We were picked up by searchlights near the Ruhr and held for a considerable time; one group of lights seemed to pass us on to the next. We were high, over 22,000 feet, but the Flak was more accurate than I had ever known it and with frightening regularity we felt the bursts juddering our

► The very battered nose of a Lancaster on its belly. Note the cannon shell holes under the cockpit and the fact that at least three props were stopped on landing. Nose art is just visible between the cockpit and the nose turret.

◄ Two Ju 88 C-6s of 5./NJG 2, showing the aerials for the FuG 202 Lichtenstein BC radar on the nose. The Ju 88 C series was introduced relatively slowly and was later replaced by the Ju 88 G which began to appear in mid-1944. At this time the machine in the foreground probably carried the code R4+GN, although later in 1944 the Geschwader's operational code was reversed to '4R'.

aircraft. We were weaving through the sky, changing height and direction every fifteen seconds or so, but though we must have made their predicted fire difficult we never shook off the searchlights. Looking back, I suppose we would have done better to have turned round and used that tremendous wind to get out of the area quickly and shake them off, then try again to get through. But that never occurred to us at the time.

"Instead, the inevitable happened: there was an extremely loud bang and a lot of crunching, and the Lancaster seemed to rear up. Afterwards I learned from the mid-upper gunner that the starboard fin and rudder had been shot clean away. The pilot tried to hold her steady but it was impossible, and on the intercom he shouted to us to abandon. This took me aback rather, and I remained calmly sitting at my bench. But then the wireless operator came scrambling past me on his way to the nose escape hatch, and I got the message. The aircraft was going down out of control by that time, and the 'G' forces made it quite a struggle to reach the door. But in the end I managed it, and parachuted safely. Early the next morning I was taken prisoner."

That night the winds cast their wrath equally on both sides' aircraft, and the night fighters enjoyed little success. For the anti-aircraft gunners, on the other hand, the action marked their high point of achievement: probably 45, and possibly as many as 52, of the 72 RAF bombers lost fell to ground fire.

For the successful operation of the defending night fighters, much depended on the fighter controllers' ability to anticipate the future flight path of the bomber stream. When his judgement was faulty, as it was during Bomber Command's next attack on Germany on 26 March, the raiders enjoyed a reasonably clear run.

On that occasion the target was Essen, and the raiding force ran in over the Zuider Zee as though bent on attacking another city in central Germany. But then it turned sharply to starboard and attacked Essen from the north-west. The *Luftwaffe* controller failed to recognise the turn until it was too late, and as a result, the assembly of fighters east of the Zuider Zee waited for the bombers in vain. Although more than a hundred night fighters were airborne, few made contact with the bombers and these did not engage until the raiders were leaving the target. The only bombers seen to go down to fighter attack – four of them – fell during the return flight. The war diarist of NJG 6 plaintively recorded the reasons for his unit's failure to engage the enemy successfully that night:

► This Fw 190 A-8, 'White 9' of 1./NJG 10 shows the aerials for the FuG 217 radar mounted on the starboard wing and the anti-glare shield over the exhaust. The emblem on the cowling originated with JG 300 and symbolised the unit's 'Wilde Sau' tactics.

"The direction of the approach and return flights could not be recognised from the running commentary. Therefore it was not possible to get into the bomber stream. Due to the devious approach and the strong headwind, II./NJG 6 did not arrive at the target before the attack ended. Severe icing was reported. Twenty-one Bf 110s on Zahme Sau operations, three Bf 110s on Himmelbett, one Ju 88 on reconnaissance [to seek out the bomber stream and report on its position and heading]. Three Bf 110s ran out of fuel and crashed, and one made a belly landing."

Of the 683 bombers involved in the Essen attack only nine failed to return. Of these, three were seen to go down to *Flak*. Not the least distressing aspect of the night's action for the defenders was that it cost the *Luftwaffe* 16 night fighters, most of which crashed attempting to land at airfields in conditions of poor visibility.

Throughout the greater part of March the *Luftwaffe* night fighter force failed to distinguish itself and, for one reason or another, the bulk of its forces failed to make contact with the bomber stream. Then, on the night of the 30th, it atoned for its previous failures and now struck with awesome power. The target was Nuremberg, and 796 bombers set out to attack the city.

This raid went wrong almost from the start. As the raiders crossed the North Sea and passed over Belgium, *Luftwaffe* ground direction-finding stations plotted their track accurately from bearings of H2S radar signals. At the same time, spoof attacks by Mosquitoes on Cologne and Kassel were recognised as such by their absence of H2S signals. Thus, by exploiting the bombers' own radiations, the fighter control officer of the *Luftwaffe* 3. *Jagddivision* maintained a grip on the air situation despite strong jamming of the early warning radars. He ordered his twin-engined night fighters to assemble over radio beacon *Ida*, near Cologne, until the bombers' track became clear.

The decision to choose that particular beacon out of more than a score was merely an opening gambit, yet it would prove providential beyond the fighter control officer's wildest dreams. Had the bombers held their heading after leaving the coast, they would have passed safely clear of *Ida*. However, the briefed route turned them on to an easterly heading which took them close to the beacon and its orbiting night fighters.

Nor was that the only mischance to befall the raiders that night. The forecast winds issued to bomber crews during their pre-flight briefings were inaccurate, and some navigators took longer to discover this than others. As a result, the bomber stream had started to lose cohesion even before it reached its initial turning point, but worse was to follow as the leading aircraft thundered into Germany.

Each minute, the petrol burned in each aero engine produced about a gallon of water in the form of steam. Normally, this steam was ejected with the other exhaust gases, but on this very cold night the steam condensed into long white condensation trails which trailed behind each bomber. Moreover, it was a clear night, and the glow of the moon gave the trails a phosphorescent quality, depriving the bombers of their protective cloak of invisibility. Sergeant Bob Truman, who flew as engineer in a Lancaster of No 625 Squadron, remembered:

"You could see them clearly – all those contrails, it was fantastic. I remember thinking at the time that if they were so clear to me, they would be equally clear to the German night fighter crews if any were about; and they would be sure to get on to us."

The German night fighter crews were certainly *"about"*. As the swarm of bombers came past *Ida*, radar operators in the orbiting night fighters made contact and guided their pilots after individual bombers. As they closed on a bomber, each night fighter crew had an important duty to perform before opening fire: they had to radio their position and the bomber's heading. Soon the ether was thick with *Pauke!* calls followed by position reports and headings. *Pauke!* – literally *"Beat the kettle drum"* – was the *Luftwaffe* equivalent of the RAF's *"Tally Ho!"*; it meant the fighter had made contact with

"It was a fantastic sight in the clear moonlight, aircraft going down in flames and exploding everywhere."

the enemy and was about to engage. The radio calls assisted the ground controllers to refine their air picture, and direct other fighter units into the fray.

Thus began a running battle that was to last for more than 200 miles across Germany. As well as the night fighters joining the bomber stream, Junkers 88s from a special illuminating unit arrived and released strings of parachute flares to mark the position of the bomber stream. The flares were visible from scores of miles away, and from all over Germany night fighters converged on the bombers like moths to a flame.

It was an ideal night for the *Zahme Sau* free-hunting tactics, and during the hour that followed the night fighters exacted retribution on those who had rained such destruction on their homeland. *Unteroffizier* Emil Nonenmacher of III./NJG 2 based at Twente in Holland, piloting a Ju 88, was one of those who joined the action shortly after the initial clash.

◄ A German 105 mm Flak battery firing in unison.

▲ A Lancaster minus the rear turret, removed by a falling bomb. Collisions and damage from falling ordnance added to the nightly toll of Bomber Command aircraft and crews.

►► Inside the bomb bay of a fully loaded Lancaster. It has been armed with 13 500lb Cluster canisters of incendiaries.

▲ With visible relief, the crew of a 630 Squadron Lancaster, ME739, LE-D, disembark at East Kirkby following a raid on French rail yards in April 1944.

"With so many targets visible I could take my pick, so I chose the nearest one in front of me – a Lancaster – and went after him. He was weaving gently. I set myself up for a deflection shot, aiming at a point one aircraft length ahead of the bomber. I opened fire and saw my rounds striking it. Then I paused, put my sight on the bomber again and fired another burst. After a few rounds my guns stopped firing – I had exhausted the ammunition in the drum magazines on my cannon."

"As we climbed out of Twente we could see that a great battle was already in progress: there were aircraft burning in the air and on the ground, there was the occasional explosion in mid-air and much firing with tracer rounds. We kept on towards the scene of high activity for about five minutes, then suddenly we hit the slipstream from one of the bombers. Now we were close to the bomber stream. It seemed there was activity all around us – here an aircraft on fire, there someone firing, somewhere else an explosion on the ground. Yet it was a few more minutes before we actually caught sight of a bomber, its silhouette passing obliquely over my cockpit."

Nonenmacher was now inside the bomber stream. On that very clear night he could see more than 12 bombers around him, each leaving dense condensation trails. He tried to move into a firing position behind the first bomber he saw, but misjudged his approach and had to break away. It did not matter; there were plenty of other targets.

Nonenmacher ordered his flight engineer to replace the ammunition drums, but as the man struggled to fit new drums the bomber escaped. Nonenmacher simply picked out another Lancaster and closed on that one:

"I moved into a firing position about 100 metres astern and a little below it. By then the engineer had one of the cannon going so I pressed the firing button and saw my rounds striking the left wing. Soon afterwards, both engines on that side burst into flames. He began to lose height and we could see the crew baling out, it was so clear. The bomber took about six minutes to go down, when it reached the ground it blew up with a huge explosion."

Nonenmacher's aircraft did not carry the *Schräge Musik* installation with upward firing cannon, but several others did. One who used these weapons to good effect was *Oberleutnant* Helmut Schulte, piloting a Bf 110 of II./NJG 5:

► A Handley Page Halifax B III of the Free French 347 Squadron at RAF Elvington in Yorkshire during the winter of 1944/45. The crew have named the aircraft "Miquette" and decorated the nose with the Cross of Lorraine, symbol of the Free French Forces fighting alongside the Allied forces.

"Normally our biggest problem was to find the bomber stream, but on this night we had no trouble. I found the enemy at a height of 6000 metres. I sighted a Lancaster and got underneath it and opened fire with [Schräge Musik]. *Unfortunately* [the guns] *jammed so that only a few shots put out of action the starboard-inner motor. The bomber dived violently and turned to the north, but because of the good visibility we were able to keep him in sight. I now attempted a second attack after he had settled on his course but because the Lancaster was now very slow, we always came out too*

far in front. [After the radio operator cleared the stoppage] *I tried the Schräge Musik again and after another burst the bomber fell in flames."*

The effectiveness of the attacks made by Nonenmacher, Schulte and their comrades was fully evident to the crews of other bombers. This was the sort of running battle the *Luftwaffe* planners had in mind when they proposed the *Zahme Sau* tactic. Squadron Leader G. Graham, a Lancaster pilot with 550 Squadron, recalled:

HANDLEY PAGE HALIFAX B III

This Handley Page Halifax served with 347 Squadron from RAF Elvington, Yorkshire during 1944-45. The aircraft is in overall standard finish of Dark Earth and Dark Green over Night (black) undersurfaces. Note the French adaption of the main fuselage roundel and the Cross of Lorraine on the nose of the aircraft.

"We went in south of Cologne and were immediately met by the German fighters, I could say hundreds. It was a fantastic sight in the clear moonlight, aircraft going down in flames and exploding everywhere."

During this phase of the action, an average of about one bomber fell out of the sky every minute, in many cases on fire. Bob Truman noted: *"We saw a tremendous amount of activity, with scores of bombers going down and much air-to-air firing."*

Flying Officer George Foley, sitting in the curtained-off and isolated H2S position of a Pathfinder Lancaster, was disconcerted to hear his pilot inform the crew over the intercom: *"Better put your parachutes on, chaps; I've just seen the forty-second go down!"* And the feelings of Flight Lieutenant Graham Ross were typical of those of many a bomber captain on that night: *"I was shaken at the sight of so many aircraft going down in flames; but I was more worried at the thought that my own crew might be scared by it all, and react in some unexpected way."*

Night fighters from bases all over Germany now joined the action. The 2. *Jagddivision*, from the north, joined via radio beacons *Ludwig* and *Otto*. The 1. *Division*, from bases in the Berlin area, moved

westwards and joined via beacons *Dora* and *Ida*; the 7. *Division*, from the south, fed into the bomber stream via beacon *Otto*.

Because the raiding force was so widely spread, *Luftwaffe* fighter controllers had great difficulty in predicting the bombers' target, but if there were doubts about where the attackers were going, there were none on where they had been: the bombers' track running eastwards from *Ida* was clearly marked by the trail of wrecked aircraft burning on the ground.

Not until 01.08 hrs, two minutes before the first bombs were due to go down on Nuremberg, was the city mentioned in the *Luftwaffe* fighter's broadcast commentary. As a result of this uncertainty, the short-range *Wilde Sau* units were nowhere near the target when it finally became known, and it is doubtful whether any single-seaters went into action that night. All told, the defenders put up 246 fighters, drawn from 21 *Gruppen*, to contest the incursion.

Due to the persistent harassment from night fighters, and the high banks of cloud over the target, the attack on Nuremberg itself was diffuse and ineffective. Indeed, the bombers were so widely dispersed that when they withdrew to the west most *Luftwaffe* night fighters lost

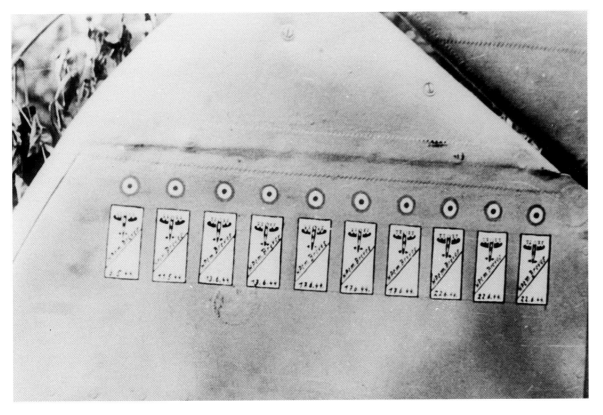

◄ The tail of Hptm. Adolf Breves' Bf 110 G night fighter showing his victory tally in June 1944. This pilot flew with Stab IV./NJG 1 and, on the night of 21/22 June, he shot down three RAF Lancaster bombers which raised his tally to ten victories. Note the meticulous book-keeping, each victory being represented by a white victory bar, within which is a silhouette of a four-engined bomber together with a note of the type destroyed and the date of the victory. Hptm. Breves later flew with II./NJG 1, and although records exist showing he was finally credited with 17 victories, it is possible he may have destroyed another in the final months of the war which was not confirmed.

contact. The scattered force of bombers provided numerous good targets for the *Flak* batteries, however, and returning RAF crews reported seeing 14 bombers go down to that cause.

That night, 94 out of the 796 bombers which had set out to attack Nuremberg, and one out of the 17 flying supplies to the French Resistance, failed to regain the shores of Britain. Twelve more crash-landed at or near their bases, bringing the total loss to 107 heavy bombers. A further 34 bombers returned with serious battle damage.

So ended the Battle of Berlin. During the 35 major attacks on German cities between 18 November 1943 and 31 March 1944, the RAF lost 1,047 aircraft and a further 1,682 returned with varying degrees of damage. The German capital had not been destroyed and Bomber Command had lost almost exactly twice the number of aircraft Sir Arthur Harris predicted in his note to the Prime Minister five months earlier. Although it had been hit hard, Germany was still very much in the war.

Whatever its outcome, the attack on Nuremberg would have seen the end of the deep penetration attacks on Germany for some months, for now the heavy bombers were required for operations to prepare the way for the forthcoming invasion of Normandy. In the night skies over their homeland, the *Luftwaffe* night fighter crews had avenged their humiliation over Hamburg the previous summer. They now stood at the pinnacle of their success, blooded and confident in their new tactics.

However, the tapestry of war is frequently woven with a thread of irony, and such was now the case. For, at the very moment that the *Luftwaffe* night defences reached the zenith of their effectiveness, their comrades battling against the daylight raiding formations were being trampled into oblivion. We shall examine these developments in the next Chapter.

◄◄ Armourers wheel a 8,000 lb 'Super Cookie' towards a waiting Lancaster.

THE NUREMBERG RAID - THE RAF PLAN

This battle order, issued by Headquarters No 1 Group Bomber Command to subordinated units on 30 March 1944, provides an insight into the detailed planning that went into the night attacks. The text of the original teleprinter signal is reproduced here, with the sole alteration that many abbreviations have been written out in full.

From Headquarters No 1 Group to Nos 12, 13 and 14 Bases and all operational stations; for information of No 11 Base, Hemswell and Headquarters Bomber Command.

Serial No: Form B Serial No 1258, Task No 1365.
Date: 30th March 1944.

Intelligence: See current Intelligence signal. A total of 796 aircraft will be attacking this target.
Aim of Operation: To cause maximum damage to the target area.
Date of Operation: Night of 30th/31st March 1944.

Forces to be Deployed from this Group: No 460 Squadron, 25 aircraft; 103 Sqn, 16 a/c; 101 Sqn, 24 a/c; 625 Sqn, 31 a/c; 576 Sqn, 16 a/c; 12 Sqn, 13 a/c; 100 Sqn, 18 a/c; 166 Sqn, 20 a/c; 626 Sqn, 15 a/c; 550 Sqn, 17 a/c.

Target: Grayling [code-name for Nuremberg].

Intelligence Required from Crews: Results of the raid with the aid of photographs.

Route: Bases – Southwold - 5150N 0230E - 5030N 0435E - 5032N 1038E – TARGET - 4900N 1105E - 4830N 0920E - 4910N 0300E - 5000N 0110E - Selsey Bill – Reading -Bases.
Timing: Zero hour will be 01.10 hrs.
Section 1 Time over target, zero hour to zero plus 3 minutes.
No 12 Base – 11 aircraft, 13 Base - 14 a/c, 14 Base - 6 a/c, plus 48 Lancasters and 46 Halifaxes of other Groups.
Section 2 Time over target, zero plus 2 to zero plus 4.
No 12 Base – 11 a/c, 13 Base - 14 a/c, 14 Base - 6 a/c, plus 48 Lancasters and 46 Halifaxes of other Groups.
Section 3 Time over target, zero plus 4 to zero plus 7.
No 12 Base - 12 a/c, 13 Base - 14 a/c, 14 Base - 2 a/c, plus 48 Lancasters and 46 Halifaxes of other Groups.
Section 4 Time over target, zero plus 7 to zero plus 10.
No 12 Base – 11 a/c, 13 Base - 13 a/c, 14 Base - 6 a/c, plus 47 Lancasters and 45 Halifaxes of other Groups.
Section 5 Time over target, zero plus 9 to zero plus 12.
No 12 Base – 11 a/c, 13 Base - 14 a/c, 14 Base - 5 a/c, plus 47 Lancasters and 45 Halifaxes of other Groups.

Other Instructions:

1. Minimum petrol load for all aircraft will be 1849 gallons.

2. Bomb loads:
Lancaster Mark IIIs – one 4000 pounder, six containers each with 150 four-pounder incendiaries, two containers each with 60 four-pounder incendiaries and eight containers each with 12 thirty-pounder incendiaries.
H2S-fitted aircraft - half: 1 x 4000 lbs, 2 x 150 x 4, 2 x 60 x 4, 13 x 12 x 30.
half: 1 x 2000lb HC, 12 x 150 x 4, 2 x 12 x 30.
ABC-fitted aircraft - half: 1 x 4000 lbs, 1 x 150 x 4, 14 x 12 x 30, 2 x 60 x 4.
half: 1 x 2000lbs, 11 x 150 x 4, 3 x 12 x 30.
Five aircraft from No 14 Base are to substitute one 4000 pounder General Purpose, fused with assorted long delay pistols, for one 4000 pounder High Capacity.

3. 24 ABC-fitted aircraft from No 101 Squadron to be spread evenly over the whole period of the attack.

4. 12 aircraft from No 12 Base, 7 a/c from 13 Base and 7 a/c from 14 Base are to transmit the winds in accordance with the instructions issued by the Group navigational staff.

5. Window—Start dropping at rate C [one bundle per minute] 5145N, 0240E.
At rate D [two bundles per minute] 4952N, 1054E.
At rate C 4900N, 1105 E.
Stop finally at 5013N, 0035E.
A total of 315 bundles to be carried per aircraft.

6. (1) The method [Pathfinder Marking] for tonight, 30th March 1944 on Grayling will be Newhaven [visual] groundmarking. If cloud obscures the target indicators, Wanganui [radar aimed] skymarking will be used as an emergency.
(2) Red target indicators will be dropped as route markers off track at position 5046N, 0606E outward bound.
(3) Pathfinders will open the attack at zero minus 5 minutes with sticks of illuminating flares and with green target indicators dropped in the target area. The aiming point will then be marked

with large salvoes of mixed red and green target indicators and kept marked with red target indicators.

(4) In addition, if cloud obscures the target indicators, the release point will be marked with flares coloured red, giving off yellow stars.

(5) The Main Force aircraft arriving early in the attack are to aim their bombs at the large salvoes of mixed red and green target indicators, if these are visible. Otherwise, all the Main Force aircraft are to aim their bombs at the centre of all the red target indicators.

(6) If cloud obscures the target indicators, the Main Force aircraft are to aim their bombs at the centre of all the flares coloured red with yellow stars, while holding an exact heading of 175 degrees (magnetic). In this case the bombsights are to be set for the aircraft's true height and air speed, but the wind control is to be set to zero. The vital importance of maintaining the correct heading requires special emphasis with regards to the Wanganui skymarking technique.

(7) Aircraft must not drop incendiaries before zero hour.

(8) Mosquitoes will carry out spoof attacks with red and green target indicators on Trout [Cologne] and Bream [Kassel]. In addition, spoof flares to imitate those released by German fighters will be dropped at approximate position 5050N 0800E.

7. Crews are to be warned that the adjustable zero hour will be in force tonight.

8. Tactics

A. Rendezvous at position 5150N 0230E at 16 - 19000 feet.

B. Cross enemy coast inbound at 16 - 19000 feet and maintain that height as far as the Rhine.

C. Then climb to 19 - 23000 feet and maintain that height on route to target and for bombing and until reaching the Rhine on return.

D From the Rhine descend to 16 - 19000 feet and maintain that height until reaching the enemy coast outbound.

E Bases are to ensure that their aircraft are spaced evenly between the altitudes laid down when over enemy territory.

F Captains are to be briefed to adhere to their ordered height, unless such adherence would interfere with their ability to carry out a successful attack.

Acknowledgement required.

[Message originated at] 13.25 hours British Summer Time on the 30th.

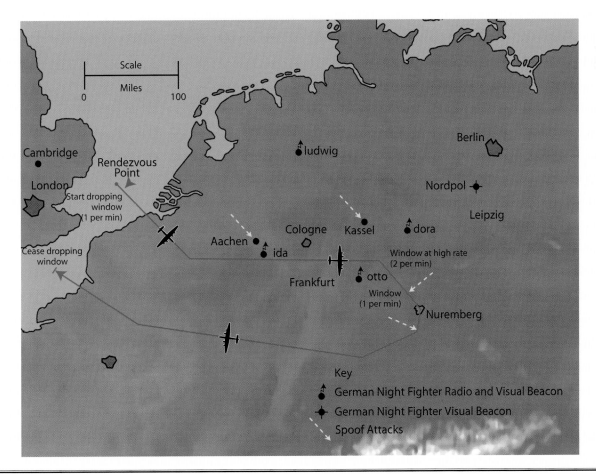

◄ The route flown by RAF Bomber Command during the attack on Nuremberg on 30/31 March 1944.

THE NUREMBERG RAID - THE LUFTWAFFE RESPONSE

Reproduced below is the translation of the War Diary of the *Luftwaffe's* 1. *Jagdkorps*,
describing the action fought on the night of 30 March 1944:

From about 22.30 hrs a force 100 Mosquitoes opened the RAF night operations; they crossed the Dutch coast and bombed the night fighter airfields at Leeuwarden, Twente, Deelen and Venlo, as well as industrial targets in the Ruhr. At the same time there appeared over the southern North Sea a smaller British force which presumably laid mines between the island of Sylt and Heligoland.

Next, the main British bomber effort developed in the Norwich area, flying on an easterly course, and turned over the North Sea on to a south-easterly course. Between 23.10 hrs and 23.50 hrs 700 bombers streamed over the coast between the mouth of the Schelde and Ostend. Passing over the Antwerp and Brussels areas they reached Liège and Florennes, where they turned onto an easterly course. The bomber stream crossed the Rhine at the Bingen/Bonn sector, and continued on to the area of Fulda and Hanau. Then the bombers took a south-easterly course over central Germany to attack Nuremberg.

Mosquitoes, which had preceded the bomber stream, tried to screen the route; they operated in the following areas: Bonn, Cologne, Kassel, Plauen, Zwickau, Nordhausen, Manheim and Frankfurt am Main. From the Nuremberg area, the return flight started at about 01.20 hrs. The bombers flew over the line Frankfurt-Stuttgart, then Brussels-Rheims and afterwards left the continent widely spread out, crossing the coast between the mouth of the Scheldt and St. Valery en Caux. The last of the returning aircraft passed over the mouth of the Somme at about 04.45 hrs.

The timely committal of the German night fighter defences prevented the large-scale British night attack from being fully pressed home. At Nuremberg there was heavy damage to residential areas, but only light damage to industry.

Operations by 1. *Jagdkorps*

FORCES COMMITTED:
Twin-engined units for pursuit [*Zahme Sau*] night fighting:
From the 3. Jagddivision
These aircraft were ordered to Radio Beacon *Ida*, and from there directed into the bomber stream: Ju 88 Gruppen from Twente, Quakenbrück, Langensalza and Langendiebach, Me 110 Gruppen from Venlo and Mainz-Finthen, I./NJG 6 subordinated from the 7. *Jagddivision* and subordinated units from the 4. *Jagddivision*. The subordinated II./NJG 6 of the 7. *Jagddivision* was directed to Radio Beacon *Otto*, and from there switched into the bomber stream. The *Gruppe* from St. Trond assembled over radar station 'Bazi', and radar station '*Murmeltier*' south of Aachen switched it into the bomber stream.

From the 2. *Jagddivision*
Gruppen from Westerland, Stade and Vechta: assembled over Radio Beacon *Ludwig*, were directed to *Otto*, then switched into the bomber stream in the area north-east of Giessen.

From the 1. *Jagddivision*
Gruppen from Erfurt, Parchim, Stendal and Werneuchen: initially flew in the direction of Radio Beacon *Otto*, then switched into the bomber stream in the areas of Radio Beacons *Otto* and *Ida*.

Single-engined [*Wilde Sau*] units for Target Defence from the 3. *Jagddivision*.

Gruppen from Rheine and Bonn: assembled over Visual Beacon *Otto*, directed to Frankfurt am Main, and landed in that area. Gruppe from Wiesbaden-Erbenheim: assembled over Visual Beacon *Nordpol*, landed in central Germany. From the 2. *Jagddivision*.

Gruppe from Oldenburg: assembled over Visual Beacon *Otto*, landed due to fuel shortage.

From the 1. *Jagddivision*
Gruppen from Ludwigslust, Zerbst and Jüterbug: assembled over Visual Beacon *Nordpol*, landed after the start of the attack on Nuremberg. Total number of sorties: 246, by single-engined and twin-engined fighters. The night fighter units of the 1. *Jagdkorps* achieved a noteworthy defensive success.

The Prerequisites for the above were:
The early identification of the main bomber stream, and recognition of its heading after leaving the bases in Britain.

The ordering off the ground of all twin-engined fighters, at the same time as the bombers left Great Britain heading for the western frontier of the Reich.

The approach by the bomber stream over the Rhein-Main area, that is to say through the centre of the area occupied by the German night fighter bases. As a result all the twin-engined night fighters were able to engage in good time and with sufficient range in hand.

The airborne search equipment SN-2 was unjammed by the enemy, making possible the use of pursuit night fighting methods.

Good visibility at height and a light night, so that the bombers could sometimes been seen at distances of up to 1,000 metres.

The first bombers were shot down in the area Liège-Bonn-

Koblenz. These and the ones later shot down burned like torches, and assisted incoming night-fighters to find the bomber stream.

The long pursuit, running from the Rhine onwards:

The chance overflight by the bomber stream of Radio Beacons *Ida* and *Otto*, which happened to be in use as assembly beacons for the twin-engined fighters.

The single-engined night fighter units were not involved in the successful defence, because they did not go into action over Nuremberg; they were, moreover, unable to take part in the pursuit due to their lack of airborne search equipment. The operations of the single-engined night-fighter units on 30/31 March were confined to the defence of Frankfurt am Main, and guarding against a possible attack on a target in central Germany or Berlin. It is therefore evident that for a successful target defence at night the prerequisites are: target defence fighters with long endurance, to allow flexibility in the choice of their operating areas, and also a timely and correct recognition of the target of the attacking force. These prerequisites were not available to the German command on the night of 30/31 March. The British bomber stream made several changes of course, and this and the decoy operations by Mosquitoes prevented an early recognition of the target for the attack. On 30/31 March the General commanding the 1. *Jagdkorps* was comparatively late in recognising that the British attackers were going for the city of Nuremberg. The bomber stream, harassed by the German defences, arrived piecemeal and took a long time to go into action. As a result, for a long time the General surmised that the attacking force was committed to another target; while the situation was thus

in doubt, the single-engined fighters used up their fuel.Losses to the Enemy:

101 bombers shot down for certain, and 6 probables. On 31 March British radio gave losses as 94 bombers.

Own Losses:

5 aircraft; 5 more aircraft with more than 60 per cent damage [considered write-offs]. Personnel losses: 3 dead, 1 wounded and 8 missing.

Weather:

Holland, Ruhr and Frankfurt areas: cloudless. Southern Germany: 10/10 cloud cover from 500 metres to 3,500 metres. Generally good visibility at high altitude. Half moon.

Special Points: *Oberleutnant* Becker, a *Staffelkapitän* in NJG 1, shot down 7 British bombers on the night of 30/31 March.

▼ This Bf 110 G-4 of 6./NJG 1 was photographed at Düsseldorf-Kaiserswerth in October 1944. Pictured with the aircraft is the pilot, Uffz. Gustav Sarzio, and his W/T operator, Heinz Conrands. Their machine was coded G9+JP and was lost in the evening of 4 November 1944 when it was shot down over Mönchengladbach, possibly by an RAF Mosquito. Sarzio, who had five victories at the time, was wounded, but Conrands was killed.

9

BATTLE OF ATTRITION
BY DAY

November 1943 - March 1944

"Total war is not a succession of mere episodes in a day or a week. It is a long,

drawn-out and intricately planned business, and the longer it continues the

heavier are the demands on the character of the men engaged in it."

General George Marshall

As described in Volume One, October 1943 marked a significant turning point in the USAAF's strategic bombing campaign against Germany. Following the heavy losses suffered in its series of deep penetration raids by day, culminating in the second attack on Schweinfurt, the Eighth Air Force drew back to lick its wounds. During November, December and January the force restricted itself to relatively shallow penetration attacks on targets in north-west Germany, Belgium, Holland and France.

The Eighth Air Force had given top priority to increasing the size of its fighter component, and this move now bore fruit. During the final quarter of 1943 the number of combat units in the VIIIth Fighter Command trebled. By mid-December it possessed eight fully operational groups of P-47s and two of P-38s. Also there was a single group equipped with the P-51B Mustang which was working up for action. In all, the force possessed about 550 long-range escort fighters.

The possession of sufficient fighters with the range to escort bombers flying deep into Germany did not, however, necessarily mean that the VIIIth Fighter Command's equipment problems were entirely solved. The escorts needed to be fast and manoeuvrable enough to take on their *Luftwaffe* opponents at least on even terms. The twin-engined P-38 Lightning was worst off in this respect. Although it could out-turn and out-run the enemy fighters at medium and low altitudes, at high-altitude its performance was less impressive. And it was at high altitudes that most of the actions would be fought.

The P-47 Thunderbolt had the opposite problem, initially. While it could hold its own against the best *Luftwaffe* fighters above 20,000 feet,

below that altitude it was at a disadvantage. As a result, pilots were loath to pursue enemy fighters diving away to escape. The answer was to fit a water injection system to the Thunderbolt's engine, which cooled the fuel-air mixture drawn into the cylinders and for short periods provided an increase of up to 300 hp. Modified P-47s began to appear in November 1943, and the change transformed this fighter into an altogether more aggressive opponent.

The great hope for the future was the North American P-51B Mustang fitted with the Rolls-Royce Merlin engine. At the main fighting altitudes of 20,000 feet and above it was more than 30 mph faster than either the Focke-Wulf Fw 190 A or the Messerschmitt Bf 109 G, and it could out-turn and out-dive both of them. The fighter had an internal fuel capacity of 269 US gallons, and with two 62 Imp.Gal. drop tanks it promised to have sufficient range to provide full-route protection for bombers attacking targets almost anywhere in Germany. Yet at first, the new variant of the Mustang had its share of teething troubles, and some months would elapse before it achieved its full potential.

As well as more and better escorts to ward off the German fighters, the B-17s and B-24s began carrying radar counter measures systems to reduce the accuracy and therefore the effectiveness of the enemy *Flak*. During the latter part of 1943 the day bombers, like their counterparts in the RAF operating at night, began dropping 'Window' in large quantities. As in the case of the night bombers, however, the foil strips

◄◄ B-17G Flying Fortresses of the 381st Bomb Group, based at Ridgewell in Suffolk, on course for another target in occupied Europe.

► Early in 1944 the US Fifteenth Air Force, based in Italy, began large-scale attacks on the Reich from the south. This had the effect of extending still further the already overstretched German defensive forces. Here, Liberators of the Fifteenth Air Force are seen crossing the Alps on their way to attack the aircraft factories at Wiener Neustadt on 12 April.

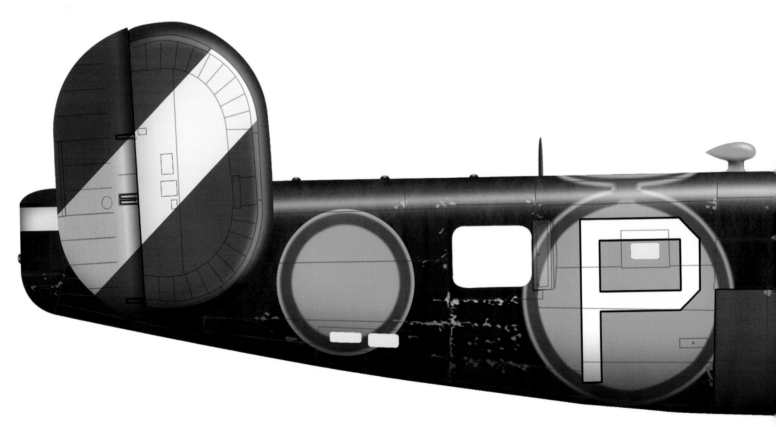

provided cover for the aircraft coming behind rather than the one that had dropped it, leaving the aircraft at the head of each formation exposed. To overcome that weakness, an increasing number of the day bombers carried the APT-2 'Carpet' transmitter, which radiated jamming on the frequencies used by the *Würzburg* fire-control radar.

As well as these improvements in equipment at the end of 1943, there was a significant improvement in the USAAF's strategic position. From November 1943 the US Fifteenth Air Force began attacking targets in southern Europe, initially from bases in North Africa. Soon afterwards the heavy bomber units began shifting to bases in central Italy.

The Fifteenth Air Force launched its first large scale attack into Germany on 2 November 1943, when 139 B-17s and B-24s with an escort of 72 P-38 Lightnings struck at the Messerschmitt assembly works at Wiener-Neustadt, south of Vienna. Despite the new direction of the attack the defenders reacted strongly, and 11 heavy bombers were lost.

With the effectiveness of their attacks compounded by the size and capability of the fighter escort, and the

◄ One factor which prevented the Italian-based strategic bombers from operating to their full potential was the condition of many airfields during spells of poor weather. In this photograph, a B-24 taxies across its partially flooded airfield in Italy. (IWM)

ability to attack targets in Germany simultaneously from both the north and the south, the US Eighth and Fifteenth Air Forces made ready to launch the next phase in their campaign. Their resources were great and increasing, but no less so was the commission they were now asked to carry through. As General 'Hap' Arnold, the Commander in Chief of the USAAF, stated in his simple New Year's Day message to his field commanders for 1944: *"Destroy the enemy air forces wherever you find them, in the air, on the ground and in the factories."*

The target for the new series of attacks was to be the German aircraft factories, repair centres and aircraft

CONSOLIDATED B-24D LIBERATOR, 790th BOMB SQUADRON, 467TH BOMBARDMENT GROUP

'Pete the POM Inspector' (formerly 'Heaven Can Wait') was an assembly ship serving with the 790th Bomb Squadron, 467th Bombardment Group based at Rackheath, England, 1944. These war-weary aircraft were painted in high-visibility markings to provide visual guides for the large numbers of US bombers as they formed their complex formations over England. Once their task was complete, the assembly aircraft peeled away from the formation and returned to base. The reference to POM Inspector was directed at those officers assigned to carry out Preparation For Overseas Movement Missions (POM). Preparation for overseas movement was more than an exercise in moving from one place to another; it was also a test of how much attention had been given by a unit to readiness in the past.

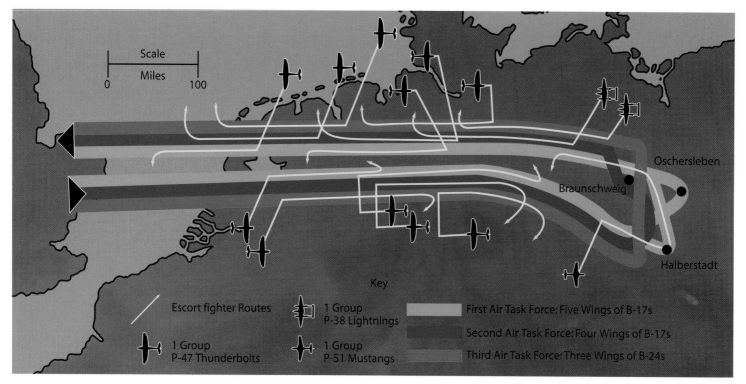

Key

╱	Escort fighter Routes	
✈	1 Group P-38 Lightnings	
✈	1 Group P-47 Thunderbolts	
✈	1 Group P-51 Mustangs	

First Air Task Force: Five Wings of B-17s

Second Air Task Force: Four Wings of B-17s

Third Air Task Force: Three Wings of B-24s

▲ Map showing the layout of the bomber force, and also the route flown during the Eighth Air Force attack on aircraft production plants at Halberstadt, Braunschweig and Oschersleben on 11 January 1944. The map also shows the planned timetable for the rendezvous of each batch of escorting fighters. Note that the strongest part of the escort supported the bombers during their withdrawal phase, when it was necessary to protect bombers that had suffered battle damage and were limping home. In the event, high cloud prevented implementation of the escort plan during the 11 January attack, and along most of the route the bombers lacked fighter cover. Nevertheless, that deployment of the escorting fighters can be regarded as typical for the period. Compared with the evasive routing flown by the RAF night raiders, the tracks of the day bombers were almost straight. One aim of the escorted daylight attacks was to force Luftwaffe fighters into battle, and evasive routing would only have hindered this.

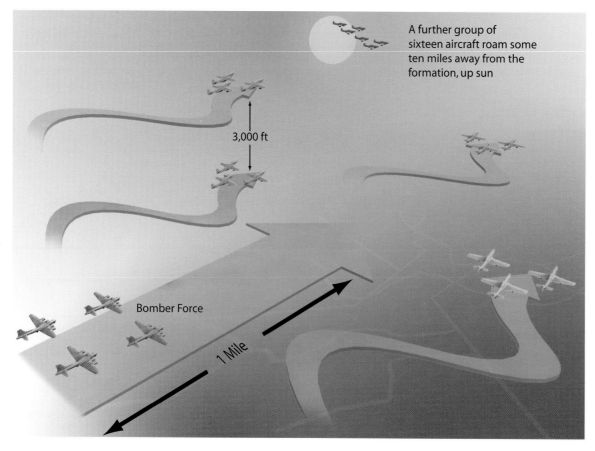

A further group of sixteen aircraft roam some ten miles away from the formation, up sun

3,000 ft

Bomber Force

1 Mile

◀ Typical deployment of a US fighter Group of 48 aircraft to escort a force of bombers. Since the bombers cruised somewhat slower than the fighters, the latter had to weave continually to maintain the same rate of advance. Two flights, each with eight fighters, flew on either side of the bomber formation to guard its flanks. Two more flights flew top cover, some 3,000 feet above the bombers. Two further flights flew about a mile in front of the bombers, in position to break up head-on attacks. A further four flights of fighters flew about ten miles up-sun of the bombers, to be in position to meet a likely direction of attack.

storage parks. The raid was intended to serve a two-fold purpose in reducing the overall effectiveness of the *Luftwaffe*. By destroying its aircraft on the ground, and also the means of replacing them, it would reduce the strength of the force in the long-term. Moreover, since the *Luftwaffe* could not allow such attacks to pass unchallenged, it would be drawn into a lengthy battle of attrition against an enemy that had far greater resources.

For the *Luftwaffe*, its successful defensive actions of October 1943 seemed to bode well for the future. If it could inflict such losses on the raiders as a matter of course, it seemed likely that the daylight bombing campaign could be stopped in its tracks.

As described in Volume one, a white hope for the medium-term future was the twin-engine Messerschmitt Me 410 fitted with the 50 mm calibre BK 5 heavy cannon. With this high velocity weapon the aircraft could sit about 1 km behind the US bomber formations, outside the effective range of the defensive crossfire, and pick off individual bombers. Flight tests at the trials establishment at Oberpfaffenhofen were successful, and the first batch of modified Me 410s would soon be ready.

For the longer term future, the *Luftwaffe* placed great hopes on the Messerschmitt Me 262 jet fighter. The Messerschmitt company was in the process of tooling up to mass produce this aircraft and it was confidently expected that the first combat units would be ready for action by the following spring. This revolutionary new aircraft had a maximum speed of 870 km/h, fast enough to outrun the fastest US escort fighter, and its armament of four 30 mm cannon was powerful enough to tear apart the strongest heavy bomber.

The first of the large-scale escorted attacks on the German aircraft industry was mounted on 11 January 1944, when 663 B-17s and B-24s set out to bomb the Fw 190 production centre at Oschersleben, the Junkers factory at Halberstadt, and factories producing Messerschmitts near Braunschweig. The incursion was certain to draw a strong reaction from the defenders, and the escort plan called for eleven groups of P-47s and two groups of P-38s to cover the bombers during their flights to and from the targets, while the single available group of P-51s would provide support for as long as possible during the time the bombers were over the target area. In addition, six squadrons of RAF Spitfires were to furnish cover for the bombers' withdrawal.

On paper the escort plan was sound, but it failed to allow for the changeable European weather. Over the North Sea and Holland the escorts found the overcast solid up to 22,000 feet in places. The majority of fighter groups turned back after they failed to make contact

▲ Two Messerschmitt Bf 110 G-2 destroyers of 3./ZG 76. They are fitted with underwing twin 21 cm air-to-air mortar tubes and their spinners carry rings in their Staffel colour of yellow.

with the bombers they were supposed to protect.

In the end, of the imposing force of fighters that should have been available, it was left to a single squadron of P-38s and the group of 49 P-51s to provide what cover they could. As had been intended, moreover, the raid drew a powerful German fighter reaction, but many bomber formations now lacked fighter protection and they suffered accordingly, sixty heavy bombers were shot down, a loss equal to that suffered during each of the two disastrous attacks on Schweinfurt. However, the raiding forces were much larger than during the earlier raids, and the Eighth Air Force could take even this heavy loss in its stride.

On 29 January a force of over 800 US bombers with fighter escort attacked Frankfurt am Main, and on the following day a similar force went for Braunschweig. One German pilot who took off to engage the latter attack was *Unteroffizier* Hans Seyringer, now a comparatively experienced fighter pilot with his own apprentice wing-man to teach the tricks of battle. His *Gruppe*, I./JG 27, which was based at Wiesbaden and equipped with Bf 109 Gs, scrambled as the raiders came in over the North Sea and intercepted the bombers as they came in over Holland. As Seyringer later recounted:

"Our Gruppe manoeuvred into a firing position for a massed attack from the rear. There was heavy defensive fire from the bombers whilst we closed in, and we had losses even before we were able to fire back. When we were in firing range I opened up on one B-17, holding my fingers on the firing button until I had closed to within about 350 metres. I saw several of my shells

THE P-51B MUSTANG COMPARED WITH ITS ADVERSARIES

The arrival in the skies over Germany in early 1944 of large numbers of long-range American fighters, sealed the fate of the *Luftwaffe* by enabling the USAAF to establish a degree of air superiority over the German homeland which it held to the end of the war. The superiority of the American fighter force was due in large measure to better pilot training and, later, the greater numbers of fighters in operation; for while the *Luftwaffe* had no shortage of fighters, after the autumn of 1944 it lacked the fuel and the trained pilots to operate them to full effect. Air superiority was also due to the superlative performance of the Merlin-engined P-51B Mustang fighter.

The fact that the Mustang could escort bombers to Berlin and beyond was proof of the remarkable range performance of this unique fighter, yet that would have counted for little had the type been ineffective when confronted by enemy fighters. How did the Mustang compare with the Messerschmitt Bf 109 G and the Focke-Wulf Fw 190 A, the two types which bore the brunt of the defensive battle? Combat reports provide only part of the answer, because unrelated factors such as pilot training, numbers involved and the tactical situation can distort the assessment.

Fortunately, exhaustive battle trials carried out by the RAF Air Fighting Development Unit at the end of 1943 between a P-51B and captured examples of German fighters allow us to know in great detail how these types compared. However, it is necessary to give a caveat against treating these figures too literally, for whereas the P-51 used in the trials was a brand new machine in peak condition and with full maintenance back-up, the German fighters had been captured several months earlier and their performance fell short of the latest sub-types employed in Reich air defence units.

The relevant sections of the subsequent AFDU report are reproduced below:

BRIEF COMPARISON WITH THE Fw 190 (BMW 801D ENGINE)

Maximum Speed
The Fw 190 is nearly 50 mph slower at all heights, increasing to 70 mph above 28,000 ft. It is anticipated that the new Fw 190D might be slightly faster below 27,000 ft, but slower above that height.

Climb
There appears to be little to choose in the maximum rate of climb. It is anticipated that the Mustang will have a better climb than the new Fw 190D. The Mustang is considerably faster at all heights in a zoom climb.

Dive
The Mustang can always out-dive the Fw 190.

Turning Circle
Again, there is not much to choose. The Mustang is slightly better. When evading an enemy aircraft with a steep turn, a pilot will always out-turn the attacking aircraft initially because of the difference in speeds. It is therefore still a worthwhile manoeuvre with the Mustang when attacked.

◄ The P-51B Mustang, whose superb performance dominated the crucial air battles over Germany during the first half of 1944. The example shown was the personal mount of Captain Don Gentile, one of the top-scoring pilots in the 4th Fighter Group.

Rate of Roll

Not even a Mustang approaches the Fw 190.

Conclusions

In the attack, a high speed should be maintained or regained in order to regain the height initiative. A Fw 190 could not evade by diving alone. In defence a steep turn followed by a full throttle dive should increase the range before regaining height and course.

Dog-fighting is not altogether recommended. Do not attempt to climb away without at least 250 mph showing initially. Unfortunately there is not enough information on the new Fw 190D for any positive recommendations to be made.

BRIEF COMPARISON WITH THE Me 109G

Maximum Speed

The Mustang is faster at all heights. Its best heights, by comparison, are below 16,000 ft (30 mph faster, approximately) and above 25,000 ft (30 mph increasing to 50 mph at 30,000 ft).

Maximum Climb

This is rather similar. The Mustang is very slightly better above 25,000 ft but inclined to be worse below 20,000 ft.

Zoom Climb

Unfortunately the Me 109G appears to have a very good high-speed climb, making the two aircraft similar in a zoom climb.

Dive

On the other hand in defence the Mustang can still increase the range in a prolonged dive.

Turning Circle

The Mustang is greatly superior.

Rate of Roll

Not much to choose. In defence (in a tight spot) a rapid change of direction will throw the Me 109G's sight off. This is because the 109G's maximum rate of roll is embarrassing (the slots keep opening).

Conclusions

In attack, the Mustang can always catch the Me 109G, except in any sort of climb (unless there is a high overtaking speed). In defence, a steep turn should be the first manoeuvre, followed, if necessary, by a dive (below 20,000 ft). A high-speed climb will unfortunately not increase the range. If above 25,000 ft keep above by climbing or all-out level flight.

COMBAT PERFORMANCE WITH LONG-RANGE TANKS

Speed

There is a serious loss of speed of 40-50 mph at all engine settings and heights. It [i.e the Mustang] is, however, still faster than the Fw 190 (BMW 801D) above 25,000 ft, though slower than the Me 109G.

▲ Captain Don S. Gentile of the 4th Fighter Group manages a smile for the official cameraman next to his aircraft in early 1944. Born on 12 June 1920, the son of Italian immigrants to the USA, Gentile was awarded many decorations for his outstanding wartime service during which he was accredited with 19.83 confirmed victories.

Climb

The rate of climb is greatly reduced. It is outclimbed by the Fw 190 and the Me 109G. The Mustang is still good in a zoom climb (attack), but is still outstripped (defence) if being followed all the way by the Fw 190 and definitely outstripped by the Me 109G.

Dive

So long as the tanks are fairly full, the Mustang still beats the Fw 190 (BMW 801D) and the Me 109G in a power dive.

Turning Circle

The tanks do not make quite so much difference as one might expect. The Mustang can at least turn as tightly as the Fw 190 (BMW 801D) without stalling out, and therefore definitely more tightly than the Me 109G.

Rate of Roll

General handling and rate of roll are very little affected.

Conclusions

The performance of the Mustang is greatly reduced when carrying drop-tanks. Half-hearted attacks could still be evaded by a steep turn, but determined attacks would be difficult to avoid without losing height. It is still a good attacking aircraft, especially if it has the advantage of height.

◄   A Messerschmitt Me 410 B-2/U-2/R-4 bomber-destroyer bearing a newer but smaller version of the Wespe (wasp) insignia of ZG 1, which operated as a Reich defence unit in the spring of 1944. This aircraft carried a forward-firing armament of four 20 mm cannon, four 7.9 mm machine guns and four launchers for 21 cm mortars.

▼   An Me 410 of II./ZG 26 fitted with two WGr.21 air-to-air mortars under each wing prepares to taxi out after engine start.

▲   This Dornier built Me 410 B-2/U2 W.Nr. 710340, possibly belonging to ZG 26 in the summer of 1944, was fitted with the 'WB 151 A' gun-pack consisting of two MG 151/20 cannon fitted in the nose of the aircraft. The armament was originally meant to be the MK 103, 30 mm cannon but due to it being in short supply most Me 410 B-2/U2 variants were fitted with the twin 20 mm gun-pack.

"I immediately pulled my ripcord and the parachute opened. Then I fainted."

clean through the fuselage, carrying away some of the control runs: my machine no longer responded to the controls. Finally there was a hell of a bang in the cockpit as some of my 30 mm ammunition exploded. I decided it was high time I got out. I pulled the canopy jettison lever but nothing happened: the hood was jammed firmly in place. Despite the intense pain from the bullet wound in my foot and head wounds from splinters, I pushed myself up on my seat, fighting like a madman to force the canopy off with my back. Suddenly it came away and I was thrown clear of the plunging fighter. I immediately pulled my ripcord and the parachute opened. Then I fainted."

Seyringer awoke to find himself in hospital, suffering from back injuries and a paralysed left arm.

The appearance of the US escorts deep inside Germany, particularly the high-performance Mustangs, came as a profound shock to the *Luftwaffe* High Command. Indeed, when he received the first report that these had been sighted over Hannover, Göring ridiculed it and reprimanded the commander of the reporting centre concerned. Yet even when it was clear that the escorts were indeed penetrating that far into Germany, the *Reichsmarschall* refused to change his earlier edict that *Luftwaffe* fighters were to concentrate their attack against the bombers and leave the escorts alone unless they sought to interfere.

General Galland's plan however, was to try and defeat the US fighters while the US pilots were still inexperienced. In the event, as one *Geschwader-kommodore* remarked pungently, *"The safest flying that was ever possible, was that of an American fighter pilot over Germany."*

Emboldened by the superior performance of their fighters, and allowed to roam the skies over enemy territory almost at will, the Mustang and Thunderbolt pilots quickly developed an aggressive attitude. This was all too evident to their counterparts in the *Luftwaffe*, as one fighter pilot recalled:

"The radical change took place in January 1944; all of a sudden the American escort fighters gave up flying top cover and remaining aloof until we tried to attack their bombers, and regularly began swooping down on us whenever they got the chance. No longer was it a case of their bombers having to run the gauntlet of our fighters, but of our having to run the gauntlet of both their bombers and their fighters."

By the third week in February the US Eighth Air Force had expanded to an operational strength of 19

▲ A close-up of a pair of 21 cm launch tubes for the WGr.21 air-to-air mortar, mounted under the port wing of an Me 410.

strike the bomber, but it did not go down. As I broke away I noticed that my wingman had vanished; an inexperienced pilot, he did not have the iron nerves necessary for our butchers' task."

Seyringer scanned the sky for his missing wingman, but without success. Then he spotted a couple of P-47s above him. They obviously had not seen him, and this seemed a good opportunity to launch a surprise attack. Seyringer pulled his Messerschmitt round and headed after his unsuspecting foes. As he closed in, he loosed off a short but accurate burst at one of them. Its engine burst into flames and it went down, but the German pilot had little time to savour his success, for the next thing he knew, his victim's wingman was on his tail and pumping bullets into the Messerschmitt:

"My engine caught fire, and several of his rounds passed

groups of B-17s, eight groups of B-24s, eight groups of P-47s, two of P-38s and two of P-51s. Meanwhile, the Fifteenth Air Force in Italy had increased to eight groups of B-24s, four of B-17s, three of P-38s and one of P-47s. The US Army Air Force now had a total of some 2,500 bombers and 1,200 fighters in position to attack targets in Germany and occupied Europe.

To meet this powerful threat the *Luftwaffe* day fighter force in Germany and the occupied territories had available only some 870 single-engined fighters and about 130 twin-engined fighters. These had now to do battle with an enemy that enjoyed technical, tactical and numerical superiority.

On the morning of 20 February the skies over northern Europe were sufficiently clear for the Eighth Air Force to hurl almost its entire operational strength against the German aircraft industry: more than a thousand heavy bombers were despatched to attack 12 aircraft-production centres, mostly in the areas around Braunschweig and Leipzig. Covering this ambitious enterprise was the entire operational fighter strength of the Eighth Air Force plus five groups borrowed from the

▲ On 6 March 1944, P-51 Mustangs with twin drop tanks ranged as far as Berlin, placing ever more strain on the Jagdwaffe's defensive capabilities. Here a pair of P-51Bs of the 363rd FG – both carrying drop tanks – take off for another escort mission from either Rivenhall or Staplehurst in the spring of 1944.

◄ A mortar fired from a Luftwaffe fighter narrowly misses a B-17 of the US Eighth Air Force over Germany.

THE COMBAT BOX FORMATION

The US daylight bombing tactics were centred around the concept of the Combat Box formation, with the heavy bombers so positioned to combine their firepower and give best chance of warding off attacks from enemy fighters. Typically, in the early months of 1944, a box formation comprised 21 heavy bombers flying in three-aircraft Vees divided into three squadrons: the lead squadron with six aircraft, the low squadron with six and the high squadron with nine. The high and the low squadrons flew on opposite sides of the lead squadron, so that when seen from a distance the box formation took the form of a letter 'V' pointing in the direction of flight but tilted at 45 degrees.

The spacing of bombers in the box formation depended upon several conflicting requirements. The bombers needed to be sufficiently close to concentrate their defensive firepower and prevent enemy fighters from picking off single aircraft. On the other hand they needed to be sufficiently far apart so that no more than one bomber suffered damage from an exploding rocket or shell, no matter where it detonated. A spacing of two wingspans – about 200 feet – between adjacent bombers gave the best compromise between these conflicting requirements.

▲ Me 410s of II./ZG 76 in formation. Note the fuselage chevrons on the fuselage of the aircraft nearest to the wing of the camera aircraft. This denotes the markings of the Gruppenkommandeur.

tactical Ninth Air Force, a total of 835 fighters.

This time the escort plan succeeded brilliantly, and only 21 heavy bombers out of that enormous force failed to return. During this action the P-47 – which still made up the backbone of the US long-range fighter force – operated for the first time with the new 165 gallon capacity drop tank. This allowed the fighters to go deeper and spend longer over Germany than ever before. When *Luftwaffe* fighters attempted to hit the

bombers when escorts were present, they came in for a rough handling. For example, as about 24 Messerschmitt Bf 110 bomber destroyers of III./ZG 26 moved into position for a rocket attack on one of the combat wings, Thunderbolts of Colonel Hubert Zemke's 56th Fighter Group bounced them from out of the sun and shot down 18.

The Eighth Air Force was over Germany in strength again on the 21st, and yet again on the 22nd when bombers of the Fifteenth Air Force joined in the attack on the aircraft industry. On the 23rd the weather prevented the Eighth from operating, but for the defenders there was no respite since the Fifteenth still attacked from the south. On the 24th there was a co-ordinated attack from both the north and the south, and another on the 25th. Then, on the 26th, the weather broke and upset US operations far more effectively than the *Luftwaffe* ever could. The so-called 'Big Week' was over.

During those six days of intensive operations the USAAF flew more than 3,800 heavy bomber sorties over Germany. In the course of these operations 226 heavy bombers, 6 per cent of the force committed, failed to return. The escorting fighter units lost 28 aircraft.

A total of 23 German airframe and three aero-engine plants suffered varying degrees of destruction and during February 1944 the number of combat aircraft delivered to the *Luftwaffe* was 20 per cent less than in January – 1,671 aircraft compared with 2,077. At the time Allied intelligence officers believed, from the patchy information available, that the German aircraft industry had suffered far more heavily than that. It was, however, to prove a resilient target, and by dispersing the work amongst factories all over Germany and introducing programmes for the rapid repair of plants which had been hit, production was resumed much more quickly than had been thought possible.

During February, the *Luftwaffe* day fighter units defending Germany lost 355 aircraft destroyed or missing, and a further 155 suffered damage. With effort, those aircraft could be replaced, but fighters were useless if there was nobody to fly them, and it was the aircrew losses during Big Week which were to prove the more serious to the *Luftwaffe* in the long run. During February 1944 the Reich air defence force lost 225 aircrew killed or missing and a further 141 wounded. Together these amounted to about one-tenth of its effective strength in flying personnel, many of whom had considerable combat experience. Replacement pilots arriving with the *Jagdgruppen* had only about 160 hours flying time compared with more than double that figure for their

◄ An Me 410 moving into position to deliver a rocket attack on a bomber formation is itself under attack from a US escort fighter.

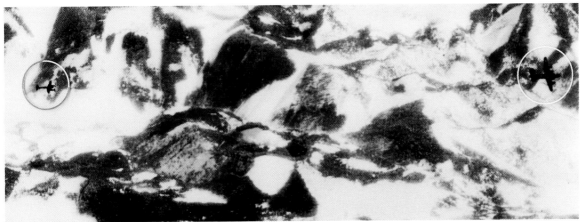

◄ There was no quarter given to stragglers. An Me 410 (circled, left) closes in to finish off a Fifteenth Air Force B-24 (circled, right). The latter had been forced out of formation on the homeward flight over the Alps on 23 February 1944, after the attack on Steyr, and was shot down soon afterwards.

American opponents. The balance of effectiveness was slowly but inexorably tilting away from the *Luftwaffe*.

Following up its success during the Big Week operations, the USAAF planned a series of strikes on another target the enemy fighter force could be guaranteed to defend with all its available strength: Berlin. With sufficient Mustangs to cover its assault, the Eighth Air Force could now *"come in"* on Sir Arthur Harris' attack on the capital.

The first large-scale daylight attack was to have been launched on 4 March, but as the bombers headed over the North Sea it became clear that the weather conditions were unsuitable. A recall signal was broadcast to the force, but two bomber groups failed to receive it and they and their escorting fighters continued on to the target.

Of the 29 aircraft that took part in the first daytime heavy bomber attack on the city, five failed to return. It would be one of the very few occasions when the US escorts suffered heavier losses than the bombers: 23 fighters failed to return. Hardest hit was the 363rd Fighter Group, which was bounced by the Messerschmitt Bf 109 Gs of II./JG 1 and lost eight Mustangs.

The next maximum-effort strike, and the first to reach Berlin in strength, took place on 6 March. A total of 812 B-17s and B-24s Liberators were assigned to hit three important production centres on the periphery of the capital. The 1st Bomb Division, with 301 B-17s, was to attack the VKF ball-bearing factory at Erkner. The 2nd Bomb Division, with 249 B-24s, was to bomb the Daimler-Benz aero-engine plant at Genshagen. The 3rd

▲ Bf 110 bomber-destroyers of III./ZG 26 preparing to intercept a formation of US heavy bombers attacking Sorau, Cottbus and Rostock on 11 April 1944. The Bf 110s concentrated their attacks on B-17s of the 13th and 45th Bomb Wings, and shot down the majority of the 25 bombers lost by those units that day.

JG 11 and JG 54. Once airborne, the fighters assembled into *Gruppe* formations and headed for the force assembly point above Lake Steinhuder near Hannover.

Accompanying the bombers during the initial penetration were 140 P-47s. In numerical terms, they outnumbered by a sizeable margin the defending fighters rising to engage the bombers, yet the arithmetic of the ensuing engagement would not be on their side. Whereas the US escort fighters had to protect the force as a whole, the *Luftwaffe* fighters could focus their attack on a single Combat Wing formation.

Luftwaffe controllers at the 3. *Jagddivision* headquarters at Stade vectored the German battle formation into position for a head-on attack, and at 11.55 hrs the formation leader, *Hauptmann* Rolf Hermichen, sighted the enemy. It was sheer bad luck for the bomber crews involved that the formation under threat was not that at the head of the bomber stream, where more than half the escorts were concentrated. Instead the blow fell on the B-17s of the 13th Bomb Wing, which was about midway down the bomber stream and had little fighter protection. Lieutenant Robert Johnson of the 56th Fighter Group was flying in a P-47 to one side of the Wing when he suddenly noticed the enemy formation closing in fast:

"I was on the left side of the bombers and going 180 degrees to them when I noticed a large box of planes coming at us at the same level. There were about 40 or 50 to a box, and I saw two boxes at our level and one box at 27,000 or 28,000 feet. I called in to watch them, and then that they were Fw 190s. There were only eight of us..."

The Thunderbolts did their best to to disrupt the attack, but the German pilots simply ignored them as they charged into the bombers.

A head-on attack on a bomber required a high degree of skill from the fighter pilot, if it was to succeed. The aircraft closed on each other at 182 metres per second, which allowed only a brief half-second burst from 460 metres before the attacker had to ease up on the stick to avoid colliding with his target. For experienced pilots like fighter ace *Hauptmann* Anton Hackl, who led the Fw 190s of III./JG 11 that day, that short burst was invariably sufficient. As he later commented to this writer:

"One accurate half-second burst from head-on [on a four-engined bomber] and a kill was guaranteed. Guaranteed!"

Bomb Division, with 262 B-17s, was to strike at the Bosch electrical equipment factory at Klein-Machnow.

The attack required a lengthy penetration into enemy airspace, 1,125 km from the Dutch coast to Berlin and back. Escorting it was a total of 691 fighters: P-38 Lightnings, P-47 Thunderbolts and P-51 Mustangs.

At 11.00 hrs, seven minutes after the leading US bombers crossed the Dutch coast, the first *Luftwaffe* fighter units began taking off: 107 Messerschmitt Bf 109s and Focke-Wulf Fw 190s drawn from JG 1,

◄ ▲ An increasingly familiar sight in Germany as the air battles became more ferocious: the burial of a Luftwaffe pilot. The overburdened German fighter training organisation proved quite incapable of making good the heavy pilot losses suffered during the succession of hard-fought battles over the Reich.

During the action on 6 March, Anton Hackl would be credited with the destruction of two heavy bombers.

Feldwebel Friedrich Ungar of *Jagdgeschwader* 54, flying a Bf 109 G, selected a B-17 and lined up on it, then saw his rounds explode on one of the engines with pieces flying off the bomber:

"There was no time for jubilation. The next thing I was inside the enemy formation trying to get through without ramming anyone. Nobody fired at me then, they were too concerned about hitting each other. When we emerged from the formation things got really hot; we had the tail gunners of some 30 bombers letting fly at us with everything they had. Together with part of our Gruppe I pulled sharply to the left and high, out to one side. Glancing back I saw the Fortress I had hit tip up and go down to the right, smoking strongly."

Sergeant Van Pinner, top turret gunner in a B-17 of the 100th Bomb Group, recalled that during the massed head-on attack he had far more targets than he could possibly engage:

"There were fighters everywhere. They seemed to come past in fours. I would engage the first three but then the fourth would be on to me before I could get my guns on him. I knew our aircraft was being hit real bad – we lost the ball turret gunner early in the fight . . . "

Following that initial head-on attack, mortally wounded heavy bombers began sliding out of formation. Lieutenant John Harrison of the 100th Bomb Group gazed in disbelief as aircraft around him began to go down:

"One accurate half-second burst from head-on and a kill was guaranteed. Guaranteed!"

◄ Adolf Galland was appointed Inspector of Fighters in November 1941, and rose to the rank of Generalleutnant. He held that position until he was dismissed early in 1945 following his outspoken criticism of decisions made by Reichsmarschall Göring and other senior officers. Galland ended the war leading the Me 262 unit Jagdverband 44 into action.

► Luftwaffe fighter aces compare notes after an action against a US raiding force. Hauptmann Hugo Frey, Staffelkapitän of 7./JG 11, bareheaded in the left foreground, was killed by bombers' return fire during the action on 6 March 1944 when his victory score stood at 32 victories. The Kommodore of JG 1, Oberst Walter Oesau wearing the forage cap, was killed during a fight with P-38 Lightnings on 11 May 1944, at which time he had been credited with 123 victories. Major Anton Hackl, with his back to the camera, would go on to lead JG 11 and survived the war credited with 192 victories.

▼ The Bf 109 G-6 'Kanonenboot' of Major Ludwig Franzisket, Gruppenkommandeur of I./JG 27, in flight somewhere over Austria or southern Germany in early 1944. The aircraft has a white rudder indicating a unit leader's aircraft, the green fuselage band of JG 27, double chevrons in black forward of the Balkenkreuz and the emblem of I./JG 27 on the cowling which has a yellow underside. A veteran of North Africa, Franzisket was appointed Gruppenkommandeur of I./JG 27 in the summer of 1943 and was engaged in the Reichsverteidigung. On 14 October, he claimed two B-17s during the Schweinfurt raid. On 12 May 1944, he was hit by return fire from a bomber formation and was badly wounded. Despite this, he baled out of his Bf 109. Following recovery from his wounds, Franzisket led fighter leaders' courses from 1 October 1944. On 15 December 1944, he rejoined JG 27 and was appointed Kommodore on 30 December. Franzisket was credited with 43 victories all claimed in the Mediterranean or the Western Front.

"The engine of one Fort burst into flames and soon the entire ship was afire. Another was burning from waist to tail. It seemed both the pilot and co-pilot of another ship had been killed. It started towards us out of control. I moved the squadron over. Still it came. Again we moved. This time the stricken Fortress stalled, went up on its tail, then slid down."

After their firing runs, the defending fighters split into twos and fours and curved around to attack the formation a second time. The action lasted about ten minutes, and it ended in a swirling dogfight between fighters as the US escorts converged on the scene. Then, as the defending fighters exhausted their ammunition, they dived away from the fight and headed for home. Twenty B-17s were shot down in that first encounter.

Even as the initial action was drawing to a close, a second large formation was assembling over Magdeburg to engage the raiders. The core of this battle formation comprised a powerful force of 42 Messerschmitt Bf 110 and Me 410 bomber-destroyers from ZG 26 and ZG 76. Covering these, though they were also expected to engage the bombers, were seventy Bf 109s and Fw 190s from JG 3, JG 302 and some smaller units.

For a second time, a large force of German fighters charged headlong into a formation of US bombers. The sight of so many of the enemy fighters closing rapidly from ahead reminded Captain Ed Curry, bombardier in a B-17 of the 401st Bomb Group, of his vulnerability:

"Sitting in the nose of the B-17, one felt terribly exposed. The nearest thing to it is that dream where you are walking down the road with no clothes on; that was what it felt like when the battle began. You knew the glass around you wasn't worth ten cents for protection, the smallest round or fragment would go clean through it."

Yet help was at hand. This time the blow was aimed at the head of the bomber stream, which enjoyed the protection of 80 P-51s from the 4th and 354th Fighter Groups. The escorts were present in sufficient numbers, in the right place, to blunt the German attack.

◄ Bf 109 Gs of III./JG 27 drawn up ready for action at their base at Wiesbaden/Erbenheim in the spring of 1944. (IWM)

▼ Emblem of I. Gruppe JG 1

Lieutenant Nicholas Megura, flying a P-51 of the 4th Fighter Group watched the approaching German formation:

"Twelve-plus smoke-trails were seen coming from 12 o'clock and high, 30 miles ahead. 'Upper' [the Group leader] positioned the Group up sun, below condensation height, and waited. Trails finally positioned themselves at nine o'clock to the bombers and started to close. Six thousand feet below the trails were 20-plus single-engined fighters in line abreast, sweeping the area for 20-plus twin-engine rocket-carrying aircraft. 'Upper' led Group head-on into the front wave of enemy aircraft."

The Mustangs' spoiling action forced several twin-engined fighters to abandon their attacks, while others held their course and launched their hefty 21 cm

▲ The Fw 190 A-4, W.Nr. 581. of Lt. Eberhard Burath carried the chevron and bar of the Gruppenadjutant of I./JG 1 and was adorned in the distinctive black and white striped cowling of the Geschwader.

FOCKE-WULF FW 190 A-4, W.NR. 518
Lt Eberhard Burath,
Gruppenadjutant of I./JG 1, April 1943

► The twelve victory markings displayed on the 354th Fighter Squadron's P-51B-5 nicknamed 'Woody's Maytag' was flown by Capt. Robert R. Woody represents ten enemy aircraft claimed in the air and two on the ground. However four of the former were shared victories, so his total in the air was actually seven with his claims being made between 5 April through 24 April 1944.

mortars at the bombers. The salvoes of rockets scorched past several bombers, frightening their crews but detonating too far away to cause serious damage to any of them.

As the bomber-destroyers emerged from the rear of the US bomber formation, other Mustangs pounced on them. The nimble escorts did great execution, shooting down 14 of the big twin-engined fighters in quick succession.

Behind the heavy fighters came the single-engined fighters, 70 Bf 109s and Fw 190s. *Leutnant* Hans Iffland of JG 3, flying a Bf 109, recalled:

"During the firing run everything happened very quickly, with the closing speed of about 800 kilometres per hour. After firing my short burst at one of the B-17s I pulled up over it; I had attacked from slightly above, allowing a slight deflection angle and aiming at the nose. I saw my rounds exploding around the wing root and tracer rounds from the bombers flashing past me. As I pulled up over the bomber I dropped my left wing to see the results of my attack and also to give the smallest possible target at which their gunners could aim. Pieces broke off the bomber and it began to slide out of the formation."

The air battle in front of Berlin also lasted a little over

BOEING B-17F FLYING FORTRESS, "MISS OUACHITA" 42-3040

Serving with 91st Bomber Group USAF Bassingbourne, England early 1944. This aircraft was lost on February 22nd 1944 during an attack on the Luftwaffe airfield of Guetersloh in Germany. The aircraft was shot down by Major Heinz Bar of II./JG 1 in a Fw 190.

ten minutes. Thanks to the Mustangs' efforts, however, bomber losses this time were considerably lighter than during the previous engagement. Only seven bombers were shot down or damaged and forced to leave the formation, to be finished off later as stragglers.

It was shortly after 13.00 hrs, and the surviving bombers closed formation as they moved on the enemy capital. In each of the three Bomb Divisions the squadrons moved into line astern as the leaders commenced their bombing runs, but now the weather intervened to protect the targets. At first it had seemed that the lead bombardier in each formation could make a visual bomb run, but at the critical moment, when they were committed to this course of action, cloud drifted in to obscure the aiming points. By then it was too late to shift to a radar-controlled bomb run.

No aircraft in the 1st Division hit its primary target at Erkner, and the attackers unloaded their bombs mainly on the Köpenick and Weissensee districts of the city which were clear of cloud. It was a similar story for the 3rd Bomb Division, which missed the primary target at Klein-Machnow and bombed Steglitz, Zehlendorf and other districts.

Only a few Liberators of the 2nd Bomb Division ran in to attack their primary target, the Daimler-Benz aero-engine works at Genshagen. The remaining B-24s

▲ A B-24 Liberator of the 445th Bomb Group shot down by Flak near Berlin during the 6 March action.

attacked secondary targets in and around the capital.

The defence of targets in these areas was the responsibility of the *Luftwaffe* 1. *Flak Division*, with four *Flak Regiments* equipped with more than 400 guns of 88 mm, 105 mm, and 128 mm calibre. These were positioned so that for the bombers to reach their targets, they had to fly through an inferno of anti-aircraft fire. To quote Ed Curry again:

"I'd been to Oschersleben and the Ruhr, but I'd never seen Flak as heavy as that they had over Berlin. It

▲ Major Hans Kogler, the commander of III./ZG 26, led the head-on attack by destroyer units operating against a US formation flying towards Berlin on 6 March 1944.

► An example of a large 128 mm Flak gun - a key element in the defence of the Reich's cities..

wasn't just the odd black puff, it was completely dense; not just at one altitude, but high and low. There was a saying that you see the smoke only after the explosion; but that day we actually saw the red of the explosions. One shell burst near us, and we had chunks of shell tear through the radio room and the bomb bay."

Lieutenant Lowell Watts, piloting a B-17 of the 388th Bomb Group, was another of those who had cause to remember the effectiveness of the Berlin *Flak*. His formation began its bombing run on the Oranienburg district.

"Then the Flak hit us. They didn't start out with wild shots and work in closer. The first salvo they sent up was right on us. We could hear the metal of our plane rend and tear as each volley exploded. The hits weren't direct. They were just far enough away so they didn't take off a wing, the tail, or blow the plane up; they would just tear a ship half apart without completely knocking it out. Big, ragged holes appeared in the wings and the fuselage. Kennedy, the co-pilot, was watching nothing but the instruments, waiting for the tell-tale indication of a damaged or ruined engine. But they kept up their steady roar, even as the ship rocked from the

►► "Flak you could walk on" was a phrase often used by returning bomber crews. This is the sight that greeted the B-24s of the 2nd Bomb Division as they passed over the Spandau district of Berlin during the attack on the city on 6 March 1944.

nearness of the Flak bursts.

"The Flak was coming up as close as ever, increasing in intensity. Above and to the right of us a string of bombs trailed out from our lead ship. Simultaneously our ship jumped upwards, relieved of its explosive load as the call 'Bombs away!' came over the interphone. Our left wing ship, one engine feathered, dropped behind the formation. Shortly afterwards, it seemed like a long time, the Flak stopped. We had come through it and all four engines were purring away."

Unless they saw an enemy aircraft fall out of formation in a spectacular manner, those manning the guns had little idea of the effect their fire was having. Serving with a double-battery of Heavy *Flak Abteilung* 422 at Marwitz, south of Oranienburg, 15-year-old *Luftwaffenhelfer* Werner Synakiewicz tracked a passing bomber through the telescopes of his rangefinder. During the engagement his unit's sixteen 88 mm guns fired more than a hundred rounds. He watched as the shells detonated in exactly the right place, just below the aircraft, but the gunners' repeated salvoes seemed to have no effect at all. The bombers, seemingly made of steel and impervious to the fire, droned on as if nothing had happened. Synakiewicz had no idea how terrifying it was to be on the receiving end of such a bombardment.

The *Flak* knocked down only four bombers, but it damaged several others sufficiently to force them to leave the formation. Nearly half the bombers that reached Berlin collected *Flak* damage of some sort or other.

As the bombers emerged from the *Flak* zones, 14 Messerschmitt Bf 110 night fighters from NJG 5 followed them at a safe distance like so many vultures, looking for lone stragglers that they could easily finish off. They had not bargained on the presence of Mustangs so deep inside German territory, however, and the US escorts pounced on the lumbering night fighters and despatched ten of their number within the space of a few minutes; the survivors beat a hasty retreat.

As the bomber formations left the target area, scores of wounded machines trailed behind them as their crews sought to make their way home. Flight Officer Bernie Dopko, piloting a B-17 of the 388th Bomb Group, had both of his starboard engines wrecked by *Flak*. He shut both down and feathered the propellers, but no longer able to keep up with its formation, the lone bomber came under attack from fighters and suffered further damage. Also, the bomber's rear gunner received severe head injuries. Dopko recalled:

"I remember a head-on pass with the bullets raking our fuselage – the very same ah-ah-ah-ah noise we used to make as kids when we played at dogfighting."

▶ A B-17 of the 94th Bombardment Group on its way to Berlin.

"As the Germans were circling for another pass, I manoeuvred the plane as best I could to appear that we were out of control and headed down to the deck. I guess it worked, as the attack was broken off and we levelled out below 50 feet."

That left Dopko and his crew some 350 miles inside enemy territory, alone and at low altitude. On its two remaining engines the badly damaged aircraft could reach only 115 mph in level flight, and it had insufficient power to climb to a safer altitude. But from then on fortune smiled on the crew. The defences ignored the lone, low-flying aircraft, which was allowed to complete its laborious journey back to England.

Other US pilots resorted to different measures to get home. During a lengthy dogfight with enemy fighters near the target, Lieutenant Rod Starkey of the 357th Fighter Group ran his P-51's Merlin engine at maximum war

▶ A photograph taken from the starboard gun position on a B-17 of the 303rd Bombardment Group shows a Bf 109 coming into attack.

emergency power for much longer than laid down in the manual. In the end, even that redoubtable piece of engineering issued a protest and started to lose power. Each time Starkey advanced the throttle, the engine would suddenly quit; each time he retarded the throttle, the engine would also quit. He decided his best chance was to join one of the bomber formations heading westwards away from the target. That move was fraught with its own dangers, however, for any single-engined machine nearing a bomber formation could expect to be regarded as hostile and treated accordingly. From experience, Starkey knew full well that the bombers' gunners were liable to shoot first and ask questions later. So the P-51 pilot closed on the bomber formation with the utmost caution:

"Everything had to be done slowly. You went in sideways showing your silhouette, never approaching the bombers from behind, above, or in any manner that could be thought threatening, but taking plenty of time and

showing the silhouette of the wings. I was able to get in underneath the wing of a B-17 and flew back to England, not escorting the bombers but with the bombers escorting me."

For the time being the defending fighters had spent their force, and during the first half-hour of the withdrawal there was a lull in the fighting around the bombers. During that time fresh squadrons of Thunderbolts arrived to relieve the Mustangs, most of which were low on fuel and ammunition.

The action around the bombers resumed at 14.40 hrs, when *Luftwaffe* single-engined fighters that had taken part in the noon action returned to the fray after being refuelled and re-armed. Other fighters came in from units based in France and Belgium, which had missed the earlier fighting.

Several more bombers were shot down, before more US escorts arrived to drive off the attackers. One of the

▲ Major Heinz Bär pictured examining B-17 F 'Miss Ouachita' of the 91st Bomb Group which he shot down on 22 February 1944. Heinz Bär was credited with 220 victories of which 21 were heavy bombers, but was killed post-war when the light aircraft he was piloting crashed. At the time of this photograph, Bär had been with 6./JG 1 for some two months, arriving from a fighter training school in the south of France. Despite his experience and victory score, he was posted to the unit as an ordinary pilot on account of his differences of opinion with Göring. Note that Ofw. Leo Schuhmacher, the NCO standing behind Bär, is wearing a US flight jacket, a coveted trophy.

'THE BLOODY HUNDREDTH'

As mentioned elsewhere, the 100th Bomb Group was hit hardest during the action on 6 March 1944, losing 15 of the 36 B-17s it sent out. Most of those losses occurred during the initial head-on encounter with German fighters. The unit had suffered heavy losses during other missions, and as a result it gained the grim sobriquet 'The Bloody Hundredth'. Many of that unit's members believed – and some still believe – that the *Luftwaffe* had a long-standing grudge against their particular Bomb Group. They believed that the enemy fighter pilots sought out the bombers bearing the unit's D-in-a-Square tail marking and made a point of attacking those. Rumour in the USAAF had it that the grudge originated when one of the unit's B-17s suffered damage, left its formation, and came under repeated attack from German fighters. The bomber lowered its undercarriage – a recognised sign of surrender – and the German fighters moved into close formation to escort the bomber to an airfield. At that point the B-17's gunners opened fire at one of the fighters and shot it down. The bomber was then shot down.

Whatever the truth of the story of the apparently surrendering B-17, it is clear that the rumours of a *Luftwaffe* grudge were unfounded. When interviewing German fighter pilots, this writer made a point of asking if any US bomber unit tail marking, and in particular the D-in-a-Square, held any significance to them. All answered in the negative. When told the reason for the question, the most common reaction was amusement. It should be pointed out that during the action on 6 March 1944, when the 100th Bomb Group suffered its heaviest loss, the German fighters attacked from head-on. From that angle the bombers' tail markings could not be seen until the fighters had completed their attacks.

Adolf Galland summed up the general feeling on this matter when he told this writer: *"When they reached an American formation my pilots had something better to do than look at the tails of the bombers before they decided whether to attack!"*

▲ Taken from a B-17, this photograph shows a Bf 110 heavy fighter coming into attack a bomber formation.

THE BLOOD-LETTING

The year 1944 was one of steady decline for the *Luftwaffe* day fighter force, which proved quite unable to make good the losses in personnel it suffered at the hands of the American escorts. The translated document reproduced below, from the Ic (Intelligence) department of the office of the *Luftwaffe* Inspector General of Fighters (*Generalmajor* Adolf Galland), gave the day fighter force's claims and losses in aircraft and personnel during the first six months of 1944. A point of interest is the so-called 'Daventry Figure' quoted at the end of each month's list. This gave the losses admitted by the Allies and broadcast over the BBC overseas service transmitter at Daventry, figures accepted by the Germans as being accurate. Comparison of the 'certain successes' and the Daventry figures reveals an average German overclaim during the large-scale day battles of almost 50 per cent. However, the Daventry figures refer only to those aircraft which failed to return to friendly territory and exclude those which subsequently crashed there. It should be also mentioned that Allied overclaiming during these hard-fought actions was much higher than 50 per cent. Yet that mattered little, for the aim of the daylight attacks – the destruction of the *Luftwaffe* as an effective fighting force – was successfully achieved.

Gruppe 1 (IC)   **Kladow-Hottengrund 17.8.44**

Inspector General of Fighters

Large-scale Incursions into the Reich Area (by day), January-June 1944

Month	Days with large incursions	Own single-engined sorties	Own twin-engined sorties	Certain	Successes Probable	Daventry
Jan	9	2467	1294	288 (+28 Flak)	89 (+13 Flak)	227
Feb	12	3591	808	529 (+120 Flak)	154 (+17 Flak)	388
Mar	18	3347	400	355 (+119 Flak)	71 (+37 Flak)	405
Apr	18	4470	541	554 (+163 Flak)	122 (+40 Flak)	577
May	19	4558	291	550 (+224 Flak)	67 (+36 Flak	456
June	11	1082	562	156 (+92 Flak)	32 (+21 Flak)	163
Totals	**87**	**19515**	**3896**	**2432 (+746 Flak)**	**535 (+164 Flak)**	**2216**

Own Losses

Month	Dead	Personnel missing	Wounded	Destroyed	Aircraft missing	Damaged
Jan	133	27	104	209	24	107
Feb	171	54	141	309	46	155
March	115	104	103	269	87	163
April	209	61	125	302	51	151
May	210	66	186	419	68	243
June	114	27	58	144	22	75
Totals	**952**	**339**	**717**	**1712**	**298**	**894**

►► Streaming white glycol vapour from a punctured cooling system, a Bf 109 goes down before the guns of a US escort fighter. In an increasingly common sight in the skies over Germany by late 1943, the Bf 109 G-6 of Uffz. Robert Pautner of 9./JG 26 falls prey to the P-47 of Lt. Leroy Ista of the 353rd FG near Gelsenkirchen on 5 November 1943, shortly after III./JG 26 had attempted to attack B-17s of the Third Bomb Division. Pautner managed to bale out suffering from a shoulder wound.

last bombers to go down in the action was B-17 'Flakstop' of the 452nd Bomb Group. Lieutenant Alan Willis, the co-pilot, watched as a succession of *Luftwaffe* fighters come sweeping in to deliver attacks from head-on:

"I remember a head-on pass with the bullets raking our fuselage – the very same ah-ah-ah-ah noise we used to make as kids when we played at dogfighting (this particular ah-ah-ah-ah killed the tail gunner). The Nos 3 and 4 engines had been hit and evidently the oil lines had too, because the props wouldn't feather no matter how I fiddled with the switches. Next we were hit in the leading edge of the port wing, probably by a 30 mm shell which flattened out a section about 30 feet long. So now on the port side we had two engines and no airfoil, and on the starboard side an airfoil but no engines. Nos 1 and 2 engines were at full rpm, Nos 3 and 4 were windmilling and the vibration began. Wagner [the aircraft captain] and I were both at the controls, trying to hold 'Flakstop' steady. But it was like trying to hold a trip-hammer. . ."

Steadily losing altitude the Fortress continued heading west, the crew hoping against hope that they could keep it in the air long enough to reach England. But then the bomber's port wing burst into flames and its fate was sealed. The captain gave the order to bale out and Willis followed the navigator through the open bomb bay:

"I missed the bomb bay doors by an inch or so and counted to ten – leaving out three through nine – and pulled the ripcord. To my rather frantic surprise nothing happened. The snap cords pulled open the pack, but the pilot chute and the neatly folded pile of white nylon just lay there on my chest. Thinking 'It's not supposed to work this way', I grabbed handfuls of material and fed it into the wind. This worked, and the chute opened with a shoulder-rending jerk."

Soon after he landed, Alan Willis was picked up by the Dutch resistance. He would pass down the escape line, and would finally link up with US troops west of Paris in the following September.

So ended the action on 6 March 1944. Of the 814 B-17s and B-24s that set out to attack Berlin, 672 attacked primary or secondary targets in the general area of the target. On that day the German air defence system was more effective than it had ever been before, or would ever be again. Sixty-nine B-17s and B-24s failed to return, including four aircraft with serious damage that put down in Sweden. A further 60 bombers landed

at airfields in England with severe damage, and 336 more returned with lesser amounts of damage. Of the bombers that failed to return, 42 were certainly or probably lost to fighter attack, 13 fell to *Flak*, five fell to fighters and *Flak*, and five were lost in collisions with friendly or enemy aircraft. The causes of the remaining four losses cannot be ascertained. A total of 691 escorts took part in the operation, of which 11 were destroyed and eight returned with severe damage. Ten escorts fell to fighter attack and one to *Flak*.

The unit hit hardest that day, the 100th Bomb Group, lost 15 of its 36 B-17s, most of them during the first head-on clash. The 95th Bomb Group, which flew with the 100th in the 13th Combat Wing, lost eight bombers. The 388th Bomb Group lost seven B-17s and the 91st lost six. Between them, these four Bomb Groups took more than half of the US bomber losses suffered that day.

By its nature, an account of this type focuses on the units involved in the heaviest fighting, and which were therefore likely to suffer the heaviest losses. To put matters into perspective, it should be noted that the remaining 33 bomber losses were spread more or less evenly across 19 Bomb Groups. Moreover, six Bomb Groups flew on the mission to Berlin without losing a single bomber.

In contesting the incursion on 6 March the *Luftwaffe* flew 528 fighter sorties, of which 369 probably made contact with the raiders. Sixty-two German fighters, 16 per cent of those that made contact, were destroyed and 13 damaged. The twin-engined fighter units took the heaviest losses. *Nachtjagdgeschwader* 5 lost ten of the 14 Messerschmitt Bf 110 night fighters it sent up and *Zerstörergeschwader* 26 lost 11 of the 18 Messerschmitt Bf 110 and Me 410 bomber destroyers it committed. The *Luftwaffe* lost 44 aircrew killed, including two leading aces. A further 23 aircrew were wounded.

Due to the presence of cloud over the targets, the attacks on the three primary targets around Berlin all failed. Only the Genshagen aero engine plant was hit, and that was attacked by only a quarter of the force assigned to it.

The 6 March attack on Berlin gave some important pointers for the future, however. It demonstrated that from now on no target in Germany was immune from attack by day from a strong force of bombers accompanied by a powerful fighter escort. Moreover the *Luftwaffe* could ill afford the loss of 67 trained aircrew, many of whom had considerable fighting experience, in a single day.

The raiders returned to Berlin in force on the 8th, the 9th and the 22nd March; on the 15th and the 23rd they

► Camera gun stills taken from German fighter attacks showing the destruction of B-17 Flying Fortresses and B-24 Liberators. The sequence at the bottom of the page, showing Liberators under attack, was taken on 8 May 1944 by Ofw. Gerhard Marburg, formerly of Sturmstaffel 1, who shot down a B-24 that day whilst flying with II.(Sturm)/JG 4.

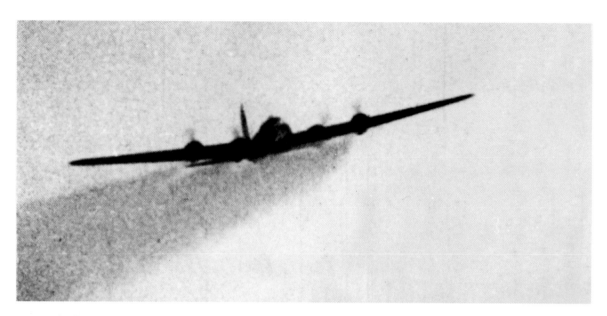

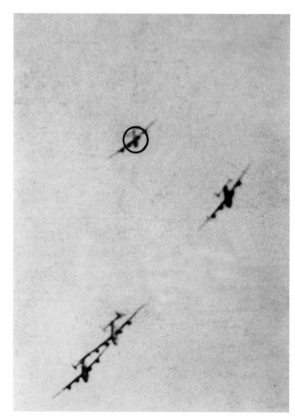

visited Braunschweig; and on the 16th they inflicted further destruction on the aircraft industry. The lumbering German twin-engined bomber-destroyers, burdened with their batteries of air-to-air mortars and heavy cannon, continued to fall as easy prey whenever they came up against the rampaging escorts. The worst drubbing of all was during the action on the 16th. As a force of 43 Messerschmitt Bf 110s was moving into position to launch its rockets at a US bomber formation near Augsburg, Mustangs of the 354th Fighter Group pounced on the would-be attackers, shot down 26 and scattered the remainder.

The *Luftwaffe* single-engined fighter force was now in a difficult position: previously the trend had been to fit these machines with increased armament so that they might more easily destroy the tough four-engined bombers, but this meant extra weight, which placed them at a disadvantage when they found themselves dog-fighting with US escorts.

Throughout March the American losses were not light, but, thanks to the vast supply and training organisations, they were bearable. For the *Luftwaffe* the position was, as we have already observed, quite different. During March the loss of trained aircrew was approximately the same as that in the previous month. The casualty list included *Oberleutnant* Egon Mayer, the commander of JG 2 and pioneer of the head-on attack, whose 102 victories included 25 heavy bombers; Oberst Wolf-Dietrich Wilcke, commander of JG 3 with 162 victories (four heavy bombers); Hauptmann Hugo Frey with 32 victories (26 heavy bombers); and Oberleutnant Gerhard Loos, 92 victories (two heavy bombers). The *Luftwaffe* had staked its all on the defence of the homeland, but it was clear this was not enough. Inexorably, the control of the airspace over the Reich was

◄ Oberstleutnant Wolf-Dietrich Wilcke, Kommodore of JG 3 and holder of the Ritterkreuz with Swords and Oakleaves, fell prey to Mustangs east of Braunschweig on 23 March 1944. Wilcke was a veteran of the Channel Front, North Africa and Russia, was an extremely respected figure within the Jagdwaffe.

being prised from the German grasp.

The end of March 1944 saw the American daylight offensive within sight of achieving its declared aim of bringing about the collapse of the enemy day fighter force. The Achilles Heel of the German wartime economy was seen to be its oil industry, and the hard-fought campaign to hit major centres of production will be described in the next Chapter.

10

THE CAMPAIGN AGAINST THE GERMAN OIL INDUSTRY

April-September 1944

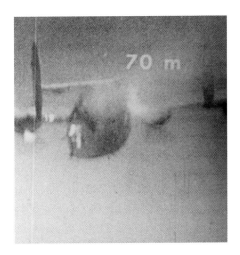

"The greatest danger lies in the threat to the fuel supply. Here the destruction of a relatively limited number

of targets would result in a complete paralysis of the Luftwaffe, all motorised units, the military

and civilian means of transportation, and the Navy."

Luftwaffe Plans Division Report, July 1944

The spring of 1944 saw German armed forces on each of the major battlefronts bracing themselves to meet expected sledgehammer blows from the enemy. In the East there were plenty of signs that the Red Army was gathering itself for the gigantic offensive, once the thaw ended and the ground dried sufficiently to allow the resumption of ground operations. In Italy, there were similar signs that the Allies were about to launch further thrusts, and in the West it was clear that preparations for the long-heralded Anglo-American invasion of north-western Europe were in their final phase. Of all the forthcoming battles, the latter was likely to be the most decisive. Should it fail, there could be no further attempt for at least a year, and large German forces would be released to re-establish the initiative in Russia.

Above all else the German High Command now needed to buy time: time to bring into service the new high performance submarines, jet fighters and bombers, and the robot bombardment weapons on which the Nazi leaders pinned their hopes of victory.

During April and May 1944, when the RAF bombers concentrated their efforts against targets in France, Holland and Belgium as part of the invasion preparations, there was a marked reduction in the previous rate and scale of the night attacks on German cities. When the bombers did strike at targets in Germany, these were almost invariably situated along the western fringe of the country through which reinforcements and supplies would pass once the land battle had been joined.

In the spring of 1944 there were few grounds for optimism among senior Luftwaffe officers, but one area of satisfaction concerned the speed and manner in which the German aircraft industry had restored production after its earlier pounding. During May 1944, deliveries of single- and twin-engined fighters to the Luftwaffe were nearly 50 per cent greater than in January; 2,213 aircraft compared with 1,550. For those charged with defending the Reich, the success of the programmes to disperse production and simultaneously to step up the number of fighters built was most encouraging. Discussing these figures with senior officers during a conference in May 1944, Hermann Göring was in a bullish mood:

"I must have 2,000 fighters in the shortest possible time, even if the battlefronts get nothing at all . . . The schools will have to make do with repaired aircraft. And then I shall want the 2,000 to be increased to 2,500. I must be in a position to meet any incursion into the Reich with 2,000 fighters. Then heaven help you if you don't send the enemy to blazes! [...] If we can stop these enemy incursions it will help the battlefronts. If the enemy is still contemplating invasion we'll give him something to think about when he suddenly finds himself confronted with 1,000 fighters within the next fortnight, just when he thinks he has settled accounts with our fighter force!"

◄◄ An Fw 190 A-8 of II./JG 300, with its red Geschwader fuselage band, landing at Löbnitz towards the end of 1944. The presence of the drop tank still in place suggests that the aircraft had not been in action.

STRENGTH OF LUFTFLOTTE REICH

31ST MAY 1944

Unit	Aircraft Type	Number Available	Number Serviceable	Unit	Aircraft Type	Number Available	Number Serviceable
Jagdgeschwader 1				Zerstörergeschwader 26			
Stab	Fw 190	2	(2)	I. Gruppe	Me 410	20	(6)
I. Gruppe	Fw 190	3	(15)	II. Gruppe	Me 410	50	(24)
II. Gruppe	Fw 190	2	(20)	III. Gruppe	Me 262	6	(1)
III. Gruppe	Bf 109	8	(21)		Bf 110	9	(9)
Jagdgeschwader 3				Zerstörergeschwader 76			
Stab	Bf 109	4	(2)	I. Gruppe	Me 410	47	(25)
I. Gruppe	Bf 109	6	(9)	II. Gruppe	Me 410	33	(0)
II. Gruppe	Bf 109	9	(23)		Bf 110	3	(2)
III. Gruppe	Bf 109	1	(9)	Nachtjagdgeschwader 1			
IV.(Sturm) Gruppe	Fw 190	4	(1)	Stab	He 219	2	(1)
Jagdgeschwader 5					Bf 110		
I. Gruppe	Bf 109	3	(36)	I. Gruppe	He 219, Me 410	33	(26)
II. Gruppe	Bf 109	4	(36)	II. Gruppe	He 219, Bf 110	21	(11)
Jagdgeschwader 11				III. Gruppe	Bf 110	17	(17)
Stab	Bf 109	4	(3)	IV. Gruppe	Bf 110	23	(14)
I. Gruppe	Fw 190	8	(20)	Nachtjagdgeschwader 2			
II. Gruppe	Bf 109	1	(14)	Stab	Ju 88	4	(4)
III. Gruppe	Fw 190	28	(11)	I. Gruppe	Ju 88	31	(21)
10. Staffel	Fw 190, Bf 109	10	(7)	II. Gruppe	Ju 88	33	(19)
Jagdgeschwader 27				III. Gruppe	Ju 88	28	(18)
Stab	Bf 109	4	(4)	Nachtjagdgeschwader 3			
I. Gruppe	Bf 109	44	(34)	Stab	Ju 88, Bf 110	3	(3)
II. Gruppe	Bf 109	24	(12)	I. Gruppe	Bf 110	26	(22)
III. Gruppe	Bf 109	26	(20)	II. Gruppe	Ju 88	37	(13)
IV. Gruppe	Bf 109	22	(16	III. Gruppe	Bf 110	29	(20)
Jagdgeschwader 53				IV. Gruppe	Ju 88, Bf 110	32	(21)
II. Gruppe	Bf 109	31	(14)	Nachtjagdgeschwader 5			
Jagdgeschwader 54				Stab	Bf 110	3	(1)
III. Gruppe	Fw 190	23	(8)	II. Gruppe	Bf 110	19	(13)
Jagdgeschwader 300				IV. Gruppe	Bf 110	18	(8)
Stab	Fw 190	2	(1)	Nachtjagdgeschwader 6			
I. Gruppe	Bf 109	29	(19)	Stab	Bf 110	2	(1)
II. Gruppe	Fw 190	32	(23)	I. Gruppe	Bf 110, Do 217	24	(21)
III. Gruppe	Bf 109	27	(25)	II. Gruppe	Bf 110	10	(8)
Jagdgeschwader 301				III. Gruppe	Bf 110	18	(13)
I. Gruppe	Bf 109	25	(21)	IV. Gruppe	Bf 110	27	(22)
Jagdgeschwader 302				Nachtjagdgeschwader 7			
I. Gruppe	Bf 109	27	(11)	I. Gruppe	Ju 88	21	(9)
Jagdgeschwader 400				Nachtjagdgeschwader 101			
I. Gruppe	Me 163	10	(0)	I. Gruppe	Bf 110, Ju 88	39	(39)
Einsatz Staffel JG 104	Bf 109	4	(4)	II. Gruppe	Do 217	38	(28)
Einsatz Staffel JG 106	Bf 109	5	(3)	Nachtjagdgeschwader 102			
Einsatz Staffel JG 108	Bf 109	12	(6)	I. Gruppe	Bf 110	39	(14)
Zerstörergeschwader 1				II. Gruppe	Bf 110	39	(16)
II. Gruppe	Bf 110	30	(15)	Nachtjagdgruppe 10	Bf 109, Fw 190, He 219, Ta 154, Ju 88, Bf 110	23	(14)

Since the previous May the formation controlling operations by units based in metropolitan Germany, *Luftwaffenbefelshaber* Mitte, had been renamed *Luftflotte Reich*. At this time the front-line strength of the *Luftwaffe* was close to the peak it would ever attain, but even so its strength fell far short of that needed to meet its many commitments. On every battlefront, and in particular over the German homeland, the *Luftwaffe* was under severe pressure.

Following the severe losses suffered since the beginning of the year; there was a particularly grave shortage of single-engined fighter units. Between them, the two major formations responsible for the defence of the homeland, *Luftflotte Reich* and *Luftflotte 3*, had only 565 of these machines serviceable. That was far too few to defend targets from attacks by raiding forces accompanied by more than 700 escort fighters. Moreover the main German fighter types available, the Bf 109 G and Fw 190, were outclassed by the latest versions of the P-47 Thunderbolt and the P-51 Mustang they engaged in combat. A force of 82 twin-engined bomber destroyers was also available to engage the daylight raiders, yet the unwieldy Bf 110s and Me 410s suffered heavy losses whenever the American escorts caught them and these units would soon be disbanded. Almost every USAAF incursion into Germany led to a full-scale air battle in which the defenders usually took a fearful mauling.

To counter the RAF night attacks, the night fighter force had 474 serviceable fighters deployed for the defence of the German homeland. In addition there was *Jagdgeschwader 300*, designated as a day and night fighter unit and supposedly able to operate in either role.

Luftflotte 3, responsible for air operations on the western front, was braced to meet the long-awaited Allied invasion of northern France and, once the invasion began there were detailed plans to transfer fighter units from *Luftflotte Reich* to buttress the defences in the west. Several landing grounds had been pre-stocked with fuel and munitions, to enable incoming units to go into action soon after arrival. Although the move would leave the homeland devoid of fighter protection, it was expected, correctly, that following the invasion the Allies would employ heavy bombers to provide support for their troops in the battle area.

Otto Saur (in charge of the new production programme): *"We shall be turning out a thousand aircraft during the next eight days alone."*
Göring: *"Every one shall go to defend the Reich."*
Galland: *"But Luftflotte 2..."*
Göring: *"My order stands!"*

The large number of fighter pilots being killed or wounded in action was a more difficult problem to solve, however. The USAAF's war of attrition against the Luftwaffe day fighter force continued unabated, and every pilot killed or seriously wounded would take no part in the forthcoming imminent battle in France. Throughout April the day bombers and their escorts fought their way through the defences to hit their targets, and for the third month running the Luftwaffe day fighter force lost more than 300 aircrew, most of them pilots. At the end of April, *Generalmajor* Galland penned a grim report to his superiors, which boded ill for the future:

"Between January and April 1944 our day fighter arm lost more than 1,000 pilots. They included our best Staffel, Gruppe and Geschwader commanders . . . The time has come when our force is within sight of collapse."

Nor would the inflow of new pilots from the Luftwaffe's training schools bring much in the way of relief, for these lacked the skills necessary to survive in combat. By mid-1944 the fighter training schools were under severe pressure to produce replacements to fill gaps in the ranks of the fighter force, and were close to chaos.

Oberfähnrich Hans-Ulrich Flade had almost completed his training as a reconnaissance pilot when he received a posting to *Jagdgruppe 106* at Reichenbach in Bavaria where he was to retrain as a fighter pilot and convert to the Messerschmitt Bf 109 G. Many trainee pilots on the course had come to Reichenbach straight from initial flying training, so Flade's level of flying experience was well above the average for students. He could see that the standard of instruction at the school was poor. Most instructor pilots had been *'flown out'* in action. They were nervous, twitchy and tired men. In many cases they had seen three or more years of almost continuous action, and had crashed or baled out several times. Because of this, and the poor initial flying training the students had received before their arrival, JGr 106 had a high accident rate. Of nearly a hundred pilots that started the conversion course with Flade, more than thirty had been killed before it ended.

▲ Fighter ace Hauptmann Heinz Knocke served with JG 1 and JG 11 on home defence operations. He was credited with the destruction of 44 enemy aircraft, of which 19 were heavy bombers.

In the hands of an inexperienced pilot the Bf 109 G could turn into a vicious animal. If the pilot opened the throttle too quickly during the take-off, or if he tried to lift the fighter off the ground before it had reached full flying speed, it was liable to enter a torque stall in which it rolled onto its back and plunged into the ground.

The conversion course on to the 'Gustav' amounted to a mere 30 flying hours on the type, barely sufficient to enable a student to take off and land safely and carry out a few simple manoeuvres. To fly an aircraft in combat, especially against a well-equipped foe, a pilot needed to be able to operate his machine to the limits of its performance envelope, but putting pilots with such a sketchy training into action against the Mustangs was to send them to near-certain death. That, however, was the fate of the majority of the graduate pilots within a few weeks of joining their operational units.

Once again, Flade was fortunate. With only 30 hours' flying on the 'Gustav', he and another graduating pilot received orders to remain with *Jagdgruppe 106* – as instructors! As can be imagined, that gave the young *Oberfähnrich* some problems, and he recalled:

"My first student was a Hauptmann, a highly decorated Ju 88 bomber pilot with more than 300 combat missions, who was now converting on to day fighters. He said to me: `Are you my instructor?' I said I was. 'Well,' he said,

▲ Major 'Sepp' Wurmheller rose through the ranks in JG 2. He was killed in a dogfight over France in June 1944, when he collided with his wingman. At the time of his death his victory score stood at 102, which included 13 heavy bombers.

► Adolf Hitler congratulating Major Wilhelm Herget during the presentation of the Oakleaves to the Ritterkreuz in May 1944. Herget then commanded I/NJG 4 and his score stood at 41 night and 14 day victories. Other prominent night fighter pilots in the line-up are Oberst Günther Radusch, nearest the camera, the commander of NJG 2 with 53 night victories, and Major Rudolf Schönert, third from the left, the commander of the trials unit NJGr 10 with 60 night victories.

'we shall have to see about that.' But the Gruppe commander confirmed what I had said, and we took off together in a two-seater 'Gustav'. That bomber pilot very soon found out for himself that the '109 G was quite different from any other type he had previously flown. In fact, he did not complete the first landing. He made a mess of it and I had to take over from the back seat and bring the machine down. That broke the ice, and from then on we got on very well."

On 6 June 1944 Allied forces punched through the German coastal defences in Normandy, and established a sizeable bridgehead in northern France. The previous day the supreme Allied commander, General Dwight Eisenhower, had confidently told his men: "If you see aircraft over you, they will be ours."

The Luftwaffe did its best to prove him wrong. Under a long-standing contingency plan, the Luftwaffe despatched almost its entire home defence single-seat fighter force to airfields in France. Fifteen *Gruppen* of fighters, with some 300 aircraft, were involved in the move. Only three *Gruppen* of single-seat fighters, two from JG 300 and one from JG 301, remained behind to mount a token defence of the homeland. Events soon separated the incoming units from their plan, however. In his book 'The First and the Last', Adolf Galland described the problems they encountered:

"When the invasion finally came, the carefully made preparations immediately went awry. The transfer of the fighters into France was delayed for 24 hours because Oberkommando West would not give the order, expecting heavier landings to be attempted in the Pas de Calais area. The Luftwaffe finally issued the order on its own authority and the transfer began.

"Most of the carefully prepared and provisioned airfields assigned to the fighter units had been bombed and the units had to land at other hastily chosen landing grounds. The poor signals network broke down, causing further confusion. Each unit's advance parties came by Junkers 52, but the main body of the ground staff came by rail and most arrived days or even weeks later."

The three hundred incoming single-engined fighters, added to the hundred or so from *JG 2* and *JG 26* already based in France, represented the largest force the Luftwaffe could reasonably have assembled to contest the invasion. Yet even that force was too weak to achieve much against the Allied air forces supporting the invasion, which outnumbered them by about 10 to 1 in fighters.

◄ Me 410s of II./ZG 26 pictured during a training sortie. In the original photograph, the barrels of the BK 5 heavy cannon are just visible.

THE PROBLEM OF SABOTAGE

By 1944 the voracious demands of Germany's fighting services had stripped the nation's industries of most men of military age. In their place came hastily trained German women, volunteers and forced labourers from nations under German occupation, prisoners of war and concentration camp inmates. To take one example, the Henschel aircraft company near Berlin had a workforce of 12,500. Of those only about 2,375 were German men; 4,000 were German women, 5,250 were volunteer or forced labourers from the occupied territories and the remaining 875 were prisoners of war or inmates from concentration camps.

It is difficult enough to maintain quality standards when the workforce as a whole is motivated to achieve that end, but when even a small part of the workforce is bent on defeating that process whenever an opportunity presented itself, it can lead to serious problems.

Feldwebel Adolf Dilg had been wounded in action earlier in the war and had been declared unfit for combat flying. During the final year of the war he served at the Arado plant at Warnemünde as a test and delivery pilot for production Fw 190s. He heard of several instances of sabotage and told this writer:

"Aircraft were sabotaged in all sorts of ways. Sometimes we would find swarf in electrical junction boxes, or sand in oil systems. On two or three occasions brand new Focke Wulfs took off for their maiden flights and as they lifted off the ground one of the wheels fell off; the pin holding the wheel-retaining ring had 'accidentally' come adrift. Once, when I was delivering an aircraft, the engine suddenly burst into flames. I baled out and the aircraft crashed into a marshy area where the water rapidly extinguished the flames. When the wreckage was examined, it was found that somebody had jammed a couple of pyrotechnic flares between cylinders Nos 7 and 9, the two at the bottom of the rear row which became hottest when the engine was running. During the delivery flight the cylinders had duly heated up, cooked off the flares, and up went the engine. Every time we had such an incident the Gestapo would make a lot of fuss, but although they would take the odd scapegoat the problem of sabotage was one we had to live with."

▶ An Me 410 of II./ZG 26 carrying the 50 mm BK 5 cannon, a modification of the weapon fitted to German tanks. This single-shot weapon was fitted with an automatic system for reloading. The Luftwaffe had placed great hopes on the BK 5, but by the time it appeared in action in the spring of 1944, the US bombers had full escort cover. As a result, the unwieldy Me 410s suffered heavy losses and achieved little. Note the telescopic gunsight set into the windscreen.

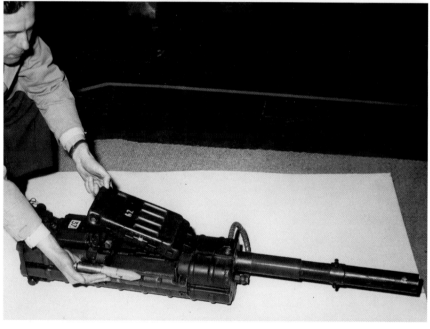

▲ The Rheinmetall MK 108 cannon carried by day and night fighters operating in the bomber-destroyer role, together with one of its destructive 30 mm rounds. The MK 108 was a blow-back operated, belt-fed cannon, using electric ignition, being charged and triggered by compressed air. Its extremely short barrel gave it its low muzzle velocity of between 500-540 metres per second with a maximum rate of fire of 650 rounds per minute. The weapon quickly earned a fearsome reputation amongst the Sturmgruppen and the Allied bomber crews who dubbed it the 'pneumatic hammer.'

As the fighter *Gruppen* arrived from Germany, their pilots found themselves pitchforked into a situation far beyond their previous experience and training. For all the problems of battling against the US raiding formations, the Reich air defence units had previously operated from permanent airfields with good facilities, and an established fighter control organisation. In the maelstrom of the battle over France it was quite different. There the *Luftwaffe* fighter units had to operate from field landing grounds, with minimal facilities and no effective ground control.

The loss of fighter pilots earlier in the year had been bad enough, but those suffered over France were far worse. Within a couple of weeks of the invasion the first fighter *Gruppen* had to be pulled back to Germany to reform after suffering heavy losses.

The crushing Allied air supremacy soon dominated the ground fighting in France. German soldiers in Normandy coined a catchphrase to describe the air situation from their viewpoint: *"If the aircraft above us are camouflaged, they are British; if they are silver, they are American. And if they aren't there at all, they are German!"*

During the weeks following the invasion, the Allied strategic bomber forces were heavily committed to supporting the land battle, but once airfields had been established in the bridgehead, the Allied tactical air forces assumed a large proportion of the army's air support needs. The heavy bombers could now return to attacks on targets in Germany.

On 8 June, just two days after the landings in France, US General Carl Spaatz issued a directive to the commanders of the Eighth and Fifteenth Air Forces. As soon as the invaders were safely ashore, the strategic bombers were to refocus their attack on the enemy oil industry. As a general arrangement, the Eighth Air Force was to attack oil refineries in central and eastern Germany, while the Fifteenth Air Force went for those in Austria, Hungary, Rumania and southern Germany. Simultaneously, RAF Bomber Command was to attack refineries in the Ruhr area.

The offensive against the German oil industry had opened less formally in mid-May, but not until after the invasion of France did it gain momentum. The effect of the repeated attacks was both immediate and devastating. Compared with its output of aviation fuel of 175,000 tons in April, before the new phase of the offensive began, the German industry turned out less than a third – 55,000 tons – in June. Unless something was done, and done quickly, the *Luftwaffe* would find itself with an abundance of aircraft but no fuel with which to fly them.

Meanwhile, what of the Messerschmitt 410 super bomber-destroyer fitted with the big 50 mm cannon? Early in May 1944, II./ZG 26 completed its conversion to aircraft carrying the new weapon and went into action. *Feldwebel* Fritz Bucholz, a pilot serving with the unit, described the weapon and its use:

"When the Gruppe went into action it was always with aircraft carrying the same armament; we did not deliver attacks in company with Me 410s carrying smaller cannon or rockets. During our operations from Hildesheim we flew without the radio operator and the rear guns. That made the aircraft about 20 kph faster, it climbed faster and was more manoeuvrable. We had a Gruppe of Messerschmitt 109 Gs assigned to escort our Me 410s, but we cruised faster than they did. So we destroyer pilots had to throttle back slightly, to enable

◄ A B-24 Liberator disintegrating under the hail of 30 mm rounds fired from close range during an attack by a Sturmgruppe. The marker on the photograph indicates the firing range at the time it was taken.

► This B-17 of the 457th Bomb Group was fortunate to return to base bearing the scars of battle. The damage is consistent with that inflicted by a hit from a single 30 mm high-explosive/incendiary shell.

► An Fw 190 A-8/R8 of Sturmbock of JG 300. The rate of attrition of these aircraft during operations was so great that often they went into action without unit identification markings, as in this example.

▲ Feldwebel Hans Schaefer of IV./JG 3 wearing the 'Whites of the Eyes' insignia on his flying jacket, denoting that he was a Sturmgruppe pilot.

▼ A close-up of the cockpit of a Focke Wulf 190 showing the 30 mm armoured glazing panels mounted in a wooden frame. These panels and the extra 5 mm steel plates fitted to the side of the cockpit were to protect the pilot during close-range attacks against formations four-engined Allied bombers.

our escorts to keep up with us!

"The BK 5 carried 21 rounds, with a compressed air system for reloading. While firing it we had to hold the aircraft very steady, because if there was any 'G' at all the feed mechanism would jam. The ideal firing range for the BK 5 was 1,000 metres, and we had markings etched on the reflector sight to assist us to judge when we were that distance from the bomber."

Fritz Bucholz's flying logbook reveals the effectiveness of the BK 5 when it functioned properly, but also its generally poor reliability. He first went into action with the new weapon on 12 May against a raiding force near Dresden, but fired two rounds without observed effect before the reloading system jammed. On the following day he was again in action with his unit, but as the cannon fighters closed on a US bomber formation they were caught by Mustangs. The escorts shot down twelve Me 410s, including that flown by Bucholz, but he baled out and landed safely. On 29 May he used the heavy cannon to shoot down a Liberator near Warnemünde, and another near Rostock on 20 June. On 7 July he was involved in a large air battle near Halle, but again the cannon's reload mechanism failed.

In the course of these operations II./ZG 26 suffered heavy losses and achieved only a meagre success rate. In mid-July 1944, the unit, together with others operating the twin-engined bomber-destroyers, disbanded and most of the pilots retrained to fly single-engined fighters.

As mentioned earlier, when German single-engined fighters engaged the US escorts they found themselves at a severe disadvantage, for the weight of armament necessary to knock down the bombers caused a severe reduction in performance. To overcome this problem the *Luftwaffe* introduced the concept of using a separate and heavily armed *Sturmgruppe* to engage the bombers, with an escort of lightly armed fighters to fend off the American escorts.

The *Sturmgruppe* was to operate the A-8 R/8 version of the Fw 190, nicknamed the *Sturmbock* (Battering Ram). This aircraft carried two 30 mm MK 108 cannon in the wings, with 55 rounds per gun. This weapon was highly destructive but it had a relatively low muzzle velocity, so it was effective only at short range. To operate the cannon to maximum effect, German pilots would need to attack the bomber formation from the rear, moving in close to the target aircraft before opening fire.

FOCKE-WULF Fw 190 A-6 'WHITE 2', STURMSTAFFEL 1, DORTMUND EARLY 1944

As they closed in on their targets, the *Sturmbock* pilots had to brave the powerful defensive crossfire from the bombers. To give them a reasonable chance of survival, the modified Fw 190 carried twice the weight of armour of the standard fighter version in the form of 5 mm sheets of steel on either side of the cockpit and 30 mm thick slabs of laminated glass on each side of the canopy. The heavier armament and armour added about 400 pounds to the aircraft and imposed corresponding reductions in manoeuvrability, maximum speed and climbing performance.

The new *Sturmgruppen* were elite units, and their pilots were all volunteers. Before being accepted into the unit every pilot had to sign a document stating that he was willing to press home his attacks on the enemy bombers to short range. If he failed to destroy the enemy bomber with his guns, he was expected to close in and destroy it by ramming. Theoretically, any pilot who signed the affidavit and failed to carry out its conditions was liable to be arraigned before a court martial on the charge of cowardice in the face of the enemy, and if convicted, could face a firing squad. Yet there was no pressure on any pilot to sign the affidavit; those who chose not to do so simply did not join the ranks of the *Sturmgruppen*.

Under the previous tactics *Luftwaffe* fighter pilots flew in pairs or in fours to attack the enemy bombers, usually from head-on. Individual pilots decided when to open fire and when to break away. In the *Sturmgruppe*, on the other hand, the tactics were much more rigid. The Fw 190s were to fly in a nine-aircraft *Staffel* formation, with the leader in the middle and the rest flying on either side of him in close echelon. Succeeding *Staffeln* followed close behind that of the leader. The *Sturmgruppe* leader was to manoeuvre his force behind a

formation of enemy bombers, then allocate each of his *Staffeln* to attack a different part of it. Each *Staffel* was to remain in position behind the bombers until the last aircraft exhausted its heavy cannon ammunition, then all the fighters were to turn away in unison.

Since the heavyweight Fw 190 would be no match for US escorts in combat, the *Sturmgruppe* was itself to be escorted into action by two *Gruppen* of lightly armed Bf 109 Gs. The latter were to be fitted with up-rated engines, and their task was to hold off the US escorts long enough for the Focke-Wulfs to move in and deliver their lethal blow.

The *Gefechtsverband* (battle formation) comprising the *Sturmgruppe* and its two escorting *Gruppen*, employed about a hundred aircraft. Since the US bomber formations might be strung out in a column up to 90 miles in length, it was clear that the escorts could

▲ Gefr. Gerhard Vivroux of Sturmstaffel 1 (right) poses for a photograph by his Fw 190 A-6 'White 2' at Dortmund in early 1944. Clearly visible are the armoured glass side panel fitted to the aircraft's canopy and the large gauntlet and lightning emblem of Sturmstaffel 1 adorning the machine's cowling.

Emblem of Sturmstaffel 1

▲ Leutnant Walther Hagenah flew during the early Sturmgruppe missions with IV(Sturm)./JG 3, when he was credited with the destruction of two B-17s and two B-24s. In the final weeks of the war he converted to the Me 262 jet fighter.

not be present in strength everywhere. The plan was to vector the *Sturmgruppe* and its accompanying fighters into the bomber stream at a point about mid-way along its length. The essence of the *Sturmgruppe* tactics was to deliver a short but extremely sharp attack against a single combat box formation. Then the Focke-Wulfs and their covering Messerschmitts were to dive away, hoping to be clear before the vengeful Mustangs and Thunderbolts arrived in the area in force.

The *Sturmgruppe* differed from a regular *Luftwaffe* fighter unit in three fundamental respects: in the type of aircraft it flew, in the tactics it employed and in the determination of the men serving in it. The first such unit to be formed, *IV./JG 3*, received its complement of aircraft and pilots in May 1944 and began training for the new role immediately. Two other *Jagdgeschwader*, *JG 4* and *JG 300*, were both earmarked to convert one *Gruppe* to the new role when sufficient *Sturmbock* aircraft became available.

The first successful *Sturmgruppe* action took place on 7 July 1944, when a force of 756 Fortresses and 373 Liberators set out from England to bomb aircraft factories in the Leipzig area, and also the nearby synthetic oil production plants at Böhlen, Leuna-Merseburg and Lutzendorf.

As the bombers droned relentlessly eastward, the control officer of the *Luftwaffe's* 1. *Jagddivision* passed a steady stream of intercept vectors to Major Walther Dahl

"From such a range we could hardly miss. As the 30 mm explosive rounds struck home, we could see the structure of the enemy bombers literally falling apart in front of us."

► Three noteworthy Sturmgruppe leaders of JG 3. From right to left Oberst Walther Dahl, a leading exponent of this tactic, Hauptmann Wilhelm Moritz commanding IV(Sturm)./JG 3 and Leutnant Oskar Romm also of that unit.

► Major Walter Dahl photographed at Finsterwalde in September 1944 whilst Kommodore of JG 300. The floral wreath around the spinner of his Fw 190 was to congratulate him on his 75th aerial victory. In total he was credited with 128 victories which included 36 four-engined bombers. On 17 September 1944 he brought down a B-17 by ramming.

leading a fully assembled *Gefechtsverband*. The latter comprised the Fw 190s of *Hauptmann* Wilhelm Moritz's *IV.(Sturm)/JG 3*, and two covering *Gruppen* drawn from *JG 300*.

Just west of Leipzig, Dahl caught sight of his quarry: box after box of bombers, advancing eastwards in column. The German formation leader swung his force through a semi-circle then led it into position behind a combat wing of B-24s which, as luck would have it, was temporarily without fighter cover.

As the *Sturmgruppe* closed in, the individual *Staffeln* moved into close arrowhead formation and were allocated to attack different parts of the bomber formation. Each German pilot selected a Liberator and advanced unswerving towards it. The bombers' gunners put up spectacular return fire, and the sky became alive with the strings of sparkling tracer rounds. The German pilots, under strict orders to withhold their fire until they saw their *Staffel* leader open up, continued their advance.

Leutnant Walther Hagenah, one of the *Sturmgruppe* pilots who saw action that day, described the mood as he closed in on the enemy bombers:

"Our tactics were governed by the performance of our wing-mounted 30 mm cannon. Although the hexogen high explosive ammunition fired by this weapon was

◄ A Bf 109 G-6 of III./JG 3, which often flew in the escort role for the Sturmgruppe operations. The aircraft is ready to scramble, with the drop tank in place and the handle for the inertia starter already inserted in the starboard side of the engine cowling.

► ► 27 July 1944: a Lancaster on a daylight raid drops its bombload on a V-1 site in France through an overcast sky.

▼ A Bf 109 G-6 of 11./JG 26 taxiing past some locally recruited construction workers on a forward airfield in the West in the summer of 1944. The aircraft is finished in the then still standard 74/75/76 scheme and has the underside of the engine cowling painted yellow.

devastatingly effective, the gun's relatively low muzzle velocity meant that its accuracy fell off rapidly with range. And since we carried only 55 rounds per gun, sufficient for about five seconds' firing, we could not afford to waste ammunition in wild shooting from long range. To be sure of bringing down a bomber it was essential that we held our fire until we were right up close against the bombers. We were to advance like Frederick the Great's infantrymen, holding our fire until we could see 'the whites of the enemy's eyes'.

"During the advance each man picked a bomber and closed in on it. As our formation moved forwards, the American bombers would, of course, let fly at us with everything they had. I can remember the sky being almost alive with tracer. With strict orders to withhold our fire until the leader opened up, we could only grit our teeth and press on ahead. In fact, however, with the extra armour, surprisingly few of our aircraft were knocked down by the bombers' return fire. Like the armoured knights of the Middle Ages, we were well protected. A Staffel might lose one or two aircraft during the advance, but the rest continued relentlessly on."

The Focke-Wulfs continued their advance until they were about 100 yards behind the bombers. Then the leader opened fire and the rest of the Sturmbock aircraft followed suit.

"From such a range we could hardly miss. As the 30 mm explosive rounds struck home, we could see the structure of the enemy bombers literally falling apart in front of us. On average, three hits with 30 mm ammunition would be sufficient to knock down a four-engined bomber. The shortest burst was usually sufficient to achieve that."

The low squadron of the 492nd Bomb Group took the full shock of the Gefechtsverband attack. One by one its Liberators tumbled out of the sky until all eleven had been shot down: the entire squadron had been wiped out. Walther Hagenah was credited with the destruction of one of the heavy bombers. For its part the Sturmgruppe lost nine fighters shot down, and three more made crash landings. Five Sturmgruppe pilots were killed, but by Luftwaffe standards of the day it had been a successful defensive operation.

Walther Hagenah went into action with his Sturmgruppe on 18 and 20 July, destroying a B-17 on each occasion, and on 3 August when he shot down a B-24.

Although the pilots had signed affidavits indicating a willingness to ram enemy bombers if other means of destroying them failed, only rarely was it necessary to adopt this course of action, for once a pilot reached a firing position close behind a bomber, he could usually achieve a kill with his heavy cannon.

Of the pilots who did carry out ramming attacks, about half escaped without serious injury. One who did

▲ Aircrew of 467 RAAF Squadron gather to celebrate the 100th succesful mission flown by Lancaster R5868 on 12 May 1944. This famous Lancaster complete with its quotation from Herman Göring on the nose, survived the war and is now preserved at the RAF Museum in London.

not was *Obergefreiter* Heinz Papenburg of *Sturmgruppe JG 4*, whose cannon jammed at the vital moment during an attack on 27 August. So he continued on and rammed the B-24. One wing of his Focke-Wulf tore away during the collision, and as the pilot jumped from the spinning fighter he struck the tail and broke both legs. The unfortunate Papenburg descended by parachute but had to take the shock of the landing on his shattered limbs.

The US counter to the new *Sturmgruppe* tactics was to send forces of fighters to sweep in front of the bombers and along their flanks. The aim was to break up the ponderous German formation before it got anywhere near the bombers. Once a *Gefechtsverband* had been scattered, there was no way it could reassemble in the face of enemy attacks and the operation had to be abandoned.

Meanwhile the debilitating attacks continued against the German oil industry. The reader may get an idea of the industry's sufferings from the events which befell one of its plants, the Meerbeck refinery situated three miles north-west of Homberg on the west bank of the Rhine. The plant produced petrol, diesel oil and wax, from coke. A synthetic oil refinery was modular in construction, and damaged sections could be removed and replaced, and bomb damage could be repaired relatively quickly. For that reason, the Allied planners knew that regular, repeat attacks would be required if a sizeable drop in production was to be maintained.

In the new offensive, Meerbeck was one of the targets allocated to RAF Bomber Command. The first attack took place on the night of 26 June, when a small force of Mosquitoes delivered a precision raid which cut production of the previous daily figure of 176 tons by

Avro Lancaster R5868, POS serving with 467 RAAF Squadron, Waddington, 1944. The nose carries the famous Hermann Göring quote "No enemy plane shall fly over Reich Territory" and the impressive tally of 100 mission symbols, later rising to 137.

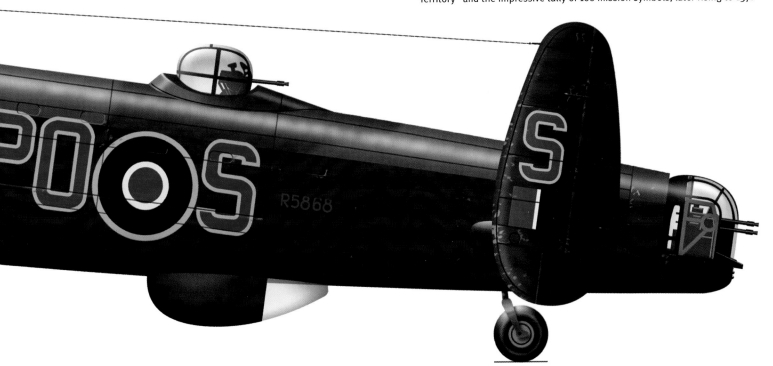

about one-third. Five days later, when the repairs were well advanced and the plant was turning out just over 100 hundred tons of fuel per day, the bombers returned. This time the attack destroyed the compressed air main and damaged all the gasholders, bringing production to a halt. By the night of 16 July, repairs enabled the plant to turn out 137 tons daily, but then a further night attack by Mosquitoes reduced daily production to 93 tons.

Four nights later, on 20 July, the RAF made its first moderately large-scale attack on the plant, with 147 heavy bombers. The bombing was accurate and four-fifths of the refinery was either destroyed or heavily damaged. Again production ceased. During this action, however, the German night fighter force provided a sharp reminder of its continuing effectiveness, and 20 heavy bombers (13.6 per cent of the force) were shot down.

Repair work was again progressing, though not sufficiently to allow production to resume, when the RAF returned yet again on 27 August. This time the raid planners at RAF Bomber Command headquarters decided to mount a potentially risky experiment. They judged that the *Luftwaffe*'s day fighter force had been depleted sufficiently to permit a daylight attack on the Meerbeck refinery. Not since the attack on the Cologne power stations in August 1941, had the RAF attempted

to mount a large-scale daylight attack on a target in the enemy homeland. A total of 243 bombers took part in the attack, supported by 16 squadrons of Spitfires carrying extra fuel tanks and operating at extreme range. The experiment paid off. Not a single bomber was lost, and the attack disrupted the repair work and prevented any resumption of production before the end of October.

In view of the losses suffered during the previous

▲ Groundcrew check trolleys of 500 lb MC (Medium Capacity) bombs just before loading up a Lancaster of RAF Bomber Command in readiness for another raid over Germany.

► The Hibernia plant seen in the latter part of the war, after the erection of nets decorated with dummy roads and houses at 'C'. The fields at 'E' were disguised as houses and roads resemble a housing estate. The road between 'E' and 'E1' had been covered by a tunnel of netting.

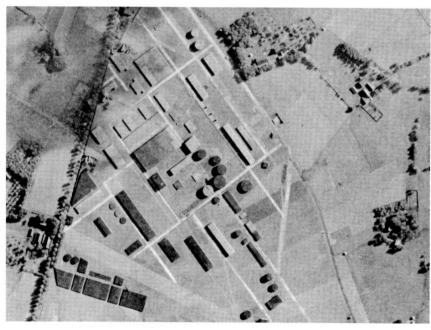

▲ Complementing the camouflage at the Hibernia plant (above) was an elaborate decoy on open ground some four kilometres away to the north, showing the main features of the real plant before it was camouflaged. By lighting fires at the critical time during night raids, such decoys could be effective in drawing bombs away from the real target.

attack at night, this result was particularly gratifying for Bomber Command. Who could have foreseen, a year before, that a situation would arise whereby a daylight attack on a target well inside Germany could be made so painlessly, while at the same time night attacks remained so costly? During the weeks that followed, daylight attacks with heavy bombers became an increasingly regular feature of RAF operations.

Recognising the inability of the *Luftwaffe's* fighter force to defend the oil industry, Flak units had to be redeployed for that purpose. Large numbers of heavy guns were moved in from other areas to turn the refineries into '*Hydrierfestungen*', or hydrogenation fortresses. In order to obtain some idea of the scale of the reorganisation, let us look at the 14. Flak Division responsible for the defence of the industrial district round Leipzig. As well as that city, the division's area of responsibility included the vitally important synthetic oil plants at Leuna-Merseburg, Böhlen and Tröglitz, Espenhain, Rositz and München.

At the beginning of May 1944 the 14. Flak Division had at its disposal 374 heavy guns: 342 of 88 mm calibre (including 54 captured Soviet 85 mm weapons which had been bored out and relined to take the standard 88 mm round), 24 of 105 mm and eight of 128 mm. Immediately after the Allied bombing campaign against the oil industry began, the energetic *Generalmajor* Adolf Gerlach was appointed to command the division. During that month both *Generalfeldmarschall* Erhard Milch and *Reichsminister* Albert Speer paid visits of inspection and impressed on him the importance of his task, each making it clear that if he failed to prevent the destruction of these important targets, the war would be as good as lost. Exploiting the power of his office, Gerlach demanded and received the highest priority for both manpower and weapons. As a result, during the months to follow, his division would nearly treble in size.

Having secured the guns and personnel he needed, Gerlach revised his units' tactics to enable them to engage the Allied bombers to maximum effect. During these attacks the bombers made large-scale use of

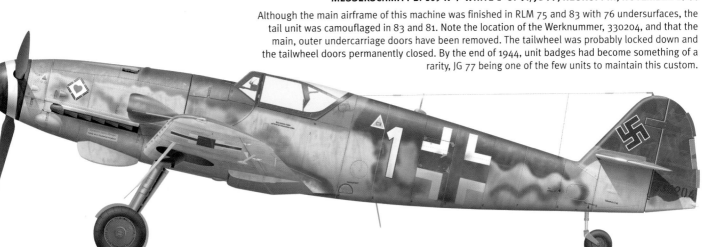

MESSERSCHMITT Bf 109 K-4 'WHITE 1' OF 9./JG 77, NEURUPPIN, NOVEMBER 1944
Although the main airframe of this machine was finished in RLM 75 and 83 with 76 undersurfaces, the tail unit was camouflaged in 83 and 81. Note the location of the Werknummer, 330204, and that the main, outer undercarriage doors have been removed. The tailwheel was probably locked down and the tailwheel doors permanently closed. By the end of 1944, unit badges had become something of a rarity, JG 77 being one of the few units to maintain this custom.

'Window' and noise jamming, to counter the gunners' *Würzburg* fire-control radars. Since most attacks on the refineries were made by day, Gerlach ordered that, whenever possible, the gunners should use optical systems to control their predicted fire; that way they would circumvent the effect of radar jamming. Smoke generators, intended to conceal the targets from the bombers, had the unwanted side effect of concealing the bombers from the Flak units, so Gerlach ordered a halt to the use of smoke screens to defend these targets, unless there were exceptional circumstances.

After some experimenting, the 14. Flak Division evolved an effective set of tactics. In a normal engagement the gun opened fire when the bombers reached the gun's maximum effective slant range (about 9,000 metres for the 88 mm shell). The usual aiming point was the leading aircraft in the combat wing formation, since it was known that this aircraft was likely to carry the lead bomb aimer for the unit. Gerlach considered it particularly important that each successive wave of bombers should be engaged during its bombing run, but that presented a problem since the US bomber formations followed each other at 15 second intervals, and even a well practised gun crew took up to 30 seconds to shift fire from one formation to the next. Gerlach therefore ordered that batteries situated to the right of the enemy formation should engage the odd-numbered waves – the first, the third and the fifth, and so on. The batteries to the left should engage the even-numbered waves – the second, the fourth and the sixth, and so on. Batteries situated on the direct line of approach should engage those waves which presented the best targets.

When the available fire control information was insufficiently accurate or complete for predicted fire, gunners were ordered to put up a box barrage just outside the bomb release line along the bombers' bearing

of approach, with the shells fused to explode at the bombers' estimated altitude. The method was extravagant in the use of ammunition, however, and it was permitted only for the defence of particularly important targets such as oil refineries.

The majority of the anti-aircraft rounds fired by the 14. Flak Division were of the normal high-explosive type, but during the summer of 1944 it received 10,000 rounds of incendiary shrapnel ammunition to conduct an operational evaluation. When these rounds exploded they hurled outwards a large number of incendiary pellets which, if they penetrated an aircraft's fuel tanks, were effective in starting fuel fires.

Generalmajor Gerlach did his work well. From the summer of 1944 until the end of the war, USAAF crews rated the oil refineries and chemical plants round Leipzig as the most hazardous places they had to attack.

In addition to the active defence measures outlined above, a series of passive measures was introduced to lessen the effectiveness of air attacks on the refineries.

▲ A Bf 109 K-4 of 9./JG 77 pictured at Neuruppin in November 1944 when the III. Gruppe was converting to the K-4. This particular machine is thought to have been W.Nr. 330204, and although shown here as 'White 1' with Hptm. Menzel in the cockpit preparing for a familiarisation flight, it is believed later to have been renumbered 'White 13'. With this latter tactical number, it is thought that this aircraft was shot down during Bodenplatte while being flown by Lt. Herbert Abendroth. The machine is shown here before unit identification bands were added, but it almost certainly had the Geschwader's green and white bands around the rear fuselage when shot down.

Where possible, vulnerable parts of these targets were 'hardened' by the construction of concrete blast walls. Also, deep shelters were built so that workers could remain at the works during attacks, emerging to extinguish any fires before they could take hold. The army released 7,000 trained engineers for employment in the repair gangs, which were also provided with unlimited slave labour. Finally, to ensure that there was no flagging in morale at the oil refineries, their work forces came under the 'special supervision' of Heinrich Himmler's feared security service.

Despite these vigorous measures, during the spring and summer of 1944 German production of oil fuels plummeted and, by design, the plants hardest hit were those producing aviation fuel. Compared with an output of 175,000 tons of aviation fuel per month in April 1944, before the campaign began, they turned out 35,000 tons in July, 16,000 tons in August and a mere 7,000 tons in September 1944.

During the intensive air operations of the summer of 1944, the *Luftwaffe* kept going on the reserve of aviation fuel accumulated before the attacks on the refineries began. However, consumption ran so far in excess of production that, by September 1944, more than half of that stock had been consumed.

Now the harsh realities of the fuel famine could be avoided no longer. Initial flying training ceased altogether; almost all the medium and heavy bomber units were disbanded; the use of aerial reconnaissance was severely limited; army support operations were permitted only in decisive situations.

The desperate shortage of fuel meant, moreover, that the *Luftwaffe* could draw no real advantage from the boost in the production of single-engined fighters that summer; in September 1944 the *Luftwaffe* took delivery of 3,802 of these aircraft. In view of the series of heavy attacks on the aircraft industry, that figure is creditably high, yet it should be stressed that the Allied aircraft production resources were far larger. Even at its peak German aircraft production was far exceeded, in terms of airframe weight alone, by the three American plants of Boeing at Seattle, Douglas at Long Beach and Consolidated Vultee at San Diego.

The *Luftwaffe*'s hopes for the retrieval of the situation over the homeland now centred on the introduction into large-scale service of the two new types of aircraft which would not make demands on the dwindling stocks of high-octane petrol: the Messerschmitt Me 163 and the Messerschmitt Me 262. Both of these types had the speed to outrun any Allied fighter, and the firepower to make short work of any Allied bomber.

The first of the new types to begin operations, the Me 163, was an unconventional tailless design powered by a rocket motor. This unusual aircraft had a maximum

◄◄ The Messerschmitt plant at Regensburg/ Obertraubling, seen after the visit by the US Eighth Air Force on 25 February 1944. Among the wrecked buildings were the assembly shops, marked at 'A'. After a series of devastating attacks on major assembly factories, fighter production was dispersed among numerous smaller facilities that were easier to conceal.

▼ P-47 Thunderbolt of the 56th Fighter Group at Boxted taxiing past a line of papiermâché 108 gallon drop tanks being readied for the next mission.

► Messerschmitt Me 163 B, C1+04, 'White 4' of Erprobungskommando 16 about to take off from Bad Zwischenahn.

▲ In the 14./EJG 2 emblem 'Baron Münchhausen' was adopted by JG 400 after the unit's living quarters were given the nickname 'Klein Zieglersdorf' after its Staffelführer, Lt. Hermann 'Mano' Ziegler.

▲ The emblem of the Me 163-equipped 1./JG 400. Translated into English, the motto reads: "Like a flea, but Oh!"

speed of 558 mph in level flight, it could climb to 30,000 feet in about three minutes and it carried an armament of two 30 mm cannon. These advantages were outweighed by the drawbacks of rocket propulsion, however. The motor ran on two special fuels: C-Stoff (a chemical combination of methyl alcohol, hydrazine hydrate and water) and T-Stoff (highly concentrated hydrogen peroxide). Both fuels required extremely careful handling, for if they ever came together they were dangerously explosive. Moreover, so great was the rocket's rate of consumption, that at full throttle the fighter exhausted the tank capacity of nearly two tons within just four minutes. Once it had exhausted its fuel, the aircraft became a glider and the pilot had to dive away and head for home. These factors limited the radius of action of the Me 163 to about 25 miles from its base, making it a target defence interceptor in the narrowest sense of the term. By the end of August a total 29 of these small fighters had been delivered to the *Luftwaffe*.

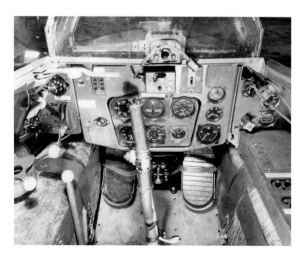

► The instrument panel of the Me 163 showing the sparse instrumentation provided for the pilot of this rocket fighter.

The second of the new high performance fighter types, the twin-turbojet Me 262, was an altogether more effective combat aircraft than the Me 163. Its maximum speed of 870 km/h and the climb to 9,000 metres in seven minutes were slightly less impressive than the figures for the rocket fighter. On the other hand, it had an endurance of over an hour, and it ran on diesel oil which was not only plentiful but also safe. The fighter's powerful built-in armament comprised four 30 mm cannon, but like any new aircraft the Me 262 had its teething troubles, mainly associated with its revolutionary new power system (see Box on page 247).

The first Allied aircraft to be menaced by the new German jet fighters were the lone high-flying unarmed reconnaissance Spitfires and Mosquitoes which, from the end of June, were used as convenient targets for the *Luftwaffe's* operational trials unit. Then, during the latter part of July, I./JG 400 moved to the airfield at Brandis near Leipzig and began operating its Me 163s against US raiding formations. On 28 July Colonel Alvin Tacon, leading a flight of Mustangs of the 359th Fighter Group escorting an attack on the Leuna-Merseburg refinery, had a brush with two rocket fighters. Afterwards he reported:

"The two I had spotted made a diving turn to the left in close formation and feinted towards the bombers at six o'clock, cutting off their jets [sic] as they turned. Our flight turned for a head-on pass to get between them and the rear of the bomber formation. While still 3,000 yards from the bombers, they turned into us and left the bombers alone. In this turn they banked about 80 degrees but their course changed only about 20 degrees. Their turn radius was very large but their rate of roll appeared

excellent. Their speed I estimated was 500 to 600 miles per hour. Both planes passed under us, 1,000 feet below, while still in a close formation glide. In an attempt to follow them, I split-S'd. One continued down in a 45-degree dive, the other climbed up into the sun very steeply and I lost him. Then I looked back at the one in a dive and saw he was five miles away at 10,000 feet."

Tacon noted that the German pilots appeared to be 'very experienced but not aggressive', yet it was clear that in the near future there would be more determined attacks on the bombers.

After reading Tacon's report, Major General Kepner, commanding the VIII Fighter Command, instructed his operational units:

"It is believed we can expect to see more of these aircraft immediately and we can expect attacks on the bombers from the rear in formations or waves. To be able to counter and have time to turn into them, our units are going to have to be in positions relatively close to bombers to be between them and our heavies. It is believed these tactics will keep them from making effective, repeat effective, attacks on the bombers..."

That was sound tactical advice: it would force the jet German fighters to run in at high speed as they sped past the escorts and closed on the slow bombers, allowing only a very brief firing pass.

Because of its limited range, a system of close control from the ground was essential if the Me 163 was to complete its interception before it ran out of fuel. These aircraft had to be scrambled at exactly the right time, and directed into a firing position. To make this possible, special ground control units were set up at Brandis and the other airfields from which the Me 163 was to operate. The system employed a Giant *Würzburg* precision radar to track the bomber formation and an *Epsilon* ground station to track each rocket fighter. The relative positions of each fighter and the bomber

▲ Uffz. Manfred Eisenmann of 2./JG 400 lost his life in this Me 163 B, W.Nr. 440013, after returning from an unsuccessful combat mission at Brandis on 7 October 1944.

MESSERSCHMITT Me 163 B

Messerschmitt Me 163 B, 'White 10', flown by Lt. Hans-Ludwig Löscher of 1./JG 400, Brandis, February 1945.

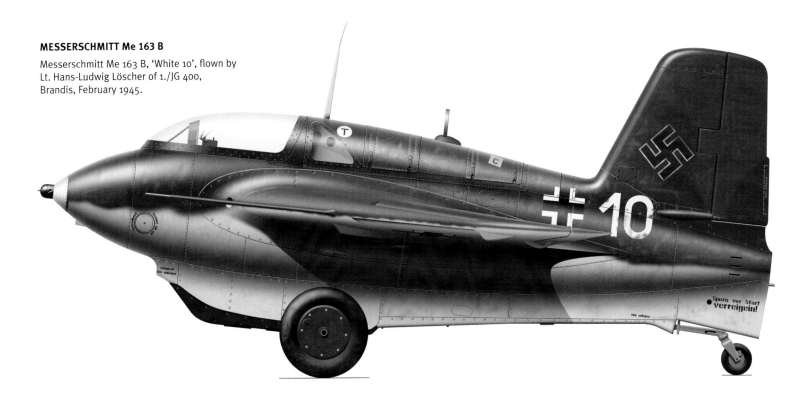

► Lt. Gustav Korff, the fighter control officer at Brandis, pictured at the plotting table from which he directed the Me 163s into action, was instrumental in developing the radar- and radio-guided interception tactics used to direct the rocket fighters to their targets. He is also reputed t o be the inventor of the vertically-firing Jägerfaust weapon which was installed experimentally on the Me 163 and used operationally for the first time on 10 April 1945 (see page 294).

► The Me 163 carried sufficient fuel for only four minutes running with the rocket motor developing full power. To assist these aircraft to reach a firing position on an enemy aircraft in that time, a special ground control unit was established beside the airfield at Brandis. At the top of the cabin were the aerials of the Epsilon device used to track the rocket fighters in flight.

formation were marked on a plotting table, enabling the fighter control officer to direct the former into position to intercept the latter.

Not until 16 August was there a real fight between the rocket fighters and a US raiding force. On that day 1,090 B-17s and B-24s, with a powerful fighter escort, set out to attack a spread of targets in central Germany. Five Me 163Bs were waiting at readiness at Brandis and on the approach of the raiders they launched into action.

Feldwebel Herbert Straznicky climbed above the bombers, then delivered a diving attack on a B-17 of the 305th Bomb Group. Sergeant H. Kaysen, tail gunner in one of the bombers, maintained an accurate fire on the rocket fighter as it closed in. When it broke away at short range, it was streaming black smoke and had suffered severe damage, causing Straznicky to bale out with splinter wounds to his left arm and thigh. He reached the ground without further injury.

Shortly afterwards *Leutnant* Hartmut Ryll attacked another B-17 of the 305th, closing in to short range. His accurate burst hit both inboard engines and flaps, and killed the ball gunner and one of the waist gunners. As he pulled away from the bomber formation, Ryll spotted a B-17 straggling behind its formation, but as he closed in to deliver the *coup de grâce*, he was seen by Lieutenant-Colonel John Murphy leading a pair of P-51s of the 359th Fighter Group. Murphy afterwards reported:

'I was escorting our bombers south-east of Leipzig at 27,000 ft when I noticed a contrail climbing rapidly up towards the bombers from behind and the port side. I recognised the contrails as being produced by a jet-propelled aircraft because of its speed [The Me 163 was a rocket propelled aircraft not a turbojet propelled aircraft as was assumed]. *Due to its speed and altitude advantage I knew I could not overtake him, but noticed a straggling B-17 to the starboard at 25,000 ft which was headed north-east of Leipzig all alone, and I headed towards him, thinking that he probably would be attacked. The 'Jettie' contrail ceased about 500 yds from the bomber, and from that point on I kept him in sight as I would any other aircraft. He passed through the bombers and down to the straggling B-17 and arrived there before I could; however, I wasn't far behind and was overtaking. After he passed the B-17 he seemed to level off, and as I closed on him I opened fire from about 1,000 ft and held it until I almost overshot. I scored a few hits on the left side of the fuselage. I pulled up to the left as sharply as I could to prevent overshooting and getting out in front of him, and lost sight of both him and my wingman. My wingman, Lt Jones, reported that the 'Jettie' flipped over on his back in a half roll, and as he did so, he scored a sufficient number of hits on the canopy to destroy him. As Jones tried to follow him through on his dive, Jones blacked out. When I completed my sharp chandelle turn to the left, I saw another "Jettie" off to my left and Jones farther off and*

MESSERSCHMITT Me 262 ENGINE PROBLEMS

During the 1940s, aeronautical engineers had to face the discomforting fact that the laws of physics imposed a speed limit of somewhere short of 500 mph on a piston-engined aircraft. The core of the problem was use of the propeller to convert rotational power into propulsive thrust. As a piston-engined aircraft neared that speed, the efficiency of the propeller fell drastically

The alternative was the turbojet engine, and engineers in Great Britain and Germany working on these for aircraft were beguiled by the obvious simplicity of this power unit. There were no propeller conversion losses, no reciprocating parts, and the turbojet engine promised to deliver much higher thrust-to-weight ratios than were possible from the piston engine/propeller combination.

Against that, however, the turbojet ran at far higher temperatures and much greater rotational speeds, and it was considerably more difficult to control than the piston engine. Those building the early turbojet engines faced a spread of new problems which, in many cases, had to be resolved from first principles.

Things were difficult enough for those designing jet engines in Great Britain, but they had the advantage of having available whatever alloying elements were required for their materials to increase their hardness and ability to resist high temperatures. Not so their German counterparts. By 1942, chromium and nickel, two of the elements usually employed in corrosion resistant and high-temperature alloy steels, were in short supply in Germany where the demands of the munitions industry exceeded availability and the stockpiles assembled earlier were steadily depleting. Only small amounts of either element could be spared for the turbojet programme and German jet engine designers were obliged to sacrifice performance so that engines could be mass-produced using alternative materials.

In the case of the Jumo 004 turbojet which powered the Me 262, Junkers engineers were forced to use substitute materials, which in some cases were not entirely suitable. For example the combustion chambers, one of the hottest parts of the engine during running, were manufactured from mild steel. To compensate for the lack of nickel, the ingredient usually added to steel to increase its resistance to corrosion, a coating of aluminium was baked on to prevent oxidisation. The lack of chromium, normally added to steel to increase its resistance to high temperatures, led to components slowly buckling during the time when the engine was running. Those components had to be replaced often, and consequently the early Jumo 004 B-1 engine had a running life of little more than ten hours between overhauls.

The engines also required very careful throttle handling to avoid the risk of engine fires, engine failure or flame outs. One particularly difficult problem throughout the aircraft's performance envelope concerned the supply of the correct amount of fuel to the engine. Too little fuel would cause a flame out, too much and the turbine blades were likely to burn out. If the engine suffered a flame out above 4,000 metres, it was necessary to descend below that altitude before a re-light was likely to succeed.

During 1943 and the first half of 1944, the Jumo 004 underwent a lengthy programme of incremental modifications to overcome its short running life and its temperamental behaviour. After much hard work, the Jumo 004 B-4 emerged, with a nominal life of ten running hours between overhauls and a total running life of 25 hours. Compared with its predecessors the new variant was also less sensitive to throttle handling and generally less temperamental. Although some control problems remained, the Luftwaffe could wait no longer. In June 1944 the design of the 004 B-4 was frozen and the production lines began tooling up to produce the engine in quantity. During September 1944 the output of production engines reached significant levels, and that month the Luftwaffe took delivery of more than 90 Me 262s.

◄ This example of a Junkers Jumo 004 A-0 jet engine, the A-022, is on display at the Luftfahrt Museum at Hannover-Laatzen. The cowlings have been partly removed to show the engine's interior detail.

lower to my right. I started down on this one, which was making rather shallow diving turns to the left. I think I must have turned with him through two turns before overtaking him. I realised that I was going to overtake him rapidly too, but I held my fire to an estimated 750 ft and held a continuous burst, seeing continuous strikes the full length of his fuselage. Parts began falling off, followed by a big explosion and more parts falling off. I could smell the strange chemical fumes in my cockpit as I followed through the smoke of the explosion. It seemed to me that a large chunk of the fuselage from the canopy on the back just popped off with the explosion."

▼ RAF fire crews dousing fires aboard 'Annie McFannie', a B-17 of the 303rd Bomb Group, which just made it back to the emergency airfield at Woodbridge in Suffolk after the mission on 5 July 1944. Note the damaged propeller of the starboard inboard engine.

Murphy followed the Me 163 down then, seeing another enemy aircraft about two miles off, broke off the chase. By now his P-51 was running low on fuel so he turned for home. At the end of his report he stated:

"My first impression when I saw the jet plane [sic] was that I was standing still. It seemed hopeless to try to attempt to overtake them, but my actions were prompted by a curiosity to get as close to them as possible. I believe that will be the reaction of every pilot that comes in contact with them. Another thing that is very noticeable is that their speed varies considerably, but it's hard to realise this until you find yourself rapidly overtaking them."

From German records it seems clear that the first Me 163 claimed by Murphy and Jones was Ryll's: he was killed. The second Me 163 may have been Straznicky's after he baled out; it is known that this aircraft exploded before it struck the ground. Without having yet scored a kill, the rocket fighter unit had lost its first two aircraft in combat.

Just over a week later, on 24 August, the rocket fighter scored its first victories when eight Me 163Bs took off from Brandis to engage a large force of B-17s approaching the Leipzig area. *Feldwebel* Siegfried Schubert and his wingman climbed to about 32,500 feet, but their ground controller failed to bring them within visual range of the bombers. Both fighters throttled back to idling power to conserve fuel and descended in a high-speed glide, searching for the enemy. They were below the bombers' level when their pilots finally sighted their prey: B-17s of the 92nd Bomb Group. The two Me 163s immediately engaged full

THE MESSERSCHMITT Me 262 AND ADOLF HITLER'S EDICT

In May 1944, the Me 262 was still undergoing its early service trials when Adolf Hitler issued his much-publicised edict calling for the aircraft to be employed initially only in the high-speed fighter-bomber role. This order was not as unreasonable as some commentators have judged it, however, and it is necessary to examine Hitler's motives.

Since the autumn of 1943 Hitler was increasingly concerned about the Anglo-American preparations to invade north-west Europe in the spring of 1944. If the Allies established themselves ashore in strength, the German Army would have to fight simultaneous campaigns in the East and the west, its recurring nightmare. Hitler and his senior army commanders were agreed on the importance of defeating the Allied seaborne invasion at the earliest possible stage and, as an element of his counter-invasion strategy, Hitler wanted to have a force of between 50 and 100 high-speed attack aircraft which could bomb and strafe the first waves of troops as they struggled ashore. If these attacks delayed the consolidation of the beachheads, and if German troops delivered rapid counter-attacks before this was achieved, it might be possible to hurl the invaders into the sea with heavy losses. However, the likely scale of Allied fighter cover over the beachhead meant that only a jet aircraft would be fast enough to penetrate to the landing area and deliver these attacks. In a conversation with Willi Messerschmitt, the *Führer* had been assured that the Me 262 could easily be modified to carry two 250 kg bombs, and from then on the aircraft featured prominently in Hitler's anti-invasion plans; this was the 'Blitzbomber' he sought to defeat the invasion.

There can be little doubt that the Me 262 did indeed possess the performance to carry out the task Hitler envisaged, and severe difficulties were experienced at Omaha Beach, one of the four landing operations on D-Day. Had there been the added harassment of scores of jet aircraft bombing and strafing the troops as they landed, this may well have caused that landing to fail.

Generalfeldmarschall Erhard Milch, responsible for aircraft production programmes, also saw the importance of the Me 262 as a fighter-bomber, but unaware of the strength of Hitler's feelings on the matter, he concentrated his efforts on getting the pure fighter version into service urgently.

Matters came to a head on 23 May 1944 when Hitler summoned Göring, Milch and other senior *Luftwaffe* officers to a conference at his headquarters at Berchtesgaden, to discuss aircraft production. When the progress of the Me 262 fighter came up, the *Führer* asked, "I thought the 262 was coming as a high-speed bomber? How many of the 262s already manufactured can carry bombs?" Milch replied that to date none yet had been modified for the purpose and that the aircraft was being manufactured exclusively as a fighter. There was an awkward silence, and then Milch confessed that the Me 262 could not carry bombs unless there were changes to the design.

At that Hitler excitedly interrupted his *Generalfeldmarschall*: "Never mind! I wanted only one 250 kg bomb." Then the *Führer* became increasingly agitated, stating that the aircraft's designer himself had assured him that the Me 262 could easily carry bombs, yet none of the aircraft produced so far could do so; the Allies might at any time launch their invasion and he lacked the weapon on which he had pinned his hopes. Hitler then rounded on the *Luftwaffe* officers present and embarked upon a lengthy monologue on the shortcomings of their service during the recent battles. He then dismissed everyone apart from Hermann Göring, and after delivering a fierce critique of the *Reichsmarschall*, finally, told Göring he was making him personally responsible for ensuring that the Me 262 was introduced into service in the fighter-bomber role as rapidly as possible. Until further notice, all new Me 262s coming off the production lines were to be delivered only to fighter-bomber units.

Erhard Milch was the first casualty of the *Blitzbomber* row. He had lost Hitler's confidence, and in the weeks that followed he was stripped of all his various offices. In retrospect, it is surprising that the Führer did no more than that.

On 6 June, just two weeks after the stormy meeting at Berchtesgaden, Allied troops came ashore in Normandy. By midday they possessed four firm beachheads and the opportunity for Me 262 fighter-bombers to defeat the landings, if it ever existed, was past.

By that time, the *Luftwaffe* had taken delivery of less than 30 pre-production and production Me 262s, all of them fitted with the temperamental pre-production engines. Clearly these aircraft were unready for action. Regardless of what Hitler, Milch, Göring or Messerschmitt had or had not done, the stumbling block limiting mass production of the Me 262 for any role was the failure to bring the Jumo 004 engine to a point where it was ready for mass production.

Only towards the end of June 1944 was the Jumo 004 sufficiently developed to allow its design to be frozen and tooling-up for mass production to begin. Not until September 1944 did production engines start to emerge from the factories in reasonably large numbers, at which point Hitler rescinded his decree that new Me 262s should be delivered only to fighter-bomber units. Within days, the first Me 262 fighter unit, *Kommando Nowotny*, received 23 aircraft fitted with production Jumo 004 engines.

The *Blitzbomber* row sent a shudder through the *Luftwaffe* High Command, following which no *Luftwaffe* officer would ever attempt to stand his ground against Hitler, on any issue. Compared with that, the edict itself concerning fighter-bombers had remarkably little effect and the delay it imposed on the fielding of the first operational Me 262 fighter *Gruppe*, equipped with aircraft fitted with production engines, was probably only about three weeks.

Early production Messerschmitt Me 262 jet fighters of the test unit Erprobungskommando 262, pictured at Lechfeld and Leipheim in Bavaria in July 1944. Much was expected from this aircraft, but problems with the reliability and running life of the revolutionary new gas turbine engines delayed the large-scale introduction of the type in front line units.

► Oblt. Fritz Müller stands on the wing of an freshly delivered, early production Me 262 (W.Nr. 170059) at Leipheim which still awaits its unit markings.

► Eight Me 262s are seen recently arrived at Lechfeld from Leipheim, now carrying the white tactical numerals of Erprobungskommando 262. The aircraft also carry yellow recognition bands on the fuselage forward of the national marking.

▼ In late 1944, a new Me 262 operational training Gruppe was formed as III./EJG 2 to prepare pilots for combat in the jet. This photograph shows Lt. Kurt Bell of III./EJG 2 flying 'White 10' in late 1944.

power and swung into position to deliver their attack. Schubert singled out the leading B-17 and fired a short burst which caused severe damage to the left wing. The bomber staggered out of its formation rapidly losing altitude, and dived into the ground.

Meanwhile, Schubert's wingman made a similarly accurate attack on another of the B-17s, which went into a spin and blew up. Two other Me 163s, piloted by *Oberfeldwebel* Peter Husser and *Unteroffizier* Manfred Eisenmann then darted in to attack the same bomber formation. Both pilots failed to score hits, but the bombers' return fire caused damage to Eisenmann's tail.

Schubert now delivered a second attack, on B-17s of the 457th Bomb Group. He scored hits on one of the bombers, which went into a spin and blew up when it reached 10,000 feet. A further pair of Me 163s then attacked B-17s of the 305th Bomb Group and shot down one bomber.

During the action the Me 163s had thus destroyed

four enemy bombers in return for one of their own damaged in combat. In each case the rocket fighters delivered their attacks so rapidly that they were safely clear of the bombers before the escorting Mustangs could intervene. *I./JG 400* had achieved its first successes in combat, though its victory total was meagre. That day was to mark the pinnacle of success for the Me 163's combat career: never in the future would the rocket fighter equal that day's victory score.

During September 1944, *JG 400* went into action on five occasions: on the 10th, 11th, 12th, 13th and 28th. The strength of the unit's reaction varied, with nine Me 163s being launched on the last missions, but in each case there were problems with the ground control system. Only a small proportion of the rocket fighters intercepted the enemy bombers, and they achieved no victories when they did so. Due to its short range, the Me 163 had to wait on the ground until the enemy aircraft came to it, yet by now the US route planners

▲ The protector protected: a Lightning of the 1st Fighter Group, having had its starboard engine knocked out by Flak near the oil refinery at Blechhammer on 7 July 1944, returns covered by the guns of the Fortresses of the 2nd Bomb Group.

► A close-up of Capt. Lee Mendenhall flying the aircraft assigned to Lt. Robert F. Hulderman of the 354th FS, 355th FG. However, neither pilot had the number of victories shown on this P-51B, serial number 42-106950, named 'The Iowa Beaut'.

were aware of the importance of Brandis, and gave it a wide berth. As a result, the rocket fighter's opportunities for action became rare.

On 24 September 1944, the *Quartermaster* General's return listed *JG 400* as having 19 Me 163s on strength, of which 11 were serviceable. By that time well over a hundred Me 163Bs had been delivered to the *Luftwaffe*, so it is clear that only a small proportion of those built were serving with front line units.

Also during September 1944, the rocket fighter programme suffered a crippling setback. Allied bombers delivered damaging attacks on the I.G. Farbenindustrie plants at Leverkusen and Ludwigshafen, which between them produced most of Germany's hydrazine hydrate, an ingredient of C-Stoff. The resultant cutback in the production of the rocket fuel would dog the Me 163 programme for the remainder of the war, for a major competitor for the limited supply was the V-1 flying bomb, which used the chemical to power its launching catapult.

Meanwhile, what of the Me 163's companion, the turbojet powered Me 262? This promised to be a far more effective all-round fighting aircraft than the rocket fighter. In September 1944 Adolf Hitler rescinded his edict that all new Me 262s should go to *Blitzbomber*

units, to counter the Allied invasion threat. Also in that month, production Jumo 004 engines became available in quantity and numerous Me 262 fighter airframes sitting around at the factories lacking engines now received production engines. That month 91 Me 262 fighters and fighter-bombers were delivered to the *Luftwaffe*.

Also in September *Major* Walter Nowotny, a fighter ace credited with 250 aerial victories, assumed command of *Erprobungskommando* 262, the Me 262 trials unit developing fighter tactics. In his honour the unit was re-designated *Kommando* Nowotny, received 23 new-build fighters with production engines and, after a hasty working-up period, was declared operational on the last day of September. We shall follow its fortunes in action in the next Chapter.

During this period, the representation and influence of the *Luftwaffe* at Hitler's headquarters fell to its nadir. One of those killed in the abortive attempt to assassinate the Führer during the previous July had been *Generaloberst* Guenther Korten, Chief of Staff of the *Luftwaffe*. His replacement was *Generalleutnant* Werner Kreipe, but from the time the latter assumed office he had frequent clashes with Hitler. *Reichsmarschall* Göring made little attempt to support his representative, and during this time was absent from Hitler's headquarters for several weeks on the pretext of a throat infection.

For the unfortunate Kreipe, matters came to a head during a conference at Hitler's headquarters at Rastenburg on 18 September. A couple of days earlier the Allies had carried out large-scale airborne landings at Nijmegen and Arnhem in Holland, with no interference from the *Luftwaffe*. Hitler used the occasion to deliver yet another savage condemnation of that service and its recent failures. When Kreipe attempted to reply to the criticisms in detail, the conversation became increasingly heated until finally Hitler dismissed him from the room. Later that day Kreipe learned that he had been ordered not to appear at the headquarters again.

Despite this rejection, Kreipe remained Chief of Staff of the *Luftwaffe*, nominally at least, until *General* Karl Koller would succeed him in the following November. In the interim, the sole *Luftwaffe* representative at Hitler's planning conferences was usually *General* Eckhard Christian. This relatively junior officer was serving with the Wehrmacht High Command, and he held no executive post in the *Luftwaffe*. As a result, there would be little or no *Luftwaffe* input to the plans for major operations then in the course of preparation. At the very time when the *Luftwaffe* was most in need of skilled and decisive leadership at the highest level, it received neither.

The six-month period between the beginning of May and the end of September 1944 had been one of unremitting decline in the effectiveness of the *Luftwaffe* home defence fighter force. Its day fighter units had suffered crippling losses in trained aircrews, losses that were unlikely to be made good since the fuel shortage had hit training particularly hard. Moreover, the USAAF was now able to send over Germany more fighters, for the most part of higher quality and with better-trained pilots, than the *Luftwaffe* could put up to defend its homeland.

The German night fighter force, too, was suffering as a result of the fuel shortage. Even against the heaviest attacks, it could rarely send up more than 50 night fighters. To compound the problem, the Allied capture of most of France and Belgium and a large part of Holland had torn a large hole in the German early warning radar cover. RAF raid planners made full use of the gap, routing bombers through it to give the defenders minimum warning of their approach.

From the end of September 1944, except on rare occasions, the Allied air fleets were able to operate over Germany by day with little interference from the *Luftwaffe*. How long this state of affairs continued would depended on how soon it took to bring the new jet fighters into action on a large scale. By night the raiders enjoyed a similar ascendancy, though there could be little doubt that the *Luftwaffe* was working hard to bring this to an end also.

In the next Chapter we shall observe how the *Luftwaffe* sought to overcome the increasingly tight Allied stranglehold on its activities.

P-51B-10-NA 42-106448 OF THE 354TH FS/355TH FG, STEEPLE MORDEN, APRIL 1944

Perfectly illustrating unit-applied camouflage, this aircraft was the second P-51B assigned to 2Lt Henry W Brown, who used it to shoot down at least three enemy aircraft in March and April 1944. In June of that year Brown received one of the first P-51Ds (44-13305) issued to the 355th FG, and 42-106448 was in turn passed on to other pilots. The aircraft endured in operational service until the end of the year, and was eventually salvaged by the 4th Strategic Air Depot in February 1945.

THE FINAL AUTUMN

September-December 1944

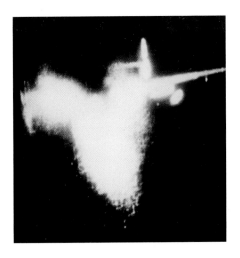

"War is an act of violence whose object is to constrain

the enemy to accomplish our will."

von Clausewitz

The late spring and the early summer of 1944 had seen further major reverses for German arms on each of the main battlefronts with their forces unable to parry any of the expected blows. In the West, they had been driven out of almost all of France and Belgium, as well as a large slice of Holland. In the South, the Allied forces had continued their relentless advance in Italy and were nearing the Plain of Lombardy. Yet even those substantial territorial losses were overshadowed by the impact of the Soviet Army's mighty summer offensive, which had ejected German forces from the remaining areas of Russia and in places advanced more than 350 miles. In the process, the offensive destroyed or severely mauled a total of 67 German Army divisions. In addition, Finland had been forced to sue for peace and Rumania and Bulgaria changed sides and were now at war with Germany. When the Soviet offensive finally ground to a halt for want of supplies, its spearhead units had established a toehold in East Prussia itself.

Even after these disasters, Adolf Hitler refused to consider a negotiated peace; and had he asked for one it is doubtful whether any terms short of unconditional surrender would have satisfied the Allies. The war would have to run its bitter course. In Germany the signs of the impending defeat were daily becoming more clear to all but the most convinced of Hitler's followers. For those who saw the realities of the situation there was despair for the future, for only a total defeat could follow the loss of a total war. The German armed forces, now fighting near or within the frontiers of their homeland, resolved to see the struggle through to its almost hopeless conclusion.

A saying popular at the time summed up the feelings of a large part of the German people: *"Enjoy the war, because the peace will be dreadful."*

Thus far the new German 'secret weapons', on which so much hope had been placed, had done little to relieve the pressure. The bombardment of London by V-1 flying bombs and the V-2 rockets had caused widespread damage, but it fell a long way short of the hoped-for devastation; the programme to build the formidable new U-boats was running far behind schedule due to the Allied bomber attacks, and several more months would elapse before the first of them was ready for action; and the new jet fighters and bombers were not yet available in sufficient numbers to have any great effect on the fighting.

Since the previous March, when the German night defences had reached their zenith of achievement with the destruction of 107 heavy bombers during the attack on Nuremberg, the effectiveness of the night fighter force had undergone a steady decline. There were four reasons for this: two of them, the fuel famine and the loss of the early warning radar stations in France and Belgium, have already been mentioned. The other two constraining influences were the compromise of most of the German electronic devices and the formation of a new force within Bomber Command to provide escort and jamming cover for the night raiders.

◄◄ A Lancaster of Bomber Command warms up its engines on a British airfield in preparation for another raid.

▶ The Jagdschloss radar, introduced in 1944, gave a considerable improvement in plotting the movements of raiding forces approaching and over German-held territory.

▶▶ The centre of Braunschweig lit up by incendiary bombs and fires, during the RAF attack on the night of 15 October 1944.

During the early morning darkness of 13 July 1944 a lone aircraft, thought to be a Mosquito, orbited the RAF airfield at Woodbridge in Suffolk and received a green clear to land light signal. The machine touched down and taxied to the end of the runway, where the crew shut down the engines and climbed out. Only when the crew truck arrived to pick the men up did it become clear that RAF Bomber Command had secured

a valuable windfall: in fact the aircraft was a Junkers Ju 88 night fighter of the latest 'G' sub-type, complete with SN-2 radar and a *Flensburg* homing device. The inexperienced pilot had taken off from his base in Holland intending to deliver the aircraft to Germany, but in error had flown a reciprocal compass heading. Bomber Command experts began an immediate examination of the prize, and within a few days the night raiders were employing tactics designed to neutralise both its electronic devices. To counter SN-2, the bombers began dropping a new type of longer 'Window' strip matched to the set's long wavelength, and to defeat the *Flensburg* homer, the 'Monica' tail-warning radar was removed from most bombers.

For those who had come to rely on SN-2 and *Flensburg* to locate the bomber streams, these moves were serious enough; yet worse was to follow for the Luftwaffe night fighter crews. Throughout the early part of 1944 a new Group had formed in Bomber Command: No 100 Group, commanded by Air Vice Marshal Edward Addison. The Group operated modified four-engined bombers to provide jamming cover for raiding forces, plus a separate force of long-range Mosquito night fighters to harry their enemy counterparts. In addition there was a special unit, No 192 Squadron, equipped with Halifaxes, Wellingtons and Mosquitoes fitted with a range of receivers with

▶ Due to the large number of unexploded bombs, the task of making them safe became a huge problem. To this end the Germans used volunteer labour from concentration camps, who in return were given extra privileges for carrying out this hazardous work.

▲ Mosquito NF. Mk 30's of No 85 Squadron on a snow-swept taxiway at Swannington in the winter of 1944. These aircraft formed a part of No 100 Group's night fighter element, which harassed its Luftwaffe counterparts during the final year of the war.

which to search the ether for the telltale signals from the latest German radars and other systems.

By October 1944, No 100 Group's heavy element comprised one squadron each of Fortresses and Liberators, and two with Stirlings that were earmarked to re-equip with Halifaxes. The Stirlings and Halifaxes each carried a battery of eight 'Mandrel' transmitters, developed versions of the device which had been in operation since the end of 1942. The Fortresses and Liberators carried two new devices intended to make the enemy night fighters' task even more difficult than it already was: 'Jostle' and 'Piperack'. 'Jostle' was a very high powered transmitter which radiated noise on the German fighter control channels – a more effective version of the earlier 'Airborne Cigar' device. 'Piperack' radiated jamming on the SN-2 radar frequencies. All of No 100 Group's jamming aircraft carried large quantities of 'Window'.

Air Vice Marshal Addison's jamming aircraft employed four basic tactics: the 'Mandrel' screen, the 'Window' spoof, close cover for the main force and target support. The 'Mandrel' screen usually comprised about eight Stirlings or Halifaxes radiating with all their jammers, orbiting at 15-mile intervals over friendly territory some way back from the front line. In that way they would blot out a sector about 130 miles wide in the German early warning radar cover in order to conceal the approach of raiding

forces. Alternatively, on nights when no major raid was planned, the same tactic was effective in luring Luftwaffe night fighters into the air to waste some of their limited supply of fuel.

The 'Window' spoof comprised ten or more aircraft flying in line abreast, each one disgorging large amounts of 'Window'. The aim was to present on Luftwaffe ground radars the appearance of a large force of bombers. It was for the perplexed Luftwaffe fighter controllers to decide whether these were real attacking forces or spoofs. There were several variations of the tactic. By sending spoofing forces on independent routes, or in front of a real actual raiding force, or splitting the spoofers away from the main force mid-way along the route to the target, it was possible to keep the defending fighter controllers guessing for many precious minutes.

To provide close cover for the raiders, the Liberators and Fortresses flew in and above the bomber stream, shielding the aircraft around them with their 'Jostle' and 'Piperack' jamming.

Finally, there were the target support operations, the most hazardous of those undertaken by No 100 Group. Sergeant Kenneth Stone who flew with the Liberator unit, No 223 Squadron, later recalled:

"The target support operations were the diciest of the lot for the bomber support aircraft and were therefore

◄ A Lancaster of No 15 Squadron, RAF. The horizontal strips on each side of the fins identified the aircraft as carrying the accurate Gee-H blind bombing system. When making daylight attacks on targets beneath cloud, aircraft without the device were ordered to formate on these aircraft and release their bombs when the Gee-H aircraft released its load.

► A Halifax of No 192 Squadron, which gathered electronic intelligence on the latest German radio and radar systems. Via Garbett/Goulding.

▲ A B-24 Liberator of 223 Squadron at Oulton, its bomb bay loaded with jamming equipment.

▲ The pressurised drum of the 'Jostle' R/T jamming transmitter in its loading pit, from which point they were hoisted into the well which previously housed the Liberator's ventral gun turret. With a power output of 2.5 kilowatts, 'Jostle' was the most powerful airborne jammer to see action in World War II.

▲ A Stirling of No 199 Squadron, one of the heavy jamming units of No 100 Group.

► A Bf 110 shot down by the RAF night fighter ace Squadron Leader Brance Burbridge while flying a Mosquito of No 85 Squadron on the night of 4/5 November 1944.

▲ Air Vice Marshal Edward Addison, the commander of the RAF's No 100 Group, was tasked with protecting night bombers from the enemy defences.

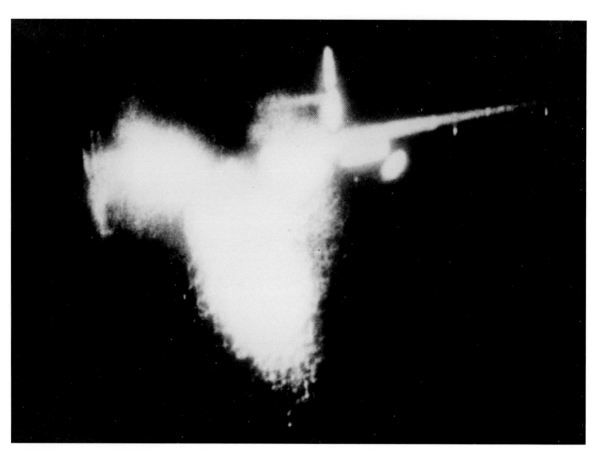

► Oberst Helmut Lent, at the time of his death in October 1944 the top scoring Luftwaffe night fighter pilot, was credited with 102 night victories and ten more by day. He joined the Nachtjagd from the Zerstörer, with whom he had flown in Poland. He became Staffelkapitän of 6./NJG 1 in January 1941, scoring his first night victory in May of that year and was then appointed Kommandeur of II./NJG 2 in November. By January 1943 he had accumulated 50 night kills, and was later appointed Kommodore of NJG 3. On the night of 15/16 June 1944, he claimed three Lancasters shot down and the following month became the first night fighter pilot to receive the Diamonds to the Knights Cross. He died following injuries suffered in a crash when he attempted to land his Bf 110 on one engine during daylight on 5 October 1944.

shared out amongst the crews in rotation. The general principle was to cover the target from five minutes before the initial marking began until five minutes after the bombing stopped. The big hazard was having to hang around while the bomber boys ran in, bombed, and got the hell out of it! Fifteen minutes seemed a long, long, time suspended over the inferno below. The support aircraft generally flew some 2,000 to 4,000 feet above the bomber stream and jammed the Flak and searchlight radars, the night fighter R/T frequencies, the night fighter radars, etc – in other words diverting the defensive forces away from the bombers during the most critical period."

With the weight of No 100 Group's trickery to back its attacks, poker-like bluff and double bluff now became regular features of Bomber Command's night operations. On the night of 4 December 1944, for example, the Command launched a four-pronged attack on Karlsruhe and Heilbronn in the south, and Hagen and Hamm at opposite ends of the Ruhr valley. But first a small force of No 100 Group aircraft ran a dense trail of 'Window' right up to the centre of the Ruhr area, then released target markers ostensibly in preparation for an attack. That spoof drew upon itself most of the *Luftwaffe* night fighters that took to the air

RECOLLECTIONS OF SOME NIGHT FIGHTER PILOTS

After the war, RAF officers interviewed some high-scoring pilots of NJG 4, including Major Heinz-Wolfgang Schnaufer (121 victories, the top-scoring *Luftwaffe* night fighter pilot) and Hauptmann Hans Krause (28 victories). The notes made during this meeting give a vivid insight into the background of the nightly battles fought over the German homeland during 1944 and 1945.

Questioned on the effectiveness of the jamming of the night fighters' radars, Schnaufer stated that it had frequently rendered his set useless. If this happened he would fly towards the strongest jamming and search visually. He remembered occasions when, if he was in the bomber stream on a moonlit night, he had had as many as 25 bombers simultaneously in view, whereas on a dark night it was rare to see more than three bombers at the same time.

When attacking with forward-firing guns, most *Luftwaffe* Experten (Experts) flew underneath the bomber to a position just ahead of it, then pulled up the nose of the fighter to rake the bomber as it flew across the line of fire. The usual point of aim was at the wing between the engines, where there was invariably a fuel tank. It was considered unwise to aim at the fuselage, because there was a risk of detonating the bomb load. On a light night, German pilots would open fire at about 200 yards, but if the night was dark, engagements from as little as 30 yards were not uncommon.

Schnaufer said he had made between 20 and 30 attacks using upward-firing cannon, and he knew that many less experienced crews used them almost exclusively. If the bomber went into a corkscrew after being attacked from below it was possible – if the manoeuvre was not too violent – for a good night fighter pilot to formate underneath the bomber and continue the attack using *Schräge Musik*. Schnaufer said he had destroyed three bombers, and Krause said he had destroyed six, in this way.

All the *Luftwaffe* pilots present agreed that a violent corkscrew, begun early, was the most effective evasive manoeuvre for the bomber. If the bomber was hit during the manoeuvre, it was usually when it was changing direction at the top. The general view was that an evading Halifax was an easier target than an evading Lancaster, though the latter usually caught fire more easily when it was hit. Schnaufer said he was impressed by the manoeuvrability of the Lancaster, and the violence of the manoeuvres flown by these aircraft never ceased to amaze him. If a bomber crew opened fire or initiated a corkscrew before they were in position to open fire themselves, experienced pilots would often break away rather than enter a long and usually fruitless chase, for once they were in the bomber stream, there was every chance they would find another bomber whose crew was less vigilant. The less experienced pilots, keen to get a kill and lacking the confidence to break away and seek other targets, would often press on with their attack regardless – and achieve nothing.

Questioned on the execution of co-ordinated attacks by one or more night fighters, as reported from time to time by returning bomber crews, Schnaufer said this was never done in NJG 4. He pointed out that it would have been very difficult for one fighter to formate on another at night, and this could have been achieved only at the expense of an efficient visual search for the bombers. He was inclined to think that when a bomber came under attack from more than one night fighter, it was the result of a coincidence.

Of the bombers shot down by the crews of NJG 4, four-fifths did not open fire or manoeuvre before being attacked. That would seem to indicate that their crews had no inkling of the approach of the night fighter. Two-fifths of the bombers shot down did not fire or manoeuvre, even after the night fighter had opened fire. Although *Luftwaffe* pilots invariably opened fire with their maximum possible firepower, there was a certain amount of competition to bring down bombers with the minimum expenditure of ammunition. Almost all of the bombers shot down by night fighters fell in flames. Schnaufer recalled two occasions when a bomber's fire had surprised him; on both occasions the fire had been accurate and he did not attempt to press his attack. On two other occasions his fighter suffered serious damage from return fire, and on many others he landed to find that his aircraft had been holed.

During the last seven months of the war NJG 4 lost about 50 fighters in action. Of these, five had fallen to return fire from the bombers, 30 to Mosquito attack, and 15 had been due to unknown causes.

"I fired a very short burst.
The whole fuselage was a mass of flame, and the Me 110
went down burning furiously, to crash in a river."

that night, and the four attacking forces bombed and withdrew with the loss of only 15 aircraft (1.7 per cent of the 892 involved). No aircraft from No 100 Group was lost.

Initially, Addison had feared that on those occasions when the spoofing forces were successful in drawing away enemy fighters, they themselves would suffer heavily; yet in the event, their loss rates were usually no greater than those of the main force. The skies around the spoofers were saturated with so much 'Window' that radar operators aboard the defending fighters found it difficult to locate the widely spaced aircraft.

In the minutes of a *Luftwaffe* conference held in Berlin on 5 January 1945, there is involuntary tribute to the effectiveness of No 100 Group's jamming and spoofing forces. The recently promoted

Generalleutnant Adolf Galland spoke of the previous magnificent achievements of the night fighter force, but those days were gone, and he added:

"Today the night fighter force achieves nothing. The reason for this lies in the enemy's jamming operations, which completely blot out our ground and airborne search equipment. All other reasons are secondary."

All of this was impressive enough, yet the jamming was only half of No 100 Group's effort in support of the bombers. The other half comprised the seven squadrons of Mosquito night fighters, which provided 'cover with teeth'. The Mosquito had a considerable performance advantage over its *Luftwaffe* counterparts and, moreover, its radar, the US-built SCR 720 (designated AI 10 in RAF service) was greatly superior

► An Me 262 in trouble. During the landing approach, once the pilot had throttled back the engines and the aircraft's speed fell away, he was committed to the landing. If he increased power in an attempt to climb away, the aircraft was liable to hit the ground before it regained sufficient speed due to the poor acceleration from the early turbojet engines. Allied fighter pilots soon discovered that after the jet fighters had taken off, they were just as helpless and vulnerable to attack as they were while landing.

▲ P-51 Mustangs of the 353rd Fighter Group preparing to take off from Raydon in Suffolk, in support of the strike on Berlin on Christmas Eve 1944.

to any equivalent in service in the *Luftwaffe*. Nor was that all, for many 100 Group Mosquitoes carried one or both of the homing devices designed to assist crews to locate *Luftwaffe* night fighters, 'Serrate IV' and 'Perfectos'. 'Serrate IV' was a modification of the earlier 'Serrate' equipment and gave bearings on signals from the SN-2 radar which now equipped most *Luftwaffe* night fighters. 'Perfectos' was a more subtle piece of knavery. It radiated pulses to trigger the identification-friend-or-foe sets carried in the *Luftwaffe* aircraft; the answering pulses from the latter then betrayed their position to the hunters.

The activities of the No 100 Group Mosquitoes were carefully co-ordinated with those of the raiding and spoofing forces. At the start of each night's operations some 20 Mosquito night fighters would fan out over enemy territory, making for night fighter airfields thought likely to become active. Once in position, they would orbit overhead for hours on end, shooting at any movement seen on the ground. Simultaneously, other Mosquitoes would orbit the fighter assembly beacons which, in the knowledge of the bombers' planned routes, were thought likely to be used. Finally, as the raiders crossed into enemy territory, yet more Mosquitoes flew on the flanks of the bomber stream ready to engage incoming enemy fighters.

One particularly successful early engagement by a

▲ Mustang P-51D, coded G4-A, 44-13691, flown by Arval Robertson of the 357th FG, which carried the name 'Passion WAGON' and an example of 'girly art' on the nose.

MESSERSCHMITT Me 262 A-1A

Me 262 A-1a 'White 4' operated by Kommando Nowotny in October 1944.

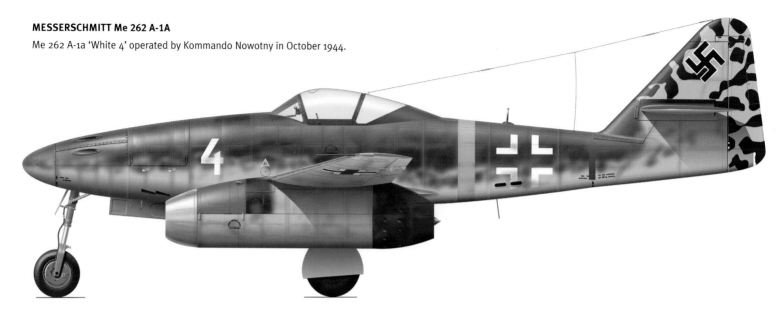

▶ This Me 262 A-1a 'White 4' operated with Kommando Nowotny and the long swept back wingspan is shown to full advantage. Note that the forward section of the port engine cowling has been changed and is still in natural metal finish.

▶ The fighter ace Major Walter Nowotny commanded the first fighter unit to operate the Me 262 jet fighter until he was killed in action with US fighters on 8 November 1944.

Mosquito of No 100 Group occurred on the night of 4 November while supporting an attack on Bochum; the pilot was Squadron Leader Bransome Burbridge, the navigator Flight Lieutenant W. Skelton. After shooting down one Ju 88 and engaging a second without success, the crew noticed a dimly lit airfield south of Cologne. As they closed on it they noticed the landing lights of an aircraft on the approach. Then, in Burbridge's words:

"A minute later we had a snap [radar] contact and fleeting visual of an aircraft above us, but were unable to pursue it. On commencing a right-hand circuit of the airfield, however, Flt. Lt. Skelton obtained a contact (on the north side of the aerodrome) at 2 miles range, 60° starboard, and at our height which was about 1,000 ft above ground. Following round the south side, we closed in to identify a Me 110. He must have throttled back rather smartly when east of the airfield for we suddenly found ourselves overtaking rapidly, horn blaring in our ears, and finished up immediately below him about 80 ft away. Very gradually we began to drop back and pulling

"..a very short burst from dead astern, 400-ft range, caused the fuselage to burst into flames."

▲ On 25 April 1944 Schwäbisch Hall was attacked by P-51 Mustangs of the US Eighth Air Force. This rare colour photograph was taken from a road outside the airfield during the raid.

up to dead astern at 400-ft range, I fired a very short burst. The whole fuselage was a mass of flame, and the Me 110 went down burning furiously, to crash in a river about 5 miles north of the airfield, which we presumed to be Bonn/Hangelar. The time was 20.32 hours, position 5048N 0712E. We flew away to the north for a few minutes, and then turned to approach the airfield again. As we did so Flt. Lt. Skelton produced yet another contact at 2 miles range, 80° to starboard. When we got in behind him he appeared to be doing a close left-hand orbit of the airfield. Again we followed him round the west and south sides, and as he seemed to be preparing to land, I selected 10 degrees of flap. I obtained a visual at 1,500 ft range: no undercarriage was visible so I took the flap off again. We identified the target as a Ju 88 and a very short burst from dead astern, 400-ft range, caused the fuselage to burst into flames. The cockpit broke away, and we pulled up sharply to avoid debris. Crosses were clearly visible in the light of the fire, and the Ju 88 dived towards the airfield. He finally turned over to starboard and exploded in a ploughed field just north of the aerodrome at 20.40 hours."

It was, however, unusual for the entire force of intruding Mosquitoes to shoot down more than five enemy night fighters in a single night; their tally of victories was in no way comparable with that of the daylight escorts, yet they had a profound effect on *Luftwaffe* night fighter operations. To avoid the seemingly omnipresent Mosquitoes, *Luftwaffe* pilots often made long cross-country flights at night at altitudes below 500 feet. Also they would take off and land on semi-lit airfields. As might be expected, those measures led to an increase in flying accidents. A tired pilot, trying to bring his aircraft down on a dimly lit

▲ This photograph shows a He 177 of KG 100 in the background, burning fiercely after the P-51 attack on Schwäbisch Hall. In the foreground are two more He 177s, one with its tail protruding from a hangar while another stands with engines running, awaiting developments.

1942 Focke Wulf 190: two 7.9 mm machine-guns and four 20 mm cannon; three-second burst, 37 pounds. This aircraft could also carry two 210 mm rockets.

1943 Messerschmitt Bf 110 Bomber Destroyer: four 20 mm cannon, two 30 mm cannon; three-second burst, 86 pounds. This aircraft could also carry four 210 mm rockets.

1944 Focke Wulf 190 Sturmbock Bomber Destroyer; two 13 mm machine-guns, two 20 mm cannon, two 30 mm cannon; three-second burst, 74 pounds.

1944 Messerschmitt 262: four 30 mm cannon; three-second burst, 96 pounds. This aircraft could also carry two 210 mm or twenty-four 55 mm rockets.

▲ The rise in Luftwaffe fighter firepower. The need to be able to destroy a tough, heavy bomber during a short firing pass led to an impressive rise in the firepower of the German fighters. The figures below give the approximate weight of ammunition fired by the guns during a three-second burst, the maximum time most pilots were able to hold their aim. Each shell symbol represents 10 lb of bullets or shells fired. In each case the figures are approximate, because the rate of fire of weapons of the same type could vary.

airfield patrolled by intruders, might misjudge his approach and crash; or a crew returning from a sortie just a little too low in marginal weather conditions, might fly into a hillside; a night fighter, its recognition equipment switched off to prevent a possible 'Perfectos' homing, might then be shot down by friendly Flak. Such losses, which were frequent, were the result of No 100 Group's operations just as much as those machines which were shot down in combat. Moreover, since the fuel famine imposed drastic limits on the number of defensive sorties that could be flown, now only the best German night fighter crews were sent into action. Each one lost produced a gap in the ranks that could not be filled.

For the daylight raiders, the new German jet

fighters represented an ongoing threat but one that seemed rarely to materialise. And when it did, these high performance aircraft flew only in small numbers. Early in October 1944 the Me 262s of *Kommando Nowotny* began operations from the airfields at Achmer and Hesepe near Osnabrück in north-west Germany.

The Allied planners soon became aware of the Achilles' Heel of the Me 262, its vulnerability when flying slowly immediately after take-off and on the landing approach. Also, a Mustang or a Spitfire with a 10,000 ft drop on the jet fighter had a decided speed advantage over it. Soon Allied fighters were mounting standing patrols over the jet fighter's bases.

On 7 October, a few days after *Kommando Nowotny* began operations, a Mustang drew the first blood. Lieutnant Urban Drew of the 361st Fighter Group was escorting a B-17 over Achmer when he noticed a couple of Me 262s taxiing out to take-off. He later reported:

"The lead ship was in take-off position on the east-west runway and the taxiing ship got into position for a formation take-off. I waited until they both were airborne and then I rolled over from 15,000 ft and headed for the attack with my Flight behind me. I caught up with the second Me 262 when he was about 1,000 ft off the ground; I was indicating 450 mph and the jet aircraft could not have been going over 200 mph. I started firing from about 400 yds, 30 degrees deflection. As I closed on him, I observed hits all over the wings and fuselage. Just as I passed him I saw a sheet of flame come out near the right wing root. As I glanced back I saw a gigantic explosion and a sheet of red-orange flame shot out over an area of about 1,000 ft. The other jet aircraft was about 500 yds ahead of me and had started a fast climbing turn to the left. I was still indicating about 400 mph and I had to haul back on the stick to stay with him. I started shooting from about 60 degrees deflection, 300 yds, and my bullets were just hitting the tail section of the enemy aircraft. I kept horsing back on the stick and my bullets crept up the fuselage to the cockpit. Just then I saw the canopy go flying off in two sections and the plane rolled over and went into a flat spin. He hit the ground on his back at about a 60 degree angle."

Leutnant Kobert, the pilot of the first Me 262 shot down by Drew, was killed in the action, but *Oberleutnant* Bley flying the other machine baled out and landed safely.

While that was happening, other Me 262s from

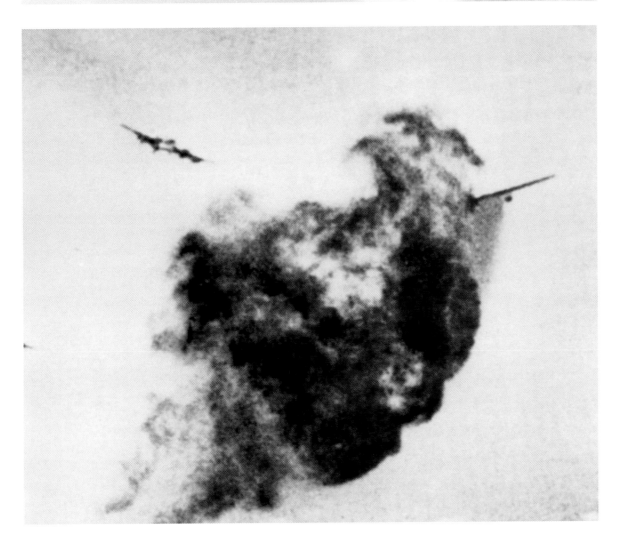

◄▼ With increasing numbers of American long-range escort fighters penetrating deep into Germany from the spring of 1944, in the ensuing combats the Luftwaffe lost many of its experienced pilots, which it found impossible to replace. These photographs show a Messerschmitt Bf 110 attempting to engage American B-17 bombers while being 'bounced' by P-47 Thunderbolts of the 56th Fighter Group, from one of whose gun cameras this remarkable footage was taken.

► This B-17 of the 398th Bomb Group returned after suffering severe Flak damage over Cologne on 15 October 1944. The bombardier was killed. The pilot, Lieutenant Lawrence De Lancey, afterwards reported: 'As soon as I recovered from the shock of the explosion I found all four engines running and the flight controls operating satisfactorily. Numbers 2 and 3 propellers were hitting the dangling nose guns, but this soon ceased. Upon making our base, because of the damage I made a high approach with power on and partial flaps. This killed the excess airspeed, making it possible to land reasonably short. I applied the brakes when the speed had lowered sufficiently, and when the brakes did quit we stopped just off the runway.'

► With the inability of its day and night fighter force to prevent the Allied incursions, the Luftwaffe was forced to expand its Flak arm. Captured weapons were pressed into service wherever possible, like this Soviet 85 mm anti-aircraft gun which had been bored out and relined to enable it to fire the standard 88 mm German round.

Kommando Nowotny were climbing to engage a formation of Liberators. Nowotny himself, *Oberfähnrich* Russel and *Feldwebel* Lennartz each claimed the destruction of a B-24. After his victory, however, Russel was caught by a pair of P-47s which shot him down, although he parachuted to safety.

Thus, during its first real action, *Kommando Nowotny* lost three Me 262s shot down and one pilot killed for the claim of three US bombers. It was not an impressive kill ratio, but it was one that would become common as the jet fighters were pitched into action against a foe with huge numerical superiority.

During those early operations, the ground crews of Nowotny's *Kommando* experienced considerable difficulty in keeping their aircraft serviceable. There were continuing problems with engine reliability, though these were not as serious as they had been with the pre-production engines, and in addition there were the myriad lesser problems to be expected when any new aircraft type is rushed into service. The Me 262 touched down at about 125 mph, much faster than any previous *Luftwaffe* aircraft, but at this stage of the war the tyres fitted to German aircraft were manufactured from reclaimed and synthetic rubber. If

"I kept horsing back on the stick and my bullets crept up the fuselage to the cockpit. Just then I saw the canopy go flying off in two sections and the plane rolled over and went into a flat spin."

▲ As the Allies drove deeper into Germany they found many aircraft construction sites. Here an American military convoy drives along a deserted autobahn where on either side of the road can be seen completed Me 262 airframes still waiting for their engines.

the fighter made a heavy landing, this often resulted in one or more burst tyres, after which the aircraft veered off the runway and usually damaged the undercarriage oleos in a high speed run over the grass. In a quite separate problem, the ammunition belts for the fighter's 30 mm cannon were liable to break if the weapons were fired during a high g turn. As a result of these and other problems, only rarely was *Kommando Nowotny* able to launch more than three jet fighters at a time against the bombers.

During its first month of operations on the western front the *Kommando* claimed the destruction of four American heavy bombers, 12 fighters and three reconnaissance aircraft. This, for the loss of six Me 262s in combat plus seven destroyed and nine damaged in accidents.

The jet fighter operations continued in this desultory manner until 8 November, when the unit suffered a grievous blow. It lost four Me 262s including that flown by Walter Nowotny, who was killed. Some mystery surrounds the death of the German fighter ace, for no Allied victory claim links with the destruction of his aircraft. Nowotny had engaged a bomber formation escorted by Mustangs

FOCKE-WULF Fw 190 D-9 FLOWN BY MAJOR GERHARD BARKHORN, KOMMODORE OF JG 6, FEBRUARY 1945

Although very few photographs of this aircraft are known to exist, some details can be confirmed such as the Stab markings and the name 'Christl' on the fuselage. Readers are recommended to Classic Colours, Jagdwaffe, Volume Five, Section 3 'Defending the Reich 1944-1945' (Classic Publications, 2005) for more information.

▲ Major Gerhard Barkhorn entering the cockpit of his Fw 190 D-9 around February 1945. At the time he was Kommodore of JG 6 but he had not fully recovered from injuries sustained in May 1944 and although at this time his aerial victories stood at 301, he did not manage to increase his tally by the end of the war. Although seen here in an Fw 190 D-9 he did not like the aircraft and much preferred the Bf 109 G. In March 1945 he left the unit to seek further medical treatment and convalescence, taking no further part in the war.

and his final radio transmission stated: *"Have just made a third kill... left engine has failed.... have been attacked again... have been hit..."* He made a further garbled transmission which was not understood, after which his Me 262 plunged into the ground with its pilot still in the cockpit.

Generalmajor Galland happened to be on a visit of inspection to Achmer that day, to discover why the jet fighter unit had not achieved more. The *Luftwaffe* fighter leader saw enough to realise that Nowotny had been given an almost impossible task. He had been charged with introducing into operational service a revolutionary new type of fighter, though many of his pilots and ground crewmen had not received a proper training. Because of the various technical problems, aircraft serviceability was poor. Moreover the unit's

bases were too close to the front line and in an area where the Allied air forces possessed massive numerical superiority.

Galland ordered the jet fighter *Kommando* to withdraw to Lechfeld in Bavaria, a quiet area where the unit could replace losses, incorporate essential modifications to the aircraft, and provide further training for its pilots and ground crews. He intended to see to it that when the Me 262 returned to the fray, it would do so in sufficient numbers and with sufficient trained personnel to make an impact on the air war. So ended the initial phase of German jet fighter operations.

Meanwhile, by the autumn of 1944, the latest Focke Wulf 190 variant, the D-9, known as 'Dora', had entered service. This aircraft had a performance matching those of the P-51 Mustang and the RAF's Spitfire XIV and in the hands of a competent pilot could match its latest Allied counterparts. The problem, as we have already observed, was that the *Luftwaffe* was becoming increasingly short of such men.

From time to time during the autumn of 1944, the *Sturmgruppen* were active and sometimes succeeded in forcing their way past the US escorts and mounting powerful attacks on individual formations. One such action occurred on 27 September, when *Major* Gerhard Michalski led the *Sturmgruppe* of JG 4 in a highly destructive attack on Liberators from the 445th Bomb Group. In a space of just three minutes the *Sturmbock* Fw 190s shot down 25 bombers and inflicted the heaviest loss ever suffered by a US bomb group in a single action. Only the last-minute arrival of Mustangs of the 361st Fighter Group prevented the total destruction of the B-24 unit. Similarly, on

6 October, a *Gefechtsverband* from JG 4 and JG 300 caught the 385th Bomb Group and shot down eleven B-17s.

On 2 November the *Luftwaffe* mounted a particularly powerful defensive effort, when it sent up 490 fighters from ten *Gruppen* to engage more than a thousand heavy bombers escorted by 873 fighters fanning out across Germany to attack the Leuna-Merseburg oil refinery and a string of rail targets.

Sturmgruppen delivered two separate attacks on that day. In the first, Fw 190s of IV.(*Sturm*)/JG 3 got through to Flying Fortresses of the 91st Bomb Group and knocked down 13, including two by ramming. Later that day, the *Sturmgruppe* of JG 4 delivered a similar attack on a combat box of B-17s from the 91st and the 457th Bomb Groups. Staff Sergeant Bernard Sitek, manning the ball turret of a B-17 of the 457th, described the action he saw unfold in front of him:

"Everything happened pretty fast, as it usually does when the Germans offer any opposition. We had been off the bomb run about ten minutes when vapour trails from fighters started to fill the sky. Friendly or enemy, was the question on everybody's mind. We soon learned the answer. They were Fw 190s and Me 109s forming up for one of those wolfpack attacks. At first it appeared that they were on the same level as our box, the high box, but as they came closer they lowered themselves for an attack on the low and the lead boxes. Every one of them followed this pattern to hit those other two boxes except the [German] leader, who must have liked the looks of one of the B-17s straggling in our box.

"I got my gun sights on him from about 600 or 700 yards as he made his attack from seven o'clock. I could almost see the bullets hit home. As he got closer I could feel his 20 mm bursts around me. At about 200 yards distance he seemed to stop dead. He rolled over and the pilot came out. In a split second the plane burst into flames and broke into several pieces. The pilot didn't wait long to open his chute. Watching his chute drift down, I could see other aircraft burning and exploding beneath me."

In all, the two US bomb groups lost 22 aircraft and, yet again, only the timely arrival of Mustangs prevented the slaughter of the entire bomber formation.

The *Sturmgruppe* units also suffered heavy losses, however. Of the 61 *Sturmbock* aircraft involved, 31 were shot down. Seventeen pilots were killed and 7 wounded.

Also that day, as a formation of B-17s neared the Leuna-Merseburg oil refinery complex, JG 400 scrambled five Me 163s from Brandis. That aspect of the defence was a complete failure, however. One rocket fighter crashed on take-off and the others were closing on the bombers when escorting Mustangs pounced on them and shot down three. The unit lost four rocket fighters destroyed and three pilots killed, without inflicting any damage on the raiders.

Of the conventional fighter units in action that day, the hardest hit was JG 27. All four of its Bf 109 *Gruppen* became embroiled in swirling dogfights with the US escorts. Although comprehensive records of the aircraft lost by the *Geschwader* appear not to have survived, they exceeded 50 and the unit lost 27 pilots killed or missing and 11 wounded. In return, it claimed the destruction of seven US fighters.

On 2 November the *Luftwaffe* as a whole exhibited the façade of air power without substance. Altogether, it lost 120 fighters shot down, with 70 pilots killed or missing and 28 wounded. The loss in a single day of 98 irreplaceable fighter pilots constituted a devastating blow and it would have severe repercussions.

US losses for the day amounted to 40 heavy bombers and 16 escorts – not a high figure considering the large number of aircraft involved, the ferocity of the action and the losses inflicted on the enemy.

The punishment meted out to the *Luftwaffe* on 2 November was bad enough, but that was only one of the four black days its fighter force suffered that month. During the US attacks on 21 November, 62 *Luftwaffe* pilots were killed or wounded. On the 26th it was 87 and on the 27th it was 51.

Oberstleutnant Dahl, commander of *Jagdgeschwader* 300, summed up the month's actions in these words:

"The flying in November 1944 was the toughest I encountered during the entire war. The odds against us were 20 to 1 and sometimes even 30 to 1. Every day we were taking casualties. Our replacement pilots had not received sufficient training and were of low quality. And more and more the fuel shortage was making itself felt."

During the autumn of 1944 *Hauptmann* Roderich Cescotti flew Fw 190 Ds with *II./JG 301*. As a secondary duty he was in charge of the unit's maintenance effort, which included obtaining fuel for the fighters. He recalled that this latter task was, *"Not so much a logistics operation, more an Intelligence battle"*.

"The flying in November 1944 was the toughest I encountered during the entire war. The odds against us were 20 to 1 and sometimes even 30 to 1."

▲ The entrance to an underground Fw 190 assembly plant a mile south of Gevelsdorf. The concrete tunnel ran almost three quarters of a mile into the mountain and both Russian and Italian POWs were used as forced labour on the site.

Cescotti would send his tankers on circuitous journeys, picking up 200 gallons in one place, 500 gallons at another. Sometimes it took as long as a week to collect the twenty tons required for a single operation by the *Gruppe*, during which the unit had to make the most stringent efforts to save the fuel it had. Teams of horses were used to tow the fighters from their dispersals to the take-off point and pilots had strict orders to shut down their engines immediately after landing and await the parties that would tow them back to their dispersals.

During the autumn of 1944 the previously laid plans for a massive expansion of production for the two conventional fighter types, the Bf 109 and the Fw 190, bore fruit. In March 1944 the *Luftwaffe* had taken delivery of 1,377 single-engined fighters and there were increases in each successive month until, in September, the *Luftwaffe* received more than double that number, 3,031.

The additional production allowed *Generalmajor* Galland (as he then was) to undertake a large-scale expansion of the single-engined fighter force: from 1,900 aircraft at the beginning of September to 3,300 aircraft in the middle of November – an increase of nearly 70 per cent. To make up for the shortage of experienced formation leaders, the individual fighter *Gruppen* now had three and in many cases four over-strength *Staffeln*, each with 10 to 15 aircraft. As well as drawing in pilots from the training schools, the force now included many experienced pilots from bomber and other units that had been disbanded.

To make the most of this increased fighter strength, Galland drew up plans for a decisive operation he termed 'The Great Blow' (*Der Grosse Schlag*). This was to be a single, overwhelming attack on a US raiding force, to be delivered at a time and place of his choosing. In preparation for this, Galland withdrew several units from action and moved them to airfields in central Germany to allow them breathing space to re-form and retrain. Galland had only limited supplies of fuel to spare, but he used this to prepare his new pilots for the intended set-piece operation.

To engage the enemy bombers on their way to the target, Galland planned to launch some 3,000 fighters. Fighters that had engaged the raiders over western Germany were then to land to refuel and rearm, and he expected to launch at least 500 for a second sortie to hit the bombers during their withdrawal. Also, about 100 night fighters were to move into position to intercept damaged bombers attempting to escape to neutral Switzerland or Sweden. Galland's intention was to shoot down between 400 and 500 bombers in a single day. It was expected to cost about 400 *Luftwaffe* fighters and between 100 and to 150 pilots, but it was thought that such a scale of losses would halt the US bombing campaign in its tracks.

In his autobiography, Adolf Galland described the detailed preparations he made for the operation:

"This was going to be the largest and most decisive air battle of the war. On November 12th 1944 the entire fighter arm was ready for action: 18 fighter groups with 3,700 aircraft and pilots, a fighter force such as the Luftwaffe had never possessed before. More than 3,000 of these were waiting for 'The Great Blow'.

"Now it was a question of awaiting favourable weather, as good weather was one of the essentials for this mass action. It was a difficult decision to hold back the defensive fighters, which were standing by in the face of the air armadas dropping gigantic bombloads daily, but contrary to my previous experience the leaders [i.e. the High Command] kept calm and did not insist on vain and costly forced action.

REPERCUSSION OF THE LUFTWAFFE DEFEAT ON 2 NOVEMBER, 1944

At a conference at Hitler's headquarters at Rastenburg on 6 November 1944, the action fought by the *Luftwaffe* four days earlier came under discussion. On that day the *Luftwaffe* had launched 305 fighters and claimed the destruction of 82 US aircraft (the real figure was 56). Of those, about 50 were credited to fighters and about 30 to Flak units. In the absence of any more senior *Luftwaffe* officer it was left to the relatively junior *General* Eckhard Christian, from the *Wehrmacht* High Command, and the even more junior *Major* Herbert Büchs, a *Luftwaffe* officer on the General Staff, to explain why their service had not achieved more during the action on 2 November. Theirs was no easy task, given the hectoring tone adopted by the *Führer*. The transcript has survived of the relevant part of the conference.

Büchs: *"There were two Sturmgruppen."*
Hitler: *"With altogether... ?"*
Büchs: *"With altogether 63 aircraft of which 61 made contact."*
Hitler: *"Right, 61."*
Büchs: *"They shot down 30 heavy bombers."*
Hitler: *"That leaves 20 over. If you take away these 60 machines from the 305, then that leaves 240 [sic]. So 240 machines made 20 kills in all, and themselves lost . . . 30 in the Sturmgruppen?"*
Büchs: *"Yes, 30 in the Sturmgruppen."* [in fact the Sturmgruppen lost 31 aircraft].
Hitler: *"And the rest lost 90. They have 240 sorties with 90 lost and 20 kills altogether."*
Christian: *"One point, the Sturmgruppen has other Gruppen with it to provide cover."*
Hitler: *"I don't give a damn about that. The covering Gruppen must shoot [at the bombers] too. It wasn't just bombers that were shot down – some [escort] fighters were too."*
Büchs: *"Yes, that's clear."*
Hitler: *"Then the result is thoroughly unsatisfactory . . . That's a very bad result. I put in 266 [sic] fighters and get 20 kills. So if I put in 2,000 I would get 200 kills. That means I just can't count on those machines producing any... and they're pouring out of the factories at the devil's own pace. They're just eating up labour and materials."*

On the evidence available from the 2 November action, it seemed to Hitler that 'The Great Blow', which Generalmajor Galland planned to launch against the US raiding formations, would incur heavy losses and was unlikely to inflict any commensurate loss on the enemy. If that was the case, he had another use for the large force of fighters that Galland had so painstakingly assembled: to support the large-scale counter-offensive he was planning in the West.

▲ This scene shows a typical, well-camouflaged Me 262 Waldwerk (forest factory) in somewhere in southern Germany just after discovery by American troops.

"The enemy began to sense the strong German fighter potential in those days, but the main object of these combats was to train the units intended for 'The Great Blow'."

In mid-November the *Luftwaffe* fighter force stood at its peak numerical strength, in readiness for 'The Great Blow'. Then, to the chagrin of senior *Luftwaffe* commanders, Adolf Hitler suddenly ordered the cancellation of the operation. The failure of the large-scale engagement against the American formations on 2 November had led the *Führer* to believe that this huge force could be better employed, as Galland explained:

"In the middle of November I received an alarming order, the whole impact of which I could not foresee. The fighter reserves were to be prepared for action on the front where a great land battle was expected in the west. This was incredible!

"On November 20th the transfer to the west was ordered, regardless of my scruples and objections . . . I must admit that even now, as I took part in the discussions for the mobilisation of the fighters in the west, it had not occurred to me that all these preparations were for our own counter-offensive. Until the very last I was kept in the dark, and only a few days before the start of the offensive in the Ardennes was I informed of the plan. Only now did I realise that the High Command from the beginning had understood something quite different by 'The Great Blow'."

Instead of being launched against US raiding formations, the huge force of fighters was to be used in a do-or-die action to support Hitler's planned major counter-offensive in the west, Operation 'Watch on the Rhein' (*Wacht am Rhein*). The plan called for a large-scale attack on Allied front-line airfields in France, Holland and Belgium, Operation *Bodenplatte* ('Baseplate'). When Adolf Galland and other *Luftwaffe* officers pointed out that the air defence training given to new fighter pilots was quite different from that required for ground attack operations, their injunctions fell on deaf ears.

Early in December the units assigned to 'Baseplate' moved up to forward airfields where the aircraft were carefully camouflaged. On the 14th, *Generalmajor* Dietrich Peltz summoned the commanders of the fighter and ground-attack Gruppen assigned to the operation to his headquarters at Altenkirchen. More than a thousand aircraft were to take part in the operation, which would involve simultaneous attacks at dawn on 16 important Allied front-line airfields.

Two days later, before dawn on 16 December, Operation *'Watch on the Rhine'* was launched but without its attendant Operation *'Bodenplatte'*. German weather forecasters had predicted that for the next several days there would be poor flying weather, with low cloud over the battle area. If poor weather precluded both sides' air forces from taking part in the land battle, that would be greatly to the Germans' advantage. The fighters assigned to *'Bodenplatte'*

remained on the ground.

On Christmas Eve the skies cleared, and German fighters and fighter-bombers were hurled into the fray. *Luftwaffe* units suffered heavy losses in the renewed bout of air fighting. In air combats the German fighter force lost 85 pilots killed and 21 wounded. Eleven *Luftwaffe* airfields used to support the offensive were bombed and suffered serious damage. On Christmas Day the *Luftwaffe* lost 62 pilots killed or wounded, and on New Year's Eve it lost 41.

In the two weeks following the Altenkirchen briefing, the *'Bodenplatte'* operation had faded into the background. Those *Gruppen* allocated to the attack on airfields were employed in supporting the offensive in other ways, and many unit commanders assumed that the airfield attack plan, like so many others, had been quietly shelved. Their surprise was all the greater when, on the afternoon of 31 December, the preliminary signal to trigger *'Bodenplatte'* clattered out on the teleprinters at each fighter unit's headquarters. The operation was to be launched at first flight the following morning, New Year's Day 1945.

12

THE BITTER END

January-May 1945

"The power of an air force is terrific,

when there is nothing to oppose it."

Winston Churchill

During the early morning darkness of 1 January 1945 the Luftwaffe pilots assigned to Operation 'Baseplate', the massed attack on Allied airfields in France, Holland and Belgium, rose from their beds early and dressed ready to receive their final briefings. By 09.00 hours the force of some 900 fighters and fighter-bombers was airborne. The previous week's battles had taken their toll and the force was not as large as originally had been planned, though it remained sizeable by any standard.

Operation 'Bodenplatte' had been carefully planned, and the attacking aircraft achieved complete surprise at nearly all their targets. Yet the low standard of flying ability of most pilots in the ground-attack role, coupled with the strength of Allied ground defences, resulted in severe losses among the attackers. There were destructive attacks on the airfields at Eindhoven, Brussels/Evere, Brussels/Melsbroek, St. Denis-Westrem and Maldegem. Elsewhere, the attackers were less effective. Some formations failed to locate their targets, at others there was confusion due to lack of co-ordination as attacking aircraft got in each other's way. The attacks on Volkel, Antwerp/Deurne and Le Culot airfields were all failures.

Operation 'Bodenplatte' cost the Allied air forces 144 aircraft destroyed and a further 62 damaged beyond repair. Those losses were serious, but at that stage of the war the aircraft holding parks were well stocked and within a few days the losses were all replaced. Allied losses in pilots during the New Year's Day attacks were minimal.

For the Luftwaffe fighter force, Operation 'Baseplate' was by far the largest single calamity it would ever suffer. No official figures appear to have survived for the Luftwaffe losses in aircraft during the operation, but probably they amounted to some 300 machines or about one-third of those taking part. From the surviving records we know that 237 German pilots were killed, missing or taken prisoner in this operation, and 18 were wounded. Among the experienced leaders lost were three Geschwaderkommodore, six Gruppenkommandeur and 11 Staffel commanders. For the Luftwaffe, these men were irreplaceable and many units would never recover their effectiveness.

From the beginning of 1945, night raiders were able to operate over Germany with little hindrance. At this time they concentrated their efforts against the oil industry and the transportation system, as well as continuing area attacks. Losses were minimal. To meet the most effective deep penetration attack in February, on the night of 13/14 when the city of Dresden was destroyed in two terrible attacks in rapid succession, the Luftwaffe put up only 27 night fighters. Of those, two were destroyed by escorting Mosquitoes and one was shot down by friendly anti-aircraft fire. Bomber Command lost only five aircraft out of the raiding force of 804, one of which was knocked down over the target by bombs falling from an aircraft above, while another crashed after it was involved in a collision near Frankfurt.

To see the pattern of a typical night operation during the closing

◄◄ In spite of the improvements in the German aircraft industry's quantity and quality, there was no real improvement in the capability of the fighter defences during the summer of 1944 due to a shortage of fuel. These wrecked storage tanks were photographed at the large Deurag and Nerac synthetic oil refinery near Hannover.

FIGHTER UNITS ASSIGNED TO REICH AIR DEFENCE

10 JANUARY 1945

By the beginning of 1945 the *Luftwaffe* had been squeezed into an area little larger than metropolitan Germany. For the Ardennes offensive, *Luftflotte* 3, based in western Germany, had been strengthened by the transfer of several single-engined fighter *Gruppen* from *Luftflotte Reich*. With a strength of 31 *Gruppen* of day fighters, it was also responsible for providing day fighter protection for targets in western Germany. For its part, *Luftflotte* Reich retained control of the bulk of the night fighter force, as well as eight day/night fighter *Gruppen* and the single Me 163 *Gruppe*.

Luftflotte 6, the strongest formation on the Eastern Front, operated from bases in East Prussia and western Poland. It was responsible for the protection of targets in eastern Germany, with five *Gruppen* of day fighters and two of night fighters.

On this date, of the more revolutionary fighter units, the only ones to fly combat missions were I./JG 400 with the rocket-powered Me 163, and NJG 11 with a few Me 262s operating in the night fighter role. These aircraft had yet to make any serious impact on operations. Although the three Gruppen of JG 7 were undergoing intensive training with the Me 262, they were not yet considered ready for action and so did not appear in the *Luftwaffe* order of battle.

Unit	Aircraft Type	Aircraft Available	Total Serviceable	Unit	Aircraft Type	Aircraft Available	Total Serviceable
Luftflotte 3				**Jagdgeschwader 26**			
Jagdgeschwader 1				Stab	Fw 190	3	(3)
Stab	Fw 190	5	(4)	I. Gruppe	Fw 190	60	(36)
I. Gruppe	Fw 190	27	(22)	II. Gruppe	Fw 190	64	(42)
II. Gruppe	Fw 190	40	(30)	III. Gruppe	Fw 190	56	(28)
III. Gruppe	Fw 190	40	(35)				
				Jagdgeschwader 27			
Jagdgeschwader 2				Stab	Fw 190	2	(2)
Stab	Fw 190	4	(3)	I. Gruppe	Bf 109	33	(24)
I. Gruppe	Fw 190	28	(23)	II. Gruppe	Bf 109	25	(20)
II. Gruppe	Fw 190	3	(2)	III. Gruppe	Bf 109	28	(23)
III. Gruppe	Fw 190	19	(6)	IV. Gruppe	Bf 109	24	(22)
Jagdgeschwader 3				**Jagdgeschwader 53**			
I. Gruppe	Bf 109	31	(22)	Stab	Bf 109	4	(1)
III. Gruppe	Bf 109	32	(26)	II. Gruppe	Bf 109	46	(29)
IV.(Sturm) Gruppe	Fw 190	35	(24)	III. Gruppe	Bf 109	39	(25)
				IV. Gruppe	Bf 109	46	(34)
Jagdgeschwader 4							
Stab	Fw 190	2	(1)	**Jagdgeschwader 54**			
I. Gruppe	Bf 109	41	(33)	III. Gruppe	Fw 190	47	(31)
II.(Sturm) Gruppe	Fw 190	25	(18)	IV. Gruppe	Fw 190	50	(39)
III. Gruppe	Bf 109	13	(10)				
IV. Gruppe	Bf 109	26	(17)	**Jagdgeschwader 77**			
				Stab	Bf 109	2	(1)
Jagdgeschwader 11				I. Gruppe	Bf 109	43	(24)
Stab	Fw 190	7	(6)	II. Gruppe	Bf 109	32	(20)
I. Gruppe	Fw 190	23	(20)	III. Gruppe	Bf 109	10	(7)
II. Gruppe	Bf 109	37	(31)				
III. Gruppe	Fw 190	42	(26)				

Unit	Aircraft Type	Aircraft Available	Total Serviceable	Unit	Aircraft Type	Aircraft Available	Total Serviceable
Luftflotte 6				**Nachtjagdgeschwader 2**			
Jagdgeschwader 51				Stab	Ju 88	8	(7)
I. Gruppe	Bf 109	36	(26)	I. Gruppe	Ju 88	41	(26)
III. Gruppe	Bf 109	38	(28)	II. Gruppe	Ju 88	28	(20)
IV. Gruppe	Bf 109	34	(24)	III. Gruppe	Ju 88	49	(26)
				IV. Gruppe	Ju 88	36	(29)
Jagdgeschwader 52							
Stab	Bf 109, Fw 190	10	(5)	**Nachtjagdgeschwader 3**			
I. Gruppe	Bf 109	34	(30)	Stab	Ju 88	6	(3)
III. Gruppe	Bf 109	42	(40)	I. Gruppe	Bf 110	48	(40)
				II. Gruppe	Ju 88	30	(23)
Nachtjagdgeschwader 5				III. Gruppe	Ju 88	37	(22)
I. Gruppe	Bf 109, Ju 88	43	(35)	IV. Gruppe	Ju 88	37	(19)
Nachtjagdgeschwader 100				**Nachtjagdgeschwader 4**			
I. Gruppe	Bf 109, Ju 88	51	(41)	Stab	Bf 110, Ju 88	5	(5)
				I. Gruppe	Ju 88	34	(17)
Luftflotte Reich				II. Gruppe	Ju 88	23	(18)
Jagdgeschwader 300				III. Gruppe	Ju 88	28	(19)
Stab	Fw 190	6	(4)				
I. Gruppe	Bf 109	57	(37)	**Nachtjagdgeschwader 5**			
II. (Sturm)	Fw 190	41	(28)	Stab	Ju 88	10	(8)
III. Gruppe	Bf 109	44	(38)	I. Gruppe	Bf 110, Ju 88	43	(29)
IV. Gruppe	Bf 109	53	(39)	III. Gruppe	Bf 110, Ju 88	66	(60)
				IV. Gruppe	Bf 110, Ju 88	51	(24)
Jagdgeschwader 301							
Stab	Fw 190	5	(5)	**Nachtjagdgeschwader 6**			
I. Gruppe	Fw 190	38	(26)	Stab	Bf 110, Ju 88	29	(23)
II. Gruppe	Fw 190	40	(38)	I. Gruppe	Bf 110, Ju 88	26	(12)
III. Gruppe	Fw 190	26	(20)	II. Gruppe	Ju 88	26	(18)
				III. Gruppe	Bf 110, Ju 88	23	(19)
Jagdgeschwader 400				IV. Gruppe	Bf 110, Ju 88	37	(29)
I. Gruppe	Me 163	46	(19)				
				Nachtjagdgeschwader 11			
Nachtjagdgeschwader 1				I. Gruppe	Bf 109, Ju 88	43	(30)
Stab	Bf 110	20	(18)	II. Gruppe	Bf 109, Ju 88	41	(23)
	He 219						
I. Gruppe	He 219	64	(45)	**Nachtjagdgeschwader 100**			
II. Gruppe	Bf 110	37	(24)	II. Gruppe	Ju 88	25	(18)
III. Gruppe	Bf 110	37	(31)				
IV. Gruppe	Bf 110	33	(24)				

▲ Despite the best efforts of the Luftwaffe's night fighter force, the fast, high-flying Mosquito bombers suffered minimal losses to the end. This example, serial LF503 of No 105 Squadron was the most famous of them all. It is seen here after completing 203 Oboe target-marking sorties during nearly two years of operations. It would complete ten more of these sorties before the conflict ended. (Lees, via Garbett/Goulding)

weeks of the war, let us examine that of the night of 3 March. That night, the RAF mounted two major attacks almost simultaneously, with the raiding forces flying a common approach path: 234 Lancasters, Halifaxes and Mosquitoes made for the synthetic oil refinery at Kamen, and 222 Lancasters and Mosquitoes made for the aqueduct in the Dortmund-Ems canal at Ladbergen. Also that night, two separate forces comprising just under a hundred Mosquito bombers launched small-scale attacks on Berlin and Würzburg.

The two heavy bomber forces received their usual support from No 100 Group. As each main force crossed over France, a 'Mandrel' screen flown by 16 Halifaxes of Nos 171 and 199 Squadrons masked its approach. In the van the attacks were twelve spoofing aircraft dropping large quantities of 'Window' to conceal the strength of each raid. Eight Flying Fortresses and Liberators of Nos

214 and 223 Squadrons flew with the bombers to provide close cover 'Jostle' and 'Piperack' protection. Elsewhere, 17 aircraft carried out a 'Window' spoof against the rail centre at Meppen, which culminated in the release of target indicators over the town. Twenty-nine Mosquito night fighters protected these incursions, patrolling the flanks of the raiders' routes. In all, 91 aircraft of No 100 Group were involved in the various actions.

At Ladbergen, ten low-flying Pathfinder Mosquitoes marked the aqueduct with red target indicators and, despite a layer of stratus cloud, these were clearly visible from the bombers flying high above. The first to attack were Lancasters of No 9 Squadron, each carrying a single 12,000-pound 'Tallboy' bomb. Then the rest of the raiders put down their loads of 1,000 pounders. A torrent of high explosive tore away the canal banks in several places, allowing the waters to drain away into the surrounding countryside. The important canal was blocked for some weeks.

The *Luftwaffe* fighter controller correctly identified the force heading towards Ladbergen, and assembled a small contingent of night fighters to meet it. The defending night fighters shot down three bombers and damaged one. At the target the raiders experienced moderate Flak which caused the loss of two more aircraft and damage to five. A further two bombers were lost to unknown causes.

Meanwhile, the detour by the Kamen attack force had passed unnoticed by the defenders, and it was not challenged by night fighters. Eight Pathfinder Mosquitoes carried out 'Oboe' marking runs on the oil refinery, and in the concentrated attack that followed the plant suffered severe damage. Production was halted. Two attacking aircraft returned with Flak damage, but

DE HAVILLAND MOSQUITO B Mᴋ IX
LF503 F:GB of No 105 Squadron, 213 Squadron, Bourne, England, 1945

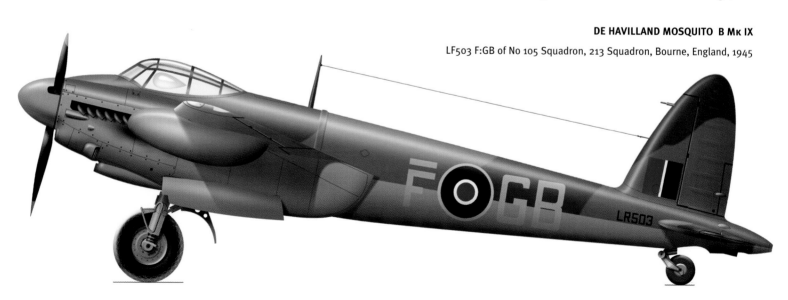

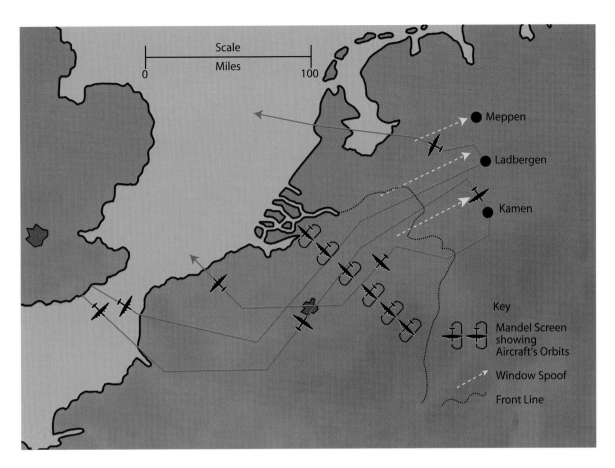

◄ The attack on Ladbergen and Kamen, on the night of 3/4 March 1945.

none was lost. That night, seven raiders and one Mosquito fighter failed to return. The remaining Mosquito fighters reported no encounters with their enemy counterparts.

Although the *Luftwaffe* night fighter arm was badly battered, it was not yet dead. By drawing on carefully husbanded reserves, it had gathered sufficient fuel to mount a final all-out blow against the night raiders. As the bombers withdrew from Ladbergen and Kamen, over one hundred German night fighters roared into the air and headed westwards in pursuit. The *Luftwaffe* was launching its long-planned Operation *Gisella*, the first large-scale intruder operation against Bomber Command's bases since the late summer of 1941.

The attack had been well planned. *Oberleutnant* Hans Krechmer, a Ju 88 radar operator with NJG 4, told this writer that a week earlier he had been ordered to join a returning bomber stream and fly with it to observe the bases in England. He and his crew were told to make a special note of the bombers' approach and landing procedures. The crew had strict orders not to engage enemy aircraft but merely to observe how they behaved. Krechmer noted that once over England, many bombers turned on their navigation lights. That would make them easy targets.

Now the constraint not to attack the bombers was lifted, and two waves of Ju 88s and He 219s swept in over the North Sea and headed for bomber airfields in Norfolk, Suffolk, Lincolnshire and Yorkshire. Twenty-seven airfields came under attack from cannon and machine gun fire and bombs, and as well as the bombers returning from Germany the intruders caught many aircraft airborne on training flights. In all, 48 RAF aircraft came under attack over England, of which 22 were shot down and eight suffered damage. The defenders claimed six intruders shot down.

From the *Luftwaffe*'s point of view *Gisella* had been a successful operation, but it would never be repeated on anything like that scale. Two weeks later, on the night of 17 March, 18 Ju 88s took off from Holland to attack bomber airfields. No heavy bomber operations had been planned for that night, however, and the intruders shot down only one aircraft on a training flight. It would be the last offensive action the *Luftwaffe* mounted against Britain during the conflict.

As the war drew to a close the *Luftwaffe* introduced a new airborne interception radar for night fighters, the *Neptun*. This equipment, a metric wavelength radar like its predecessors, had started to replace the SN-2 which now faced severe jamming. The *Neptun* radar operated on one of two frequencies, one in the 158 MHz band and one in the 187 MHz band. Until a prying aircraft of

► This two-seater Me 262 B-1a/U1 'Red 10' was handed over to British forces at Schleswig in northern Germany in 1945. The aircraft had been operated by 10./NJG 11 under Oberleutnant Kurt Welter and was the only jet Nightfighter unit to become operational before the end of the war. Only very few of the unit's Me 262s were equiped with the FuG 218 'Neptun' radar in the nose.

▲ The 'Village Inn' gunlaying radar, with the scanner dome fitted below the rear turret of a Lancaster, allowed the rear gunner to engage targets on radar indications alone. Operated in the blind firing mode, it could have made life extremely uncomfortable for the Luftwaffe night-fighter crews, but problems in producing and installing the infrared lights in the nose of each bomber to identify them as friendly could not be resolved before the war ended. As a result, 'Village Inn' could not be used to its full capability. (Garbett/Goulding collection)

No 192 Squadron picked up its signals and their significance was realised, this radar would operate without hindrance from No 100 Group's jamming. The small number of radars deployed assisted in keeping the new type secret, and it remained unjammed until the end of the conflict.

Simultaneously, to swat some of the pestilential Mosquito bombers buzzing over Germany with near-immunity at night, a small force of jet fighters was formed specially to combat them. Raised under the command of *Oberleutnant* Kurt Welter, it operated about ten Me 262s with anti-Mosquito operations beginning in earnest in January 1945, initially from Burg, about 70 miles west of Berlin. At first, the single-seat fighters, lacking radar, relied on searchlights to illuminate their prey for them, in a manner reminiscent of the *Helle Nachtjagd* tactics used in 1940 and 1941. Near the end of the war, a few two-seater trainer versions of the Me 262 fitted with the *Neptun* radar became available.

Welter's jet fighters probably accounted for most of the 13 Mosquitoes lost in the Berlin area during the first three months of 1945.

The innovations at the close of the war were not, of course, on one side alone. Several night bombers now carried the 'Village Inn' gunlaying radar fitted to the rear turret. With that device it was technically possible to engage enemy night fighters at well beyond visual range, a defence against which the *Luftwaffe* crews would have been almost helpless. Yet before unrestricted use of the blind firing technique could be permitted, it was necessary to solve the problem of recognition. To prevent large-scale errors with friendly aircraft being fired upon, every operational heavy bomber had first to be fitted with special nose-mounted infrared identification lamps which flashed the Morse recognition letters of the night. Due to delays in producing and fitting the infrared lights, the full use of radar-controlled defensive fire was not permitted before the war ended.

One interesting idea proposed by No 100 Group was to employ aircraft fitted with the 'Village Inn' radar in a 'Window' spoof, to set up the conditions for an ambush. Since the aircraft in such spoof forces flew in a widely spaced line abreast, their gunners could safely be allowed to loose off at any aircraft they detected within range of their guns. Such an ambush could have dealt an unexpectedly rough reception to any *Luftwaffe* night fighters seeking to investigate the swirling clouds of 'Window', but the war ended before that scheme could be tested in combat.

Early in 1945 *Oberfähnrich* Hans-Ulrich Flade was posted to *III./JG* 27 flying Bf 109s from Brunswick/Volkerode. Morale in the *Gruppe* was low and losses were severe: out of a strength of about twenty pilots, it was losing two or three each day. Flade recalled:

"Each morning we pilots had breakfast together, and the replacements would come in. The older pilots regarded the young newcomers as though they had only days to live – and with reason, for the standard of fighter conversion training was now so low that most new pilots flew only two or three missions before they were shot down. I remember many conversations along these lines – not exactly a cheerful subject for a young man who had just joined his first operational unit!"

Flade was in a much better position than most of the newcomers, however. Due to his retention as an instructor at the fighter conversion unit, he now had some 400 hours flying time on the Bf l09 G. That was

"Each morning we pilots had breakfast together, and the replacements would come in. The older pilots regarded the young newcomers as though they had only days to live – and with reason."

about ten times as much as the average pilot received when he came through the training system. Flade's *Gruppe* operated the G-10, G-14 and K versions of the fighter, which were lightly armed and had engines fitted with water-methanol boosting and enlarged superchargers for high-altitude operations. The intended role of the unit was to keep the escorting Mustangs busy so that other fighters could go for the bombers. During his initial sorties, Flade flew as wingman to *Unteroffizier* Rippert:

"We followed the old rules: dive as a Rotte [two] or a Schwarm [four] out of the sun, make a quick attack to break up their formation and make them drop their tanks, then climb back out of danger and assess the situation. If conditions were favourable, we would go down for a second attack. Always the escorts were so numerous that it would have been foolish to get into a

▲ The strain of continuous combat shows clearly on the faces of these pilots. These two Ritterkreuzträger were former members of JG 7 and are, on the right, Major Erich Hohagen, who ended the war with 55 aerial victories and on the left is Leutnant Klaus Neumann whose final total was 37. When this photograph was taken in April they were flying with Adolf Galland's JV 44 based at München-Riem.

◄ In a long battle of attrition, the recovery and repair of aircraft with light damage was an important factor in maintaining serviceability levels. Here a team prepares to lift a late model Bf 109 which crash-landed in Denmark after a combat in the spring of 1945.

AIRFIELD STRAFING

The German aircraft grounded for want of fuel provided fine targets to swell the scores of the US fighter pilots, who included aircraft destroyed on the ground in their victory tallies, although the ground defences often made these attacks hazardous. Making repeated strafing attacks on the same group of targets compounded the dangers, as Major Edward Giller of the 55th Fighter Group learned the hard way a few days before the conflict ended:

"I was leading Tudor Squadron on the mission on 16 April 1945. We were sweeping on ahead of the bombers in the area of Brunnthal landing ground. I had taken the squadron down to about 3,500 feet in order to be able to find any targets that might present themselves. This was the same area we had attacked on April 9th; we could see the burned out hulks of the many aircraft we had destroyed on that day. However, I could see between 10 and 15 assorted types of aircraft cached away in the woods along the autobahn and around Brunnthal, that we had apparently missed on the 9th. Since the number of targets in this area was not lucrative enough to engage the entire squadron, I released the flights to find their own targets. I broke my White Flight down into elements to cover this area. My wingman, Lt. Arnold, and I made our passes parallel with the autobahn, from south to north, clobbering the aircraft which were parked in the woods along either side of the road. My first attack was on an He 111; it started to burn in a beautiful burst of flame. Parked just beyond it was an Me 109; I put the pipper on it, getting a good concentration of hits. Just as I pulled up over it, a steady stream of black smoke began to belch forth from it. I had seen two other aircraft parked in this same area on the east side of the road during the first pass, so I went in again, making the same pattern from south to north. The first aircraft turned out to be a Ju 52 aircraft parked a little way further back from the road than the first two targets. I fired at it, pretty well covering the engines; it also burst into flames. I had to make a third pass to position myself on the fourth target which I had observed. It turned out to be a Ju 88; I came in on it in the same pattern from south to north, and although I observed many strikes all over the aircraft I could not get it to burn. As I pulled up from this last pass, a 20 mm Flak shell came in the left side of my canopy and exploded, wounding me in the left shoulder. I was dazed and bleeding rather badly, so I called my flight together and we set course for home."

▲ A gun-camera still from an Allied fighter making a low-level attack on a German night fighter airfield. The three aircraft to the right of the photograph are Junkers Ju 88 Gs while the rest appear to be Messerschmitt Bf 110s.

dogfight. On one occasion there were no Mustangs about, so Rippert led me in a diving attack on a large formation of B-17s. It was terrible! Tracer was everywhere, and I felt as though I was standing in a shower and trying not to get wet. I was so frightened that I just huddled up close to my armour plate and followed him down, content only to survive that dreadful experience."

To the very end there was no shortage of new aircraft to replace those lost. Flade recalled that if a fighter was damaged it was usually simpler to acquire a new one than to try to effect repairs:

"We simply went to the depot nearby, where they had hundreds of brand-new 109s – G-10s, G-14s and even the very latest K models. There was no proper organisation any more. The depot staff said: `There are the aircraft, take what you want and go away.' But getting fuel, that was more difficult . . ."

Meanwhile, what had become of the Me 262 jet fighters, which should have been able to restrict the almost complete freedom of action now enjoyed by the Allied aircraft over Germany? At the end of 1944, following a period of further training, the men of *Kommando Nowotny* had formed the nucleus of the first jet fighter *Geschwader*, JG 7 under *Major* Theodore Weissenberger. The first *Gruppe* to reach full strength was III/JG 7 based at Parchim to the northwest of Berlin. Its two sister *Gruppen*, I./JG 7 at Kaltenkirchen and II./JG 7 at Neumünster, were somewhat slower in receiving their Me 262s.

Early in 1945 pilots of a bomber unit, *Kampfgeschwader 54*, also began converting to the Me 262 to operate the aircraft in the fighter role. The unit was redesignated *Kampfgeschwader (Jagd) 54* and some accounts have linked this diversion of Me 262s away from pure fighter units to Adolf Hitler's earlier insistence that the type be used as a fighter-bomber. Now the issues were quite different, however. To shorten training time and save resources, trainee pilots earmarked for *Luftwaffe* single-engined day fighter units throughout the war had not received a formal training in instrument flying, whereas bomber pilots received this training as a matter of course. Following the heavy losses suffered during the previous year, the fighter force was desperately short of trained pilots, but in the summer of 1944 almost all multi-engined bomber units had had to be disbanded due to the fuel crisis. The result was a surplus of experienced bomber pilots, all of whom were

RAF BOMBER COMMAND OPERATIONS AGAINST TARGETS IN GERMANY, JANUARY 1945

This list shows the scale of RAF Bomber Command day and night operations against targets in Germany during January 1945 and also the minimal losses suffered in the course of these raids. For each date, the period runs from 08.00 hours untill 07.59 hours the next morning.

Target classification:

A = area target; 0 = oil target; T = transport system target; M = miscellaneous other target.

Daylight Attacks				Night Attacks		
Date	Target	Sorties	Missing	Target	Sorties	Missing
1	Ladbergen (T)	102	1	Dortmund (O)	123	0
				Gravenhorst (T)	152	0
				Vohwinkel (T)	146	1
2				Nuremberg (A)	514	4
				Ludwigshaven (M)	373	0
3	Castrop-Rauxel (O)	49	0			
	Dortmund (O)	50	1			
5	Ludwigshaven (T)	160	2			
6				Hanau (A)	468	6
				Neuss (T)	147	0
				Munich (A)	645	10
7	Krefeld (T)	152	0			
13	Saarbrücken (T)	158	0	Saarbrucken (T)	264	0
				Poelitz	218	2
14	Saabrücken (T)	126	0	Leuna-Merseburg (O)	573	9
				Gravenbroich (T)	139	0
				Dülmen (O)	103	1
15	Bochum (O)	63	0			
	Recklinghausen (O)	82	0			
16				Magdeburg (A)	364	17
				Zeitz (O)	328	8
				Bruex (O)	231	1
				Wanne-Eickel (O)	138	1
22				Bruckhausen (O)	286	2
				Gelsenkirchen (O)	136	0
28	Cologne (T)	153	3	Stuttgart (T)	574	9
29	Krefeld (T)	148	0			
Total		**1243**	**7**		**6572**	**99**

▲ Mustangs of the 332nd Fighter Group flying over their airfield in Italy, prior to a long-range mission.

► An Me 262 at high speed is caught briefly in the gunsight of a US fighter.

trained in instrument flying. The role of KG (J) 54 was to be that of bad weather interception, for which an ability to fly blind on instruments was essential. The ex-bomber pilots received only a sketchy training in air-to-air combat, however, and for that omission they would suffer accordingly.

On 9 February KG (J) 54 scrambled several aircraft to counter an attack by US heavy bombers against targets in central Germany. Escorting Mustangs pounced on them and shot down six Me 262s. Five of the jet fighter pilots were killed including the Geschwader commander, Oberstleutnant von Riedesel. For their part the ex-bomber pilots inflicted damage on just one B-17. Two weeks later, on the 25th, KG (J) 54 had another bad day when it lost 12 Me 262s: six in air combat, four during

an Allied strafing attack on the airfield and two in flying accidents. Thereafter the unit was withdrawn from operations to allow its pilots to receive further training.

It was late in February before the first fully-trained Me 262 day fighter Gruppe was ready to go into action. On the 21st some 15 Me 262s fought an inconclusive action with Mustangs over Berlin, without loss to either side.

Only in March 1945 did the Me 262 day fighter units start to launch large-scale attacks on the US bomber formations. On the 3rd, there were 26 Me 262 sorties in response to the US attacks on Magdeburg, Brunswick, Hannover and Chemnitz. The jet pilots claimed the destruction of seven bombers and two fighters in return for one Me 262 lost. US records list nine bombers and eight fighters lost on that day.

During the next few weeks the US heavy bombers confined their activities to targets in western Germany, beyond the reach of Me 262 units based around Berlin. Leutnant Walther Hagenah was one of the pilots posted to JG 7, and he described some of the problems facing the unit when he reached it:

"By the time I reached [the Gruppe] there were insufficient spare parts and insufficient spare engines; there were even occasional shortages of J-2 fuel. I am sure that production was sufficient and that all of these parts and engines existed, but by that stage of the war the transport system was so chaotic that things often failed to arrive at front line units."

Hagenah was an experienced fighter pilot who had received training in instrument flying, and he converted

"I was sitting right on his tail until my guns were completely empty. By that time I knew he was a dead duck and veered off to the left, pulling up just as he crashed into the ground."

to the Me 262 with little difficulty. The same could not be said, however, for other, less experienced pilots, who arrived at the jet fighter unit at the same time:

"In our unit, flying the Me 262, we had some pilots with only about a hundred hours total flying time. They were able to take-off and land the aircraft, but I had the definite impression that they were little use in combat. It was almost a crime to send them into action with so little training. These young men did their best, but they had to pay a heavy price for their lack of experience."

The next large-scale action was on 18 March, when 1,221 heavy bombers escorted by 632 Mustangs made an attack on Berlin. The *I.* and *II./JG* 7 put up a total of 37 Me 262s, many of which exploited the hazy conditions and persistent vapour trails to close on the bomber formations unobserved. During one such skirmish, four Me 262s darted out of the condensation trails to a position less than a hundred yards behind one B-17 formation and opened a withering fire which caused lethal damage to two Fortresses and serious damage to a third. In a subsequent firing pass a B-17 was seen to go down with its entire tail section shot away. The Me 262s claimed 12 US bombers destroyed, but from US records it appears that only eight heavy bombers fell to jet fighters that day. Five more were credited to Flak at the target. Three jet fighters were shot down, and two more were destroyed in a collision in bad visibility well clear of the bombers. Fighter ace *Oberleutnant* Hans Waldmann, credited with 134 victories, was killed in the collision.

On each of the following three days, the 19th, 20th and 21 March, Me 262s were again up in force, but with less success. They accounted for only three heavy bombers, while the escorting Mustangs claimed 17 of the jet fighters.

Representative of the brisk actions fought on the 21st was that by Captain Edwin Miller of the 78th Fighter Group:

Me 262 TECHNICAL FAILURE REPORTS

In January 1945 the Me 262 still suffered from a variety of teething troubles. From a few of the technical failure reports which *Luftwaffe* units submitted to the Messerschmitt company, the reader may form an impression of the problems faced:

"Oberfähnrich Schnurr had instruction to carry out an air test following an engine and generator regulator change, in Ahorn [Ahorn = Maple, code-name for Me 262] Werknummer 110564. After flying straight and level at 600 metres, the aircraft suddenly dived into the ground. Schnurr was experienced on the type and was known to be a reliable, disciplined and competent pilot. Possibly, due to a change of trim, the aircraft became nose heavy; the cause has not been ascertained.

"Oberfähnrich Ast looped Ahorn 110479 at an altitude of 4,500 metres, and went into a spin. Due to excessive speed the aircraft went out of control and crashed."

Moreover, rampaging Mustangs were seemingly always ready to cut down a wounded jet fighter that lacked the speed to outrun them. One pilot of III./JG 7 reported the loss of his aircraft on 14 January:

"At 12.32 hours (flying Ahorn 130180—Red 13), I took off as one of a pair of Ahorn aircraft to attack an Anglo-American formation of fighters and bombers. In the climb, at an altitude of about 6,000 metres, I suddenly noticed a considerable rise in the jet pipe temperature of my right engine. I turned off the fuel, and then noticed that the aircraft was losing a great deal of fuel between the fuselage and the right engine, near the landing flap. Because of this I stopped the right engine completely. After a few minutes I tried to relight it, but it began to smoke. Over the R/T I heard that enemy aircraft were making a low-level attack on Parchim, so I called the JG 7 operations room and requested permission to land at Brandenburg-Briest. I received orders to land at Neuruppin, but in that area I found several groups of enemy fighters; about 1,000 metres above and in front of me I saw three Mustangs to the left and four on the right coming towards me. I dived to avoid their attack, but nevertheless I received hits on the left wing and engine, the fuselage and the cockpit, during which I was wounded by a glancing bullet and a splinter. I pulled my machine into a bank to the right, and baled out; the aircraft crashed near Lögow, in the area of Neuruppin."

USAAF BOMBER FORMATION, ASSEMBLY AND ATTACK

The assembly of the gigantic American bomber formations called for precision flying of a high order, linked with rigid timing. In this example we follow the movement of the B-17s of the 384th Bomb Group based at Grafton Underwood, which led the attack on Berlin on 18 March 1945

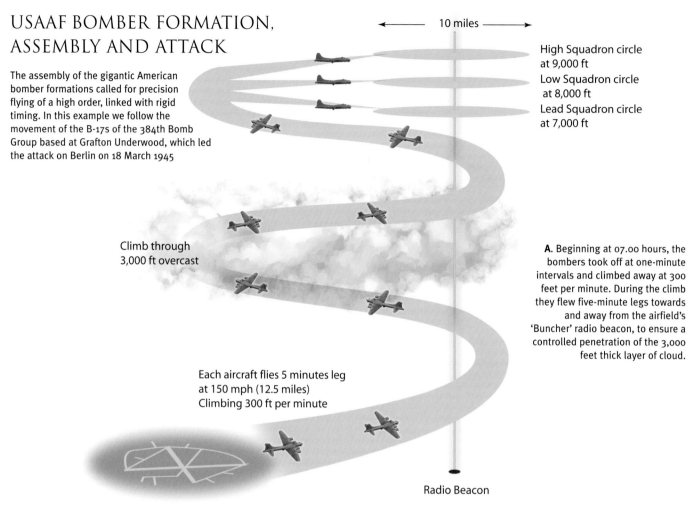

←—— 10 miles ——→

High Squadron circle at 9,000 ft

Low Squadron circle at 8,000 ft

Lead Squadron circle at 7,000 ft

Climb through 3,000 ft overcast

A. Beginning at 07.00 hours, the bombers took off at one-minute intervals and climbed away at 300 feet per minute. During the climb they flew five-minute legs towards and away from the airfield's 'Buncher' radio beacon, to ensure a controlled penetration of the 3,000 feet thick layer of cloud.

Each aircraft flies 5 minutes leg at 150 mph (12.5 miles) Climbing 300 ft per minute

Radio Beacon

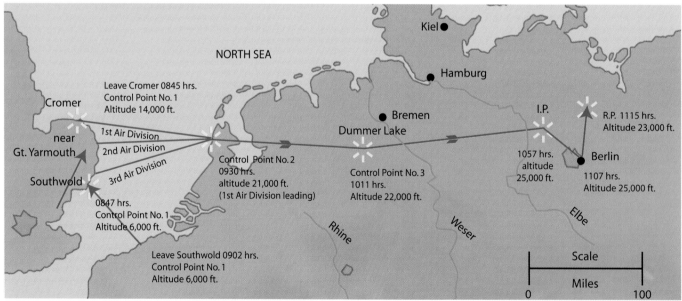

Kiel ●

NORTH SEA

Hamburg ●

Leave Cromer 0845 hrs.
Control Point No. 1
Altitude 14,000 ft.

Cromer

Bremen ●

Dummer Lake

I.P.

R.P. 1115 hrs.
Altitude 23,000 ft.

near
Gt. Yarmouth

1st Air Division

2nd Air Division

3rd Air Division

Control Point No. 2
0930 hrs.
altitude 21,000 ft.
(1st Air Division leading)

Control Point No. 3
1011 hrs.
Altitude 22,000 ft.

1057 hrs.
altitude
25,000 ft.

Berlin ●

1107 hrs.
Altitude 25,000 ft.

Southwold

0847 hrs.
Control Point No. 1
Altitude 6,000 ft.

Rhine

Weser

Elbe

Leave Southwold 0902 hrs.
Control Point No. 1
Altitude 6,000 ft.

Scale

Miles

0   100

C. To position himself at the head of the column of group formations, the 384th had to reach the Wing Assembly Point over March at exactly 08.37 hours; at two-minute intervals other groups arrived over March and slotted in behind. To allow flexibility of timing without altering the airspeed (which would have caused the formation to lose cohesion), the dog-leg turn over St Neots could be cut short or extended. There was a similar dog-leg over Watton, to allow the leading group in the Wing to reach the Divisional Assembly Point over Cromer at exactly 08.55 hours. Note that nearly two hours elapsed from the time the first aircraft took off to the time it left the coast.

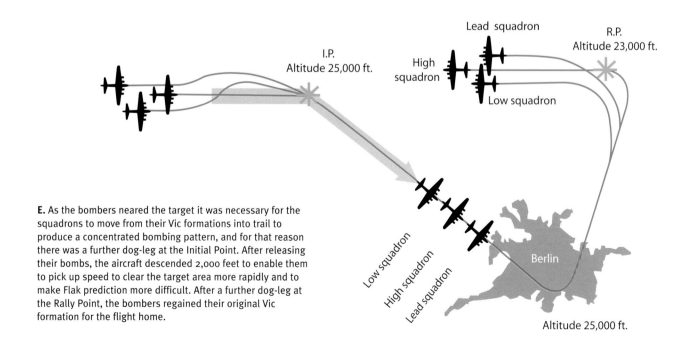

36 aircraft formed at 08.16 hrs. Proceeding on first leg at 8,000 ft.

Squadron gaining formation

To St. Neots

5 Miles

Bombers climbing to formation altitude under circle

A/D

Group leg

St. Neots

To wing assembly point at March

B. Once safely above cloud the bombers circled the beacon, forming up into lead, high and low squadrons (prior to take-off each crew had received a briefing sheet giving its position in the formation). By this stage of the war, fighter cover was available to and from the target. Since the bombers' defensive crossfire was no longer of such importance, the 36 aircraft group formation was now employed.

NORTH SEA

THE WASH

0853 hrs Cromer

1st Combat Bomb Wing

40th Combat Bomb Wing

94th Combat Bomb Wing

To 1st Air Division Assembly Point

379th B.G.

303rd B.G.

384th B.G.

1st Combat Bomb Wing

March
0837 hrs
Altitude 10,800 ft.

Watton
0843 hrs
Altitude 12,000 ft.

Scale

Miles

0   50

St. Neots

D. With the 384th BG in the van, the 1st Air Division began to cross the Dutch coast at 09.30 hours. By the time the leading bombers were past the Zuider Zee, the other two divisions, the 3rd and then the 2nd, were in position behind. When formed up, the phalanx of bombers was about 180 miles long, and comprised 916 Fortresses and 305 Liberators; a total of 632 Mustangs provided cover for this attack.

Lead squadron

R.P.
Altitude 23,000 ft.

High squadron

Low squadron

I.P.
Altitude 25,000 ft.

Low squadron

High squadron

Lead squadron

Berlin

E. As the bombers neared the target it was necessary for the squadrons to move from their Vic formations into trail to produce a concentrated bombing pattern, and for that reason there was a further dog-leg at the Initial Point. After releasing their bombs, the aircraft descended 2,000 feet to enable them to pick up speed to clear the target area more rapidly and to make Flak prediction more difficult. After a further dog-leg at the Rally Point, the bombers regained their original Vic formation for the flight home.

Altitude 25,000 ft.

► The 'Roller-Coaster' attack, employed by German jet fighters against escorted bomber formations. Operating under ground control, they were guided to a position about three miles behind and 6,000 feet above the bomber formation. The Me 262s then moved into line astern and followed their leader towards the bombers in a shallow dive, during which their speed increased to over 550 mph to enable them to penetrate the screen of escorting fighters. That speed was also too high for an effective firing pass on the bombers, however, so the Me 262 pilots continued their descent to a point about a mile behind and 1,500 feet beneath the bombers. There they made a high-g pull-up to reduce speed, then levelled off at the same altitude as the selected bomber. In the USAAF, this manoeuvre was called the 'Roller Coaster' or 'Leap Frog', because of its appearance seen nose-on. The pull-up left the Me 262 about 1,000 yards behind the target bomber, with an ideal overtaking speed of about 100 mph. If the fighter carried R4M rockets, the Me 262 pilot would ripple-fire the entire battery at the bomber from a distance of about 650 yards, then follow this with an attack on the same aircraft using the 30 mm cannon. The breakaway was usually made in a shallow climb to pass over the target aircraft to avoid falling debris.)

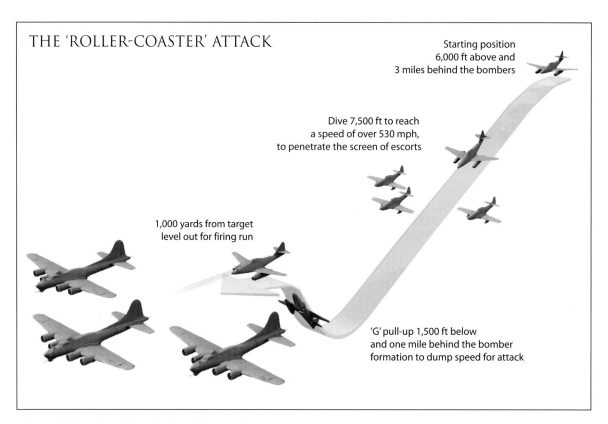

THE 'ROLLER-COASTER' ATTACK

Starting position
6,000 ft above and
3 miles behind the bombers

Dive 7,500 ft to reach
a speed of over 530 mph,
to penetrate the screen of escorts

1,000 yards from target
level out for firing run

'G' pull-up 1,500 ft below
and one mile behind the bomber
formation to dump speed for attack

► This Me 262 A-2a, coded 9K+FH, W.Nr. 111685, had originally belonged to the bomber unit KG 51, but had been transferred to JV 44. It is seen here in a woodland dispersal area off the München-Salzburg autobahn.

"We were flying escort when an Me 262 approached the rear box of bombers and began leap-frogging through the entire group, scoring several hits. He then veered off, returned, and started attacking the rear box again. By this time we were on his tail. I tried a long shot and could see strikes all over his left wing, which immediately caused him to lose speed. My wingman and I were then able to close on him and I scored several strikes on both wings and the fuselage. The Jerry then peeled out and proceeded to head for the deck, and I was following him all the time firing as we went. We broke through a scattered undercast and I was sitting right on his tail until my guns were completely empty. By that time I knew he was a dead duck and veered off to the left, pulling up just as he crashed into the ground."

During the next four days there were further pitched battles between Me 262s and US formations, yet although the US heavy bombers were the main targets for the Me 262s' attacks, they were not the only ones. By this stage of the war the RAF was also mounting large-scale daylight attacks on targets in Germany, and on 31 March, a force of 460 Lancasters and Halifaxes set out to bomb the U-boat assembly yards at Hamburg. As the bombers neared the target a small force of Me 262s delivered a sharp attack which rapidly knocked down three Halifaxes and four Lancasters in succession before the escorts drove off the assailants. Also that day, more than a thousand US heavy bombers attacked Zeitz, Brandenburg, Braunschweig and Halle, and these were also engaged by jet fighters.

Me 262 fighters flew 58 sorties on 31 March, the greatest number they would ever achieve. On the available evidence, it appears they shot down 14 Allied bombers and two fighters, for a loss of four of their number. That victory score also marked the pinnacle of achievement for the Me 262 fighter units, and it would never be surpassed. Yet, even on this most successful of days, the losses they inflicted amounted to less than one per cent of the huge Allied forces sent over Germany. The effect of the jet fighters' defence was merely a pinprick.

Early in April a new and remarkable Me 262 fighter unit entered the fray, *Jagdverband 44* (JV 44). Its commander was *Generalleutnant* Adolf Galland, recently dismissed from the post of Inspector of Fighters after a row with Hermann Göring. No doubt Göring hoped that by allowing Galland to lead the unit in action, the Allies would rid him of his troublesome but highly-decorated subordinate.

With many German piston-engined day fighter units

now grounded for want of fuel, Galland was able to draw into his unit several of the most experienced and successful fighter pilots in the *Luftwaffe*. As he later commented, *"The Ritterkreuz was, so to speak, the badge of our unit."* In addition to Galland himself, other members of the unit who held this coveted decoration were Johannes Steinhoff, Günther Lützow, Heinz Bär, Gerhard Barkhorn, Erich Hohagen, Karl-Heinz Schnell, Willi Herget, Walter Krupinski, Hans Grünberg, Klaus Neumann and Heinz Sachsenberg. During and after the war there has been much loose talk about '*crack Luftwaffe fighter units'*. The term implies a unit with more than its share of ace pilots, and the ability to draw these from other units, but arguably the only such '*crack'* *Luftwaffe* fighter unit to go into action was JV 44.

JV 44 flew its first interception mission on 5 April when it scrambled five fighters and claimed the destruction of two enemy bombers. By now, the *Luftwaffe* fighter control organisation was in tatters and even with its unique collection of talented pilots, JV 44

▲ An American photograph from April 1945 clearly showing the oval layout of München-Riem airport. JV 44 normally parked their jets along the perimeter track connecting the start platform with the airport control buildings. Careful examination of the original photograph shows that some of the aircraft parked off the southern perimeter track in the main area of bomb craters are Me 262s.

▶ Oberst Hajo Herrmann was the instigator of the 'Wilde Sau' tactics and the forming of JG 300 in his role as Inspekteur der Luftverteidigung (Inspector for Air Defence). He was awarded the Ritterkreuz as a bomber pilot with KG 4 and also flew as a Staffelkapitän with III./KG 30. Towards the end of 1944 he led the 9. Fliegerdivision and proposed the Rammkommando 'Elbe'. He ended the war with nine four-engined bomber victories and flew more than 320 bomber missions sinking some 12 ships. He spent many years as a prisoner in Russia after the war.

was unable to operate effectively. Later Galland wrote in his biography:

"Our last operation was anything but jolly, light-hearted hunting, for we not only had to battle against technical, tactical and supply difficulties, but also lacked a clear [radar] picture in the air of the floods coming from the west – a picture which was absolutely necessary for the success of an operation. Every day the fronts moved in closer from three sides, but, worst of all, our field was under continuous observation by an overwhelming majority of US fighters. During one raid we were hit three times very heavily. Thousands of workers had to be mobilised to keep open a landing strip between the bomb-craters . . .

"Operations from Riem started, despite all resistance and difficulties. Naturally we were able to send up only small units. On landing, the aircraft had to be towed immediately off the field. They were dispersed over the countryside and had to be completely camouflaged. Bringing the aircraft on to the field and the take-off became more and more difficult; eventually it was a matter of luck. One raid followed another."

With so much going against it, only rarely was *JV 44* able to fly more than half a dozen sorties or shoot down more than a couple of enemy aircraft per day. Indeed, the *'crack Luftwaffe fighter unit'* achieved so little that its entry into battle passed unnoticed by the Allied air forces.

▶ This remarkable photograph taken from another B-17 of the 97th Bomb Group shows the aircraft after a shell had exploded in the nose over Budapest in July 1944. Amazingly at least five of the crew managed to bale out before the aircraft crashed.

Had the *Luftwaffe* been able to inflict serious losses on the US heavy bomber formations even once during the previous months, it would have had something to show for the terrible losses it suffered. But that was no longer the case, and the US escort fighters had imposed their superiority in the skies over Germany.

Against this background of near-despair *Oberst* Hajo Herrmann, father of the *Wilde Sau* tactic for night fighters, submitted another radical proposal for the defence of the Reich. He now commanded the *1. Jagd Division* responsible for the air defence of central Germany, including the area around Berlin. He told this writer:

"I did not have a Sturmgruppe in my Division, but I knew about them, of course. I knew they were not effective in the long run, on account of the losses they suffered from the escort fighters. It was clear to me that no system of destroying the enemy bombers would work unless some way could be found of avoiding the escorts. The long-term answer was to use the Me 262 jet fighter. But its introduction into service would take time, and we desperately needed some means of inflicting an unacceptably high loss on one or two US raiding formations, so the attacks would cease and we would gain a breathing space to get the jet fighters into service in large numbers."

Herrmann proposed the formation of special units manned by volunteer pilots, who would be willing to destroy the US heavy bombers by ramming them. With ramming as their tactic of first resort, these fighters did not need a heavy armament. The ideal vehicle was a high altitude fighter version of the Messerschmitt Bf 109,

either a G or a K variant, carrying a single 13 mm or 15 mm heavy machine gun for self-defence. Thus lightened, these fighters could out-climb and out-run the US escorts, so they would not require fighter protection to help them get past the escorts.

When an enemy bomber formation approached central Germany, the lightweight fighters were to take off and climb to altitudes around 33,000 feet where they would be out of reach of the Allied escorts. The lightweight Messerschmitts would be vectored into attacking positions above a bomber formation. Then, with the formation in sight, each German pilot would select a bomber and dive on it almost vertically, aiming to strike his victim in the rear fuselage, immediately in front of the tail unit, where the airframe was at its weakest.

The plan required a force of some 800 ramming fighters, manned by volunteers, to engage in a single large-scale operation. If just half of the ramming attempts succeeded, the USAAF would lose 400 heavy bombers and crews in a single day. Herrmann believed it would take the USAAF several weeks to recover from such a blow. If the massed ramming attacks halted the US heavy bomber attacks for even a few weeks, that would create a breathing space for the oil industry and perhaps also for the *Luftwaffe* fighter force to stage a recovery.

Herrmann did not minimise the personal risk to those involved in the ramming operation. From available reports of rammings, he thought that maybe half of the pilots who rammed bombers would bail out successfully. The other half – about 200 German pilots – would be killed or would suffer serious injury. At first sight that might seem a callous way to use men, even if they had

▲ A Bf 109 G-6 with Erla-Haube (modified Erla hood) and a tall tail unit, probably in the summer of 1944. This machine may have belonged to JG 27 and has the wavy bar of IV. Gruppe on the rear fuselage. Beneath this, however, is what appears to be an earlier II. Gruppe horizontal bar upon which is painted the name 'Margot'. With the gradual disappearance of unit emblems, decorating aircraft with the names of girlfriends, fiancées or wives became an increasingly popular alternative.

UNITS ASSIGNED TO REICH AIR DEFENCE

9 APRIL 1945

This is the last date for which there exists a reasonably complete listing of the *Luftwaffe* Order of Battle. Since the previous January the *Luftwaffe* had undergone a further reorganisation. For Reich Air Defence the main change was that *Luftflotte* 3 had transferred the majority of its day fighter units to *Luftflotte Reich*, and was then downgraded to *Luftwaffenkommando West*. Also, *Luftflotte* 4 had withdrawn so far westwards to airfields in Austria and Czechoslovakia, that its two full-strength *Gruppen* of day fighters contributed to the defence of the homeland.

By now Allied ground forces had overrun several aircraft production centres and aircraft storage parks, while others were under threat and were being hastily evacuated. Given those difficulties, it is remarkable that the strength of the combat units had not fallen further below the January figure. Two factors helped the *Luftwaffe* to maintain its strength, at least on paper. Firstly, after the surge in production during the previous year, large numbers of aircraft were sitting in storage parks and available to replace losses. And secondly, the fuel famine restricted piston-engined fighter units to low sortie rates. Thus their aircraft spent most of the time sitting at camouflaged dispersal points some distance from their airfields, in relative safety; that greatly reduced losses.

At last, the Me 262 jet fighter was going into action in moderate numbers, but despite high production levels, only a small proportion served in the front line and the main part of the air defence system hinged on the activities of just 89 serviceable Me 262s. Whenever they went into action against a USAAF raiding force, the jet fighters were outnumbered ten-to-one or more by the swarms of escorts. Under these conditions, it is not surprising that the Me 262s achieved so little.

The *Luftwaffe* night fighter force possessed 485 serviceable aircraft, but a shortage of fuel meant that its operational capability was far lower than the numerical strength would suggest.

Unit	Aircraft Type	Aircraft Available	Total Serviceable	Unit	Aircraft Type	Aircraft Available	Total Serviceable
Luftflotte 4				Jagdgeschwader 52			
Jagdgeschwader 51				Stab	Bf 109	8	(7)
II. Gruppe	Bf 109	7	(5)	I. Gruppe	Bf 109	40	(37)
				III. Gruppe	Bf 109	32	(30)
Jagdgeschwader 52							
II. Gruppe	Bf 109	43	(29)	Jagdgeschwader 77			
Jagdgeschwader 53				Stab	Bf 109	1	(1)
I. Gruppe	Bf 109	27	(27)	I. Gruppe	Bf 109	30	(26)
Jagdgeschwader 76				II. Gruppe	Bf 109	36	(30)
Stab	Bf 109	1	(1)	III. Gruppe	Bf 109	34	(25)
Luftflotte 6				Ergänzungsjagdgeschwader 1			
Jagdgeschwader 3					Bf 109	109	(97)[1]
Stab	Fw 190	4	(4)				
II. Gruppe	Bf 109	51	(49)	**Luftflotte Reich**			
III. Gruppe	Bf 109	47	(46)				
IV. Gruppe	Fw 190	61	(56)	Jagdgeschwader 2			
				I. Gruppe	Fw 190	5	(3)
Jagdgeschwader 6				II. Gruppe	Fw 190	8	(4)
Stab	Fw 190, Bf 109	4	(4)	III. Gruppe	Fw 190	12	(9)
I. Gruppe	Fw 190	72	(59)				
II. Gruppe	Fw 190	48	(45)	Jagdgeschwader 4			
III. Gruppe	Bf 109	21	(17)	Stab	Fw 190	6	(4)
				II. Gruppe	Fw 190	50	(34)
Jagdgeschwader 11				III. Gruppe	Bf 109	61	(56)
Stab	Fw 190	4	(4)				
I. Gruppe	Fw 190	55	(53)	Jagdgeschwader 7			
III. Gruppe	Fw 190	54	(51)	Stab	Me 262	5	(4)
				I. Gruppe	Me 262	41	(26)
				II. Gruppe	Me 262	30	(23)

Unit	Aircraft Type	Aircraft Available	Total Serviceable
Jagdgeschwader 26			
Stab	Fw 190	4	(3)
I. Gruppe	Fw 190	44	(16)
II. Gruppe	Fw 190	57	(29)
III. Gruppe	Fw 190	35	(15)
Jagdgeschwader 27			
I. Gruppe	Bf 109	29	(13)
II. Gruppe	Bf 109	48	(27)
III. Gruppe	Bf 109	19	(15)
Kampfgeschwader (Jäger) 54			
I. Gruppe	Me 262	37	(21)[2]
Jagdgeschwader 301			
Stab	Ta 152	3	(2)
I. Gruppe	Fw 190	35	(24)
II. Gruppe	Fw 190	32	(15)
Jagdgeschwader 400			
II. Gruppe	Me 163	38	(22)
Jagdgruppe 10	Fw 190	15	(9)
Jagdverband 44	Me 262	30	(15)[3]
Nachtjagdgeschwader 1			
Stab	He 219	29	(25)
	Bf 110		
1. Staffel	He 219	22	(19)
4. Staffel	Bf 110	16	(15)
7. Staffel	Bf 110	16	(14)
10. Staffel	Bf 110	17	(15)
Nachtjagdgeschwader 2			
Stab	Ju 88	2	(2)
I. Gruppe	Ju 88	25	(22)
II. Gruppe	Ju 88	24	(21)
III. Gruppe	Ju 88	29	(27)
Nachtjagdgeschwader 3			
Stab	Ju 88	4	(4)
1. Staffel	Ju 88	14	(12)
7. Staffel	Ju 88	19	(16)
10. Staffel	Ju 88	20	(17)
Nachtjagdgeschwader 4			
Stab	Ju 88, Bf 110	4	(4)
1. Staffel	Ju 88	17	(9)
4. Staffel	Ju 88	28	(23)
7. Staffel	Ju 88	14	(11)

Unit	Aircraft Type	Aircraft Available	Total Serviceable
Nachtjagdgeschwader 5			
Stab	Ju 88	16	(10)
	Bf 110		
1. Staffel	Ju 88	17	(10)
4. Staffel	Ju 88, Bf 110	28	(25)
7. Staffel	He 219, Ju 88,	34	(32)
	Bf 110		
10. Staffel	Ju 88	12	(11)
Nachtjagdgeschwader 6			
Stab	Ju 88, Bf 110	17	(17)
1. Staffel	Ju 88	17	(17)
4. Staffel	Ju 88	14	(11)
7. Staffel	Bf 110	15	(12)
10. Staffel	Ju 88	15	(8)
Nachtjagdgeschwader 11			
1. Staffel	Bf 109	16	(15)
4. Staffel	Bf 109	14	(9)
7. Staffel	Bf 109	21	(19)
10. Staffel	Me 262	9	(7)
Nachtjagdgeschwader 100			
I. Gruppe	Ju 88, Fw 58	23	(20)
Kommando Bonow	Ar 234	2	(1)[4]
Luftflottenkommando East Prussia			
Jagdgeschwader 51			
Stab	Fw 190	20	(11)
I. Gruppe	Bf 109	10	(8)
III. Gruppe	Bf 109	23	(7)

Notes
[1]. Training Unit
[2]. Bad Weather Day Fighter
[3]. Approximate Figure
[4]. Experimental Night Fighter Unit

volunteered for the operation, but war is a callous business. In a military operation, the correct tactics are those that secure the aim for the lowest cost in men and materials. The aim of the *Luftwaffe* was to bring about a temporary halt to the highly destructive Allied daylight attacks that were tearing the guts out of German industry. Using conventional air defence methods, the previous attempts to halt the attacks were costing the *Luftwaffe* fighter force more than 300 pilots killed and wounded each month. And, patently, they failed in their purpose.

Herrmann's scheme therefore promised a more tangible result for the loss of fewer pilots than would fall during a month of air defence operations using conventional tactics. He wrote:

"Regardless of the scale on which the [ramming] operation is carried out, it is the most effective course open to us under present conditions. It is in no way more expensive in personnel than are ordinary operations. It will consume only one-third as many aircraft, and one-fifth to one-tenth as much fuel, as would normal operations..."

Herrmann's proposal sparked a lively debate within the *Luftwaffe* High Command, then it went before Adolf Hitler for final approval. The Führer said he would not *demand* that any German make such a sacrifice, but if *volunteers* could be found who were willing to ram the enemy heavy bombers, the scheme would have his blessing.

These various discussions took time, and above all else the Third Reich was short of time. Early in March 1945 the appeal for volunteers was posted at operational and flying training units throughout the *Luftwaffe*. The appeal simply asked for pilots willing to volunteer for a decisive operation from which there was only a small chance of returning.

There was no actual or implied pressure on individuals to volunteer, yet the appeal produced an overwhelming response, with more than two thousand pilots offering themselves for the forthcoming operation. That was more than Herrmann's plan required, and it allowed the *Luftwaffe* to reject pilots it could not afford to lose. *Reichsmarschall* Göring ruled that the majority of the ramming pilots would be students coming straight from the fighter training schools, with a sprinkling of experienced pilots to lead them into action.

On 24 March the selected volunteers began arriving at the fighter airfield at Stendal near Berlin. The next day, the pilots were told the nature of the mission for which they had volunteered. Even then, any pilots who wished to recant were allowed to do so and they were able to

leave the operation without recrimination.

The final training of pilots for the ramming operation lasted two weeks, and it fell well short of what was needed. Due to the fuel shortage, the pilots had no opportunity to handle the lightweight Messerschmitts at high altitude or in high-speed dives. Most of the available time was taken up with ground instruction on the required tactics. There were also periods of political indoctrination, with lectures on Germany's current military position and the extent to which this would improve if the planned operation went ahead as planned and succeeded.

Oberst Herrmann stressed the importance of holding back on the ramming operation until there was a large enough force to strike a decisive blow. At the end of March he wrote to Göring pointing out that mounting the attack with only 150 or 250 pilots would not achieve its intended purpose. To bring about the required halt in the bombing attacks, Herrmann asked that the operation be delayed until he had at least 650 pilots trained and ready for action.

Herrmann's arguments were sound, but it was already too late for these to carry the day. Early in April Allied troops crossed the Rhine and began thrusting into Germany. In the East, the Red Army was massing for a final assault on Berlin itself. The ramming operation had to be launched as soon as possible, using the resources to hand.

Early in April the volunteer pilots moved to the airfields around Berlin from which the operation was to be mounted: Stendal, Delitzsch, Mörtitz, Gardelegen and Sachau. Other pilots were taken to airfields near Prague in Czechoslovakia, from which a co-ordinated operation was to be flown. To avoid attracting Allied attacks on these airfields, the specially modified Messerschmitts were to be delivered there only a few hours before the operation was launched.

Operation *Wehrwolf* was launched on 7 April, the day the US 8th Air Force sent more than 1,300 B-17s and B-24s, escorted by more than 800 fighters, to attack railway marshalling yards, fuel storage areas and airfields in central Germany.

Wehrwolf suffered some last-minute glitches, of which the most serious was the late delivery of many of the specially modified fighters. As a result, the ramming operation was launched with only about 200 Bf 109s. Supporting them as they went into action were about a hundred conventional fighters, as well as about 40 Me 262s.

Since it was mounted with far fewer aircraft than Herrmann had proposed, and with pilots that had

► ► At the end, a nation laid waste. The two major targets for the Allied heavy bombers were the German cities, and the oil industry, represented here by this wrecked refinery near Hamburg.

► This aerial photograph shows the centre of Nuremberg completely devastated as were virtually all other major cities in Germany at the end of the war.

received insufficient training, the ramming operation went off in a disorganised fashion. In several cases the inexperienced pilots were unable to maintain formation on their leaders, became lost and had to break off the action. Other fighters suffered technical failures. Moreover, the 60-odd ramming fighters that had taken off from airfields around Prague were too far from the bombers' routes to engage, and these had to be recalled.

Due to the various reductions, only about one hundred ramming fighters went into action that day. The main attack fell on the B-17s of the 3rd Air Division as they passed north of Hannover. The P-47 and P-51 escorts fought a furious action to defend their charges, and the rammers failed to achieve the hoped-for overwhelmingly concentrated attack. Numerous Bf 109s were shot down; others suffered damage and had to break off the action. Only ten fighters penetrated the escort screen and delivered ramming attacks. Seven of the rammed bombers went down immediately, yet, remarkably, despite having suffered heavy damage, the remaining three B-17s were able to reach airfields in friendly territory and make normal landings.

B-24s of the 2nd Air Division also came under

attack, though their escorts fought off most attempts to reach the bombers. One Bf 109 rammed a B-24 Liberator of the 389th Bomb Group, which went out of control and crashed into the bomber next to it in the formation. The wreckage of the three machines tumbled from the sky. Another Bf 109 rammed a B-24 Liberator, but the latter regained friendly territory.

In total the US Eighth Air Force's losses on that day amounted to 17 bombers and five fighters, a loss it could easily afford to shrug off. It is estimated that the ramming force lost about 40 pilots killed during the *Wehrwolf* action. There was no attempt to repeat the operation.

In March 1945, following a resumption of production of hydrazine hydrate, there was a small-scale resurgence of Me 163 activity. On the 15th of the month, I/JG 400 launched five rocket fighters from Brandis to meet a US raiding force. No rocket fighter succeeded in getting through to the bombers, however, and escorting Mustangs claimed the destruction of one Me 163.

One factor that had prevented the Me 163 from becoming an effective bomber-destroyer was the lack of an armament system which enabled none but the most skilful of pilots to deliver an accurate burst during the

fighter's brief high-speed attacking run. Closing on a bomber at an overtaking speed of about 150 metres per second, many pilots found that as soon as they had their sight on a bomber they had to break away to avoid colliding with it.

To overcome that problem the Hasag company in Leipzig developed *Jägerfaust* (Fighter-Fist), an automatic firing system. As applied to the Me 163, *Jägerfaust* comprised five vertically mounted 50 mm gun barrels built into each wing root, each barrel loaded with a 2.2lb high explosive shell. The barrels were fired in rapid succession, triggered by a photoelectric cell which detected the shadow of the enemy aircraft passing overhead. To balance the recoil forces as each shell was fired upwards, a counterweight of similar weight was fired downwards. To use the system, the Me 163 pilot primed the *Jägerfaust*, then manoeuvred his aircraft to a point beneath the target bomber and within about 90 metres of it, attacking either from head-on or tail-on. The barrels were divided into two groups of five for firing, enabling the pilot to carry out two attacks with the available rounds.

Jägerfaust performed well during trials in which a cloth target the size of a bomber's wing was stretched between two tethered balloons to trigger the device. In the final weeks of the war about a dozen Me 163s were fitted with the system, but it was used in combat only once.

On 10 April, *Leutnant* Fritz Kelb took off to test the system when he sighted a lone B-17 straggling behind its formation near Leipzig. He delivered a high-speed attack on the bomber using the new weapon, and it went down shedding pieces.

Kelb's attack marked the virtual end of the Me 163's operational career. Although it had a sparkling maximum speed and climbing performance, it operated too close to the limits of what was possible, the chemical rocket fuels were rather too exotic for general service use, and the aircraft's short endurance allowed pilots little margin for error when they tried to engage enemy bombers. Consequently, little was achieved and it is doubtful whether, after just over eight months in combat, the rocket fighter destroyed any more than 16 enemy aircraft.

During the rest of April, the struggle between the Allied aircraft and the Me 262s reached its climax. US fighters reported 319 encounters and 234 combats with jet aircraft, in which they claimed 56 destroyed in the air

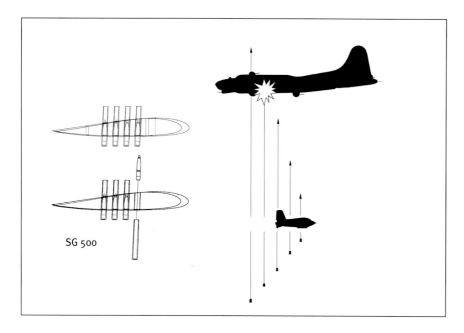

SG 500

they had to be transported by rail on a network that was being systematically cut to pieces by Allied strategic and tactical bombers.

Inexorably, the tattered remnants of the *Luftwaffe* were squeezed into the areas around Schleswig Holstein and Denmark in the north and Bavaria, Austria and Czechoslovakia in the south. On 25 April, the two arms of a Soviet pincer around Berlin met to complete the encirclement of the city. On the same day, Soviet and US armies met on the River Elbe near Leipzig to slice Germany into two. By then, *Luftwaffe* air operations had come to an almost complete halt. On 6 May, *Grossadmiral* Dönitz, who inherited the leadership of the Third Reich after Adolf Hitler committed suicide, ordered that his forces were to lay down their arms on the following day. The war in Europe was over.

So ended the Battle over the Reich, the greatest air action there would ever be. Certainly no other came close to it in terms of its length, its ferocity, the numbers of men and aircraft committed to it, and the losses suffered by both sides.

What did the strategic air attacks on Germany achieve? They did not, as their supporters had hoped, bring about a complete collapse of the German war economy without the need for an invasion by ground forces. On the other hand the bombing, and the need for the *Luftwaffe* to build up and maintain powerful Flak and fighter defences in the homeland, created

▲ The Jägerfaust weapon fitted to the Me 163 comprised five vertically mounted 50 mm gun barrels, each loaded with a single 2.2 pound high-explosive shell, built into each wing root. To balance the recoil forces when the shells were fired upward, counterweights were fired downwards. The firing was triggered by a photoelectric cell which detected the shadow of the enemy aircraft as it passed overhead. Leutnant Fritz Kelb of JG 400 scored the sole victory with this system fitted to an Me 163, when he shot down a RCAF Lancaster on 10 April 1945.

and 46 on the ground. In the course of that month, however, only 24 heavy bombers were seen to go down to attacks from jet fighters.

Despite the large numbers of Me 262s now coming off the production lines – during the first four months of 1945 the *Luftwaffe* took delivery of more than 850 of these aircraft – only a small proportion saw action. Such was the general chaos in Germany during the closing stages of the war that the majority remained on the ground for want of fuel, spare engines or spare parts. Although these existed in depots around the country,

► Lt. Friedrich 'Fritz' Kelb, served with 2./JG 400 and is seen here climbing into a Junkers-built Me 163 B, W.Nr. 190579.

progressively more serious shortages at the various battle fronts. Of these, the most notable were in radar and signals equipment, artillery and fighter aircraft.

From mid-1944, Allied strategic bombers focused their attention on the German oil industry, and we have observed the far-reaching effects of this on the *Luftwaffe*; the German Army and Navy suffered similar restrictions to their activities. Once the oil industry was under siege from the air it mattered little that the German production of aircraft (or for that matter tanks) continued to rise. Without the fuel to run them, the extra output was of little value.

Moreover, during their large-scale daylight attacks, the US raiding formations used German industry as the anvil upon which their long-range fighters hammered the life out of the *Luftwaffe*. It is

difficult to exaggerate the importance of this to the success of the Normandy invasion, and it is equally difficult to see how, without the need to combat the daylight heavy bomber attacks, the *Luftwaffe* could have been forced into the air to fight a battle that it was bound to lose. Finally, the day and night attacks on the German rail and canal systems did much to bring about the chaos which greatly assisted the Allied advances into the country. Thus, although the strategic air offensive did not prove decisive in its own right, it made a crucial contribution to the success of the overall Allied strategy.

In the next and final Chapter we shall look at the advanced new weapons the *Luftwaffe* was about to introduce into large-scale service when the war ended, and observe how effective they might have been.

▲ As the fuel crisis began to take its effect, the scene in this photograph had become a common sight on airfields across Germany by early 1945. Here pilots of II./JG 301 line up for a briefing on the perimeter track at Stendal as oxen and local civilians roll a two-seat Fw 190 S-8 trainer to or from its dispersal. Such trainers were used to convert pilots from disbanded bomber units onto fighter operations.

13

THE WEAPONS THAT CAME TOO LATE

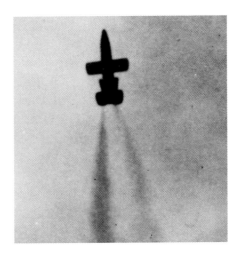

"The race is not always to the swiftest nor the fight to the strongest.

But that's the way you bet."

Attributed to Samuel Goldwyn

In this Chapter we shall examine the best of the new weapon systems the *Luftwaffe* was close to bringing into action at the time the war ended. How effective might they have been, and could they have altered the course of the air war over Europe?

The Heinkel He 162 *Volksjäger*

On 10 September 1944, the *Luftwaffe* Technical Office invited design proposals for the so-called *Volksjäger* competition. This called for a lightweight single-seat fighter with an all-up weight of 1,995 kg (less than one-third that of Me 262), using wood wherever possible in place of aluminium in its construction. The specification called for a maximum speed of 750 km/h at sea level, an operational endurance of at least half an hour and a take-off distance in still air of no more than 500 metres. The aircraft was to be armed with two 20 mm cannon each with 100 rounds, or two 30 mm cannon each with 50 rounds. Time was of the essence, and companies had to submit draft proposals within ten days. The winning design had to be ready for large-scale production by 1 January 1945.

The Heinkel design was considered the most promising and it was pronounced the winner, receiving the official designation Heinkel He 162. The fighter was a clean-lined high wing monoplane with a nacelle housing a single BMW 003 turbojet mounted mid-way along the top of the fuselage. The fuselage was of light alloy construction with a moulded plywood nose, and the wing was to be made in one piece and constructed primarily of wood, with a plywood skinning. To avoid the

jet efflux, the aircraft was fitted with twin fins and rudders, the tailplane, elevators and rudders being of metal construction while the fins were made of wood. To enable the pilot to escape from the fighter in an emergency, it was fitted with a rudimentary ejector seat designed by the Heinkel company.

Initially, two production versions of the aircraft were to be produced in quantity: the He 162 A-l bomber-destroyer with two 30 mm Mk 108 cannon rounds of ammunition, and the A-2 air superiority fighter with two MG 151 20 mm cannon.

With the acceptance of the design came an order for a thousand lightweight fighters to be delivered by the end of April 1945. To achieve such figures, planners at the *Jägerstab*, the Fighter Production Committee, had to short-circuit many accepted practices in aircraft manufacture and detailed design work, construction of prototypes and tooling up for mass production were to take place simultaneously. Final assembly of the fighter would be at the Heinkel plant at Marienehe, the Junkers plant at Bernberg and underground production facility at Nordhausen. Numerous sub-contractors dispersed throughout the country were to feed these plants with the necessary sub-assemblies and components.

On 6 December, a remarkable 90 days since the start of the programme, the fighter made its maiden flight. During the 20-minute flight test pilot Gothold Peter reached 840 km/h at 5,975 metres. In

◄◄ **This He 162 A-2, formerly of I./JG 1 and found at Leck in May 1945, was one of two examples sent to Canada and this restored example is currently on display at Rockliffe, Ontario.**

▶ He 162 A-2, 'White 23', W.Nr. 120230 was captured at Leck in May 1945 by British forces, where numerous examples of the 'Volksjäger' belonging to JG 1 were handed over intact.

▶ After the capture of Leck, this He 162 A-2 'White 3' was restored to flying condition around 15 or 16 May 1945 under the watchful eye of Oblt. Wolfgang Wollenweber, who also instructed British test pilots on how to handle the aircraft.

general, the aircraft handled well, though there was some longitudinal instability and a tendency towards excessive sideslip. Disaster struck four days later, however, when Peter demonstrated the He 162 over Vienna/Schwechat before senior Nazi party officials. During a high speed run the starboard wing came apart, the fighter rolled out of control and dived into the ground with the pilot still in the cockpit. The investigation revealed the cause of the accident to be defective glue bonding of the wooden components. The wings of subsequent aircraft were checked for bonding,

and re-stressed and fitted with a revised structure giving increased strength.

Despite the loss of the first aircraft, the He 162 programme continued with undiminished vigour. On 22 December, less than two weeks after the crash of the first prototype, Heinkel director Carl Francke took the second prototype into the air. The flight passed off without incident, although because the aircraft was fitted with the original type of wing, Francke had to restrict his speed.

The third and fourth prototypes, both fitted with the new strengthened wings, flew on 16 January 1945. Firing tests with the two 30 mm cannon revealed that the recoil forces were too great for the original nose structure to absorb. For this reason few He 162 A-1s were built, and most early production aircraft were A-2 versions fitted with two 20 mm Mauser MG 151 cannon.

By the end of January 1945, six He 162s were flying, including two production aircraft. The first *Luftwaffe* unit, *Erprobungskommando 162* based at Rechlin/Roggenthin, was formed to assist with the testing of the new fighter and speed the introduction of the type into service. The unit's commander, *Oberstleutnant* Heinz Bär, was a respected fighter leader with more than 200 aerial victories to his credit.

Flight tests revealed that the production He 162 A-2 had a maximum speed of 890 km/h at sea level, and

905 km/h at 5,945 metres. With the various modifications to strengthen the aircraft and improve handling, the original maximum all-up weight of around 1,995 kg was greatly exceeded, and at take-off the He 162 A-2 in the operational configuration weighed 2,805 kg. However, since the fighter's maximum speed exceeded the requirement by a handsome margin, the excessive weight was ignored.

During February, 46 He 162s were delivered to the *Luftwaffe*, sufficient to re-equip the first operational unit, I./JG 1, which gave up its Fw 190s and withdrew to Parchim to convert to the jet fighter. During March, further production He 162s arrived at Parchim, but by now Allied ground forces were thrusting deep into Germany from both the east and the west. For *Luftwaffe* flying units the situation had become increasingly chaotic with each day that passed, and severe shortages of spare parts and aviation fuel at the airfields delayed the conversion of I./JG 1 into an effective jet fighter unit.

On 7 April, Parchim airfield came under attack from US bombers and suffered heavy damage, forcing the He 162 unit to move to the nearby airfield at Ludwigslust. There the operational work-up continued with about 15 He 162s. After less than a week the unit moved again, to Leck near the Danish border.

During the work-up, He 162 pilots had orders to avoid enemy aircraft whenever possible. Allied fighters conducted offensive sweeps over German-held territory, however, and such contacts were inevitable. On 15 April, *Leutnant* Rudolf Schmitt, a pilot straight from training making his fourth flight in the He 162, encountered a Spitfire but successfully avoided combat.

After an RAF pilot was taken prisoner and told his captors that he had been shot down by a jet fighter, *Feldwebel* Günther Kirchner was credited with scoring the He 162's first aerial victory on 19 April. Although the 2nd Tactical Air Force lost several aircraft that day, it is not possible from British records to confirm or refute the

▼ Very few operations were flown by the He 162 A-2s of 1./JG 1 before the end of the war, and when British forces captured Leck airfield, they discovered the unit's aircraft lined up in neat rows on either side of the runway. These machines carry the badge of the unit, a black diving eagle on a yellow shield with a white diagonal band.

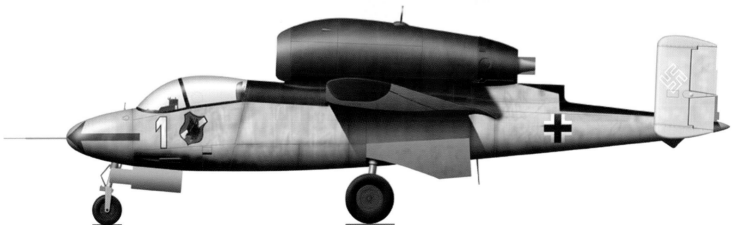

HEINKEL He 162 A-2 OF 1./JG 1, LECK, MAY 1945
Although most He 162s carried the standard camouflage scheme allocated to the type, the dividing line between the upper and lower surface colours varied widely. The red arrow marking was common to the He 162 but its significance is unknown.

▲ Test pilot Lothar Siebert boarding the Natter for its first manned test flight on 28 February 1945 which ended in his death.

were lost in flying accidents. On 24 April *Hauptmann* Paul-Heinrick Dähne, commander of I. *Gruppe*, was on a training flight over Leck when his aircraft was seen to turn and yaw violently, then break up and crash, killing the pilot. The war ended before the cause of the crash could be determined.

On 26 April *Unteroffizier* Rechenbach was credited with the destruction of an unspecified enemy aircraft and had his victory confirmed by two independent witnesses. Again, that was a day when the 2nd Tactical Air Force lost several aircraft over enemy territory and the claim cannot be confirmed or refuted from British records.

On 30 April *Leutnant* Alfred Dürr ran short of fuel and was killed when he attempted an emergency landing on a strip of autobahn near Lübeck. The fighter's short endurance was a constant source of difficulty, and it is known that the unit lost at least one other pilot to this cause.

The same *Leutnant* Schmitt who had earlier ejected from an He 162, claimed the destruction of a Typhoon near Rostock on 4 May, and this time there is clear verification of the victory from British records. The 'Typhoon' was in fact a Tempest of No 486 Squadron piloted by Flying Officer M. Austin, who parachuted to safety and was taken prisoner. The fact that the novice German pilot had shot down one of the RAF's best piston-engined fighters illustrates the Heinkel's formidable potential.

On 5 May a cease-fire was declared in north-western Europe, and when British troops arrived at Leck the next day, they found 31 He 162s drawn up in neat rows on either side of the runway. In total, the *Luftwaffe* accepted delivery of about 120 He 162s. Possibly half as many again were collected from the factories by service pilots, and a similar number were awaiting flight-testing or collection.

Oberleutnant Emil Demuth flew the He 162 with I./JG 1, and he told this writer that, in his opinion, it was a first class combat aircraft, much faster than any Allied machine he had encountered. Demuth was an experienced fighter pilot credited with 16 previous victories, however, and in the hands of less experienced pilots the jet fighter was a potential death trap. During the three-week period between 13 April and the end of the war, I./JG 1 lost 13 aircraft and ten pilots, at least one, possibly three, of these losses being due to enemy action. The rest resulted from flying accidents, mostly due to engine flame-outs and pilot error and, as at least one of the unit's He 162s suffered a structural failure in flight, there may have been more.

claim that one of them was shot down by an He 162. Shortly afterwards, however, Kirchner also became the first He 162 pilot to lose his life in action when his aircraft crashed and he was killed. The loss of the German jet fighter can be confirmed from British records, however, for during a strafing attack on Husum airfield, Flying Officer Geoff Walkington, flying a Tempest of No 222 Squadron, reported encountering an unidentified jet aircraft with twin fins and a single engine – obviously an He 162. Walkington pursued the enemy machine, but was unable to close the distance until the German pilot made the fundamental mistake of entering a sweeping turn to starboard, which allowed the Tempest to close to within firing range. Walkington scored hits and saw the German aircraft spin into the ground.

On 20 April, *Leutnant* Rudolf Schmitt ejected from an He 162, to make what is believed to be the first and perhaps the only successful emergency use of the jet fighter's ejector seat. Schmitt's flying logbook has survived and confirms his escape, though it makes no mention of whether an enemy aircraft was involved. The logbook gives the duration of the flight as 25 minutes, which was close to the maximum for the new fighter at low altitude. Possibly the inexperienced pilot had become lost and ran out of fuel.

I./JG 1 came under the control of *Luftflotte Reich* on 23 April and received clearance to commence combat operations, but due to its over-hasty development, the He 162 retained some nasty vices in service and several

The He 162 had its good points, but this was not the fighter to inflict severe losses on the massive Allied air fleets. It was not an easy machine to fly, and was rather beyond the abilities of the novice pilots intended for it. Moreover, the knowledge that it was liable to break up in flight produced a marked reluctance to explore the limits of its manoeuvrability. Worst of all, its value in air-to-air combat was marred by the novel engine layout which severely restricted the pilot's view in the all-important six o'clock position, i.e. above and to the rear. If enemy fighters were thought to be in their area, He 162 pilots would have felt extremely vulnerable to surprise attack from the rear.

The Bachem Ba 349 *Natter* Target Defence Fighter

The *Natter* (*Viper*) was the brainchild of Erich Bachem of the Fieseler company. The semi-expendable rocket-powered interceptor could be regarded as a manned surface-to-air missile, intended to provide daylight point defence for important targets. It was also the world's first practical design for a vertical take-off and landing fighter (the former under rocket power, the latter by parachute).

The mode of operation was as follows. The two and a half ton *Natter* was to take off vertically from a railed launcher. During the boost phase the control surfaces were locked in the fore-and-aft position. Following the release of the exhausted booster rockets, the flight controls unlocked and the climb continued under autopilot. The *Natter* accelerated to about 650 km/h in its near-vertical climb, and when the fighter neared the altitude of the enemy bomber formation, the pilot took control. He levelled out the machine, then manoeuvred into a firing position on one of the enemy aircraft. From a range of about 200 metres he ripple-fired the battery of unguided rockets in a single attack, then dived away. When the rocket motor ran out of fuel, it cut out and the pilot continued his gliding descent.

At about 1400 metres the pilot released his seat harness, then slipped the catches that held the nose cone in place. The entire nose section in front of the pilot, including the windscreen, then fell away. As it parted company from the rest of the machine, a cable released the recovery parachute attached to the rear fuselage. When the parachute opened, the rear part of the aircraft decelerated sharply and the pilot's weight carried him safely clear of his seat. He then completed the rest of his descent by parachute.

After the flight, the re-usable parts of the *Natter*, i.e., the rocket motor, the autopilot and a few other

◄ The Bachem Natter semi-expendable vertically-launched rocket fighter was intended to provide point defence for important targets. As described in the text, the pilot was to launch his battery of unguided rockets in a single firing pass on a bomber. He would then dive away, bale out of the machine and return to the ground by parachute. The rear section of the Natter, containing the rocket motor, autopilot and other valuable items of equipment, would also descend by parachute for later reuse. The rest of the aircraft would be scrapped.

items, were to be removed. The remaining pieces were scrapped.

Two armament options were considered for the *Natter*, each involving salvoes of unguided rockets. One scheme envisaged 33 folding-fin 55 mm R4M rockets, the other 24 *Föhn* 73 mm spin-stabilised rockets.

In 1944, Bachem submitted his proposal for a semi-expendable interceptor to the *Luftwaffe* Technical Office, and the latter placed an order for 50. The semi-expendable fighter received the official designation Bachem Ba 349.

Detailed design work on the *Natter* began in August 1944. The machine had a wingspan of just under 4.25 metres, and a cruciform tail. Power came from a 2,040 kg thrust rocket motor, with four booster rockets which in total delivered a similar thrust during the ten seconds following launch.

The launcher for the *Natter* comprised a 24 metre high vertical structure, with three channelled rails to hold each wing tip and the lower fin. The launcher

pivoted at the base so that it could be lowered to the horizontal to allow the fighter to be loaded into place by a crane.

In November 1944 the *Natter* underwent its initial flight tests, towed to 5,500 metres by a Heinkel 111 bomber. The pilot found the aircraft extremely stable in flight, with the controls crisp and effective throughout the speed range between 700 km/h and 200 km/h. As the aircraft passed through 900 metres the pilot initiated the escape procedure, and he and the rear part of the *Natter* completed their separate descents by parachute. Next came a series of unmanned vertical launches before the *Natter* was judged ready to make its first manned flight.

On 28 February 1945, *Oberleutnant* Lothar Siebert boarded a *Natter* to conduct its first manned flight under full rocket power. The diminutive interceptor roared off its launcher and, at the end of the boost phase, the four boosters fell away and the interceptor continued its vertical climb. Then, shortly after the aircraft passed 450 metres, observers on the ground saw the cockpit canopy fall away. The nose tilted and the aircraft continued its climb at a shallow angle on its back, arcing across the sky before it smashed into the ground with Siebert still in the cockpit. The subsequent investigation failed to determine the cause of the accident, but there were suspicions that the canopy had not been properly locked in place and the pilot had been knocked unconscious when it came away. That theory did not explain why the aircraft deviated so violently from the intended vertical climb under autopilot control, however.

Despite the loss of the pilot during the first manned launch, there was no shortage of volunteers willing to fly the novel interceptor. By the end of March the aircraft had completed three successful manned test flights, and an operational evaluation of the *Natter* could now begin.

Early in April an operational air defence site was set up at Kirchheim near Stuttgart, with launchers for ten *Natter*. The diminutive rocket fighters and their pilots stood to each day, ready to engage the next enemy bomber force to come within range. In the event an American tank unit reached the area before the bombers, and to prevent capture, the rocket fighters and their launchers were blown up.

Although deployment at Kirchheim came just too late for the *Natter* to be launched operationally, it is easy to see the pitfalls of the concept for the *Natter's* radius of action was even less than that of the Me 163 rocket fighter, which had difficulty enough reaching an attack position before the fuel ran out. Until the Bachem 349

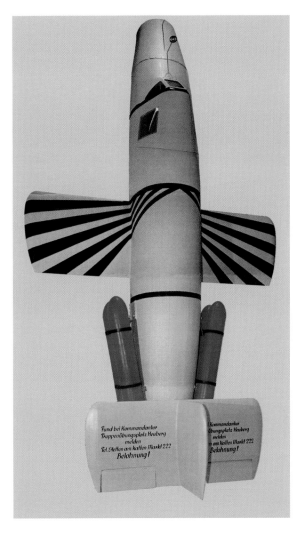

◄◄ A dramatic view of a Bachem Natter during launch.

◄ This example of the Bachem Ba 349 Natter, is currently on display at the Deutsches Museum in Munich.

was deployed at a large number of sites, the Allied air attack planners could easily have routed the bomber formations so that they did not come within reach of the *Natter*.

In retrospect, for all its novelty, it is difficult to see how the interceptor could have achieved much. Pilot training would have posed a major problem. Given the dangers to life and limb, it seems unlikely that individual pilots would have had more than a couple of training launches to familiarise themselves with the system. For the rest of the time every launch would have been an operational launch, bringing new meaning to the term 'on the job training.'

The Dornier Do 335

The Dornier Do 335 was a piston-engined fighter of novel configuration, with one engine in the nose driving a conventional tractor propeller and another in the rear fuselage driving a pusher propeller. As well as giving a cleaner aerodynamic shape to the aircraft, the unusual power plant arrangement enabled the aircraft to fly on

► This two-seat example of the Do 335 A-12, W.Nr. 240121, was found in the Dornier assembly hall at Oberpfaffenhofen and shows two American officers examining the aircraft. In the background, still under construction, are two single-seat Do 335 B protoypes.

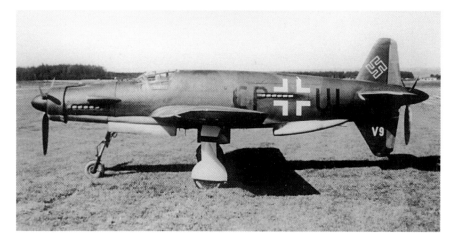

▲ The newly completed Do 335 V9, W.Nr. 230009, coded CP+UI, represented the definitive prototype for the initial production model of the 'Arrow'. It made its first flight on 29 June 1944 with Flugkapitän Quenzler at the controls. During the last days of the war this machine was flown out of the Rechlin test centre by a pilot trying to reach Switzerland but due to inaccurate compass reading, the pilot baled out over Allied-controlled territory and was taken prisoner.

one engine with none of the unpleasant handling problems associated with asymmetric flight. Over the years, many hundreds of aircraft have been destroyed in crashes following attempts to make asymmetric landings, so that was no small advantage. To prevent the rear propeller striking the ground during take-off or landing, the aircraft was fitted with a cruciform fin with a sprung bumper at the base of the lower fin.

The Do 335 had a maximum speed of 474 mph and a range in excess of 800 miles on internal fuel. It was, moreover, remarkably agile for so large an aircraft. It was planned to build the type in large numbers for the fighter-bomber, escort fighter, bomber destroyer and night fighter roles. Construction of the Do 335 suffered a major setback in March 1944, when much of the production tooling was destroyed in an attack on the Dornier plant at Manzel. The company went on to establish a new production line at its Oberpfaffenhofen works, but when US forces overran the area in April 1945

◀ Test installation of the Ruhrstahl X-4 air-to-air guided missile, fitted to a Focke-Wulf Fw 190 fighter.

only 13 of the twin-engined fighters had been completed.

The bomber destroyer variant of the Do 335 was to have carried an armament of two 30 mm MK 103 high velocity cannon and two MG 151 20 mm cannon. With a maximum speed of around 470 mph, it was significantly faster than all except the latest Allied piston-engined fighters it was likely to meet in combat. With its hefty armament and long range it might have been a worthy successor to the twin-engined Bf 110 and Me 410 bomber destroyers that saw action against the US formations in 1943 and the early part of 1944. For all that, however, it was unlikely to have been ready for service until the autumn of 1945.

The First Generation Anti-Aircraft Guided Missiles: *Wasserfall, Schmetterling* and X-4

By the end of the Second World War, three types of guided missile, the surface-to-air *Wasserfall* and *Schmetterling* and the air-to-air X-4, were in production for the *Luftwaffe*. In describing these weapons, some commentators have grossly overestimated their capabilities, likening them to their modern counterparts, so it is necessary to ask, had those first-generation missile systems seen action, could they have had any serious major effect on the course of the air war?

The *Wasserfall* (Waterfall) was designed by Werner von Braun and his team at the Peenemünde research establishment. The weapon was an approximately half-

◀ The X-4 joystick control unit, fitted in the cockpit of an Fw 190.

scale version of the V.2 bombardment missile, and like its predecessor it was launched vertically. At launch the missile weighed 3,810 kg, of which 235 kg was the warhead. At burnout the weapon reached a maximum speed of 2,700 km/h, which gave it a maximum slant range of about 25.75 km. To assist manoeuvring, the

◀◀ The Peenemünde Wasserfall surface-to-air missile was a scaled-down version of the V.2 bombardment missile which was to have entered service late in 1945. The cruciform wings midway along the body enabled the missile to manoeuvre in flight to follow the commands of the ground controller.

▲ These two photographs show the X-4 V59 being tested at the Travemünde test site. The test aircraft was a specially equipped Ju 88.

►► When the US 9th Army captured the 150 year old salt mine at Egein, Austria they found a complete production line of He 162 jet fighters. One of the workers is talking to Allied soldiers about the aircraft.

to sit on its launcher at readiness for long periods of time. To overcome the problem, the Peenemünde team developed a new rocket motor which ran on visol (vinyl isobutyl ether), using fuming nitric acid as the oxidant, and which produced a thrust of 7,711 kg for 42 seconds. *Wasserfall* was placed in production, with the delivery of the first operational rounds scheduled for October 1945.

The Henschel Hs 117 *Schmetterling* (Butterfly) was far smaller and simpler than the *Wasserfall* and was intended to intercept aircraft flying at low (above 1,500 metres) and medium altitudes. The missile was 4.26 metres long, had a wing span of 1.98 metres, and weighed 440 kg at launch. The BMW 558 rocket motor used Tonka (a mixture of xylidine and triethylamine) as fuel and fuming nitric acid as oxidant, and developed 381 kg of thrust for 35 seconds. Take-off was from an inclined ramp, assisted by two jettisonable booster rockets which provided an additional 1,746 kg of thrust for four seconds. After launch, the missile accelerated rapidly to about 1,100 km/h, then the booster rockets fell away and the missile's sustainer motor ignited. Its speed then fell to 865 km/h which was maintained by an automatic system. The *Schmetterling* had a maximum effective slant range of about ten miles, and its warhead weighed 41 kg.

The *Schmetterling* used a similar radio command guidance system to the *Wasserfall*. By the end of 1944 the missile had completed its initial firing trials and it was ordered into full production. The planned production rate of 150 missiles per month was scheduled to be attained during March 1945, with the aim of establishing three operational missile batteries in the late spring, but Allied bombing proved such plans to be grossly over-optimistic and no production rounds were completed before the war ended.

The third German anti-aircraft guided missile, the air-to-air *Ruhrstahl* X-4, had a cigar-shaped body 1.98 metres long with cruciform wings mid-way along the body and at the rear. At launch the X-4 weighed 60 kg, of which 19.95 kg was warhead, and it was intended that one of these missiles would be carried under each wing of the Messerschmitt Me 262. Power came from a BMW 448 rocket motor, which used the same fuels as those fitted to the *Schmetterling* to develop 110 kg of thrust for 17 seconds. On that thrust, the missile reached a maximum speed at burnout of about 900 km/h and its maximum effective range was about 2,750 metres.

Like the two ground-launched weapons described above, the X-4 used optical CLOS guidance, but the guidance signals were transmitted down thin wires

Wasserfall had cruciform fins set mid-way along its 7.92 metre long body.

The *Wasserfall* was what would now be called an optical command-to-line-of-sight (CLOS) weapon. That is to say, throughout its flight a human operator tracked a flare in the rear of the weapon by means of a sighting telescope. A small joystick controller, part of the *Kehl* radio guidance system, generated the appropriate up, down, left or right command signals and transmit these to the missile in flight. The *Strassburg* receiver in the missile picked up the signals, and applied the relevant movements to the control surfaces. The operator steered the missile's tracking flare until it appeared to be superimposed on the target, then endeavoured to hold the missile there until it impacted.

The propulsion system of the V.2 bombardment missile ran on alcohol and liquid oxygen. Once the tanks for the latter were filled, it was important to fire the weapon as soon as possible or the liquid oxygen would start to boil away and leak into the atmosphere. Obviously that system was unsuitable for an air defence weapon like the *Wasserfall* which, by its nature, needed

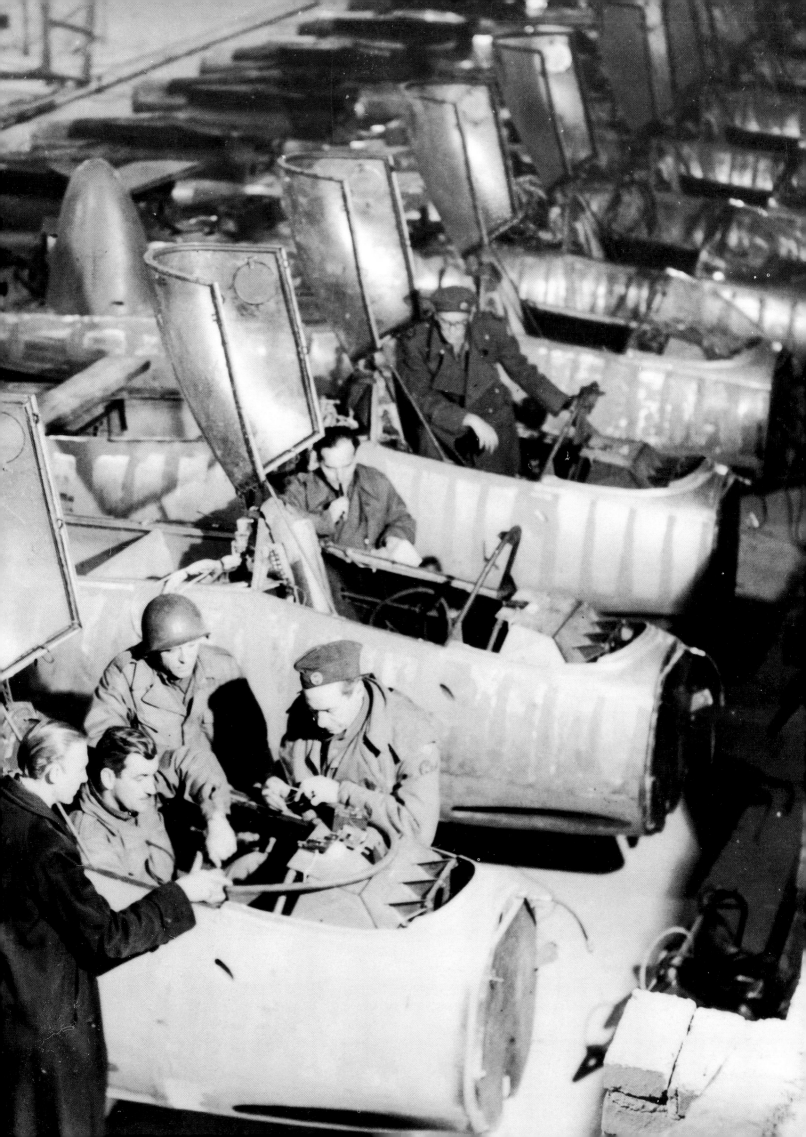

► After the occupation of German airfields the Allies sifted through the remaining aircraft and all scrapped aircraft were collected together into vast scrap dumps. This photograph of three Ju 88 tails was a typical sight.

which unreeled from bobbins fitted to its wings. The pilot of the launching aircraft operated a joystick controller to transmit the appropriate CLOS signals to guide the missile on to the target.

Mass production of the X-4 began in January 1945, and by the war's end Ruhrstahl had turned out more than a thousand missile airframes. However, although production of the rocket motors was well under way at the BMW works at Stargard, a bombing attack destroyed the factory and a large stock of completed motors. Production did not resume before the war ended.

In the light of what we now know about anti-aircraft guided missiles, it is clear that those three first-generation weapons were naïve in their tactical concept. Since they did not home automatically on their targets, the missile operator had to guide them throughout their flight. He needed to have both the target aircraft and the missile flare continuously in view and if darkness, cloud, smoke, haze or the sun intervened, there was little chance of a successful engagement.

Another major weakness of these weapons was that they lacked a proximity fuse to detonate the warhead when the missile was within lethal range of its target. Although German engineers had produced a range of designs for proximity fuses – using acoustic, infrared, magnetic or radar methods – none was ready for production when the war ended. Thus, in their initial

forms, these missiles had to score a direct hit with an impact-fused warhead if they were to destroy an aircraft. This greatly reduced their chances of achieving a kill.

A further significant problem lay with the variants of the *Kehl* and *Strassburg* radio command guidance systems fitted to the initial versions of the *Schmetterling* and *Wasserfall*. These were similar to the system fitted to the Henschel 293 anti-ship missile, which had been in action since the summer of 1943 and which by 1945 was well known to the Allies. It was vulnerable to electronic jamming, and the Allies had produced suitable jamming systems to counter it.

The wire guided X-4 air-to-air missile was invulnerable to electronic jamming, though it had problems unique to itself. The weapon had a maximum speed of only 900 km/h, so the engagement might take as long as 20 seconds. During that time the Me 262 pilot needed to fly straight and level to hold his position behind the target bomber, while he concentrated his attention on steering the missile until it impacted. If Allied escort fighters were about, delivering an attack with the X-4 would have been a highly risky undertaking.

None of the German anti-aircraft missile systems went into action, but in this writer's view, none of them was ever likely to achieve a single shot kill probability greater than about 20 per cent, and it could have been a

◄ The above photographs show he Berlin centimetric airborne interception radar, fitted to a small number of Ju 88 G night fighters and tested in action during the final weeks of the war. Although the new radar gave a considerable improvement in performance compared with earlier types of German airborne interception radar, it was much inferior to the latest Allied equipment in this class.

▲ The Kulmbach centimetric surveillance radar formed part of the Egerland Flak control system and was intended to guide the Marbach precision radar on to targets. Although the new radar was more difficult to jam that the earlier Würzburg and Manheim radars, by the spring of 1945 the western Allies had manufactured and tested types of 'Window/Chaff' and electronic jammers to counter it.

◄ The Marbach centimetric wavelength precision radar which, with the Kulmbach, made up the Egerland Flak control system.

lot less. On that basis, it is difficult to believe these weapons could have done anything to dent the Allies' all-pervading air supremacy.

German Radar Developments

Early in 1945, the first German centimetric-wavelength radars were ready to enter large-scale production for the *Luftwaffe*. The *Berlin* airborne interception radar had been installed in a few Ju 88 night fighters and had been tested in action. Prototypes existed of the *Egerland* Flak control system, which comprised the *Kulmbach* surveillance radar and the separate *Marbach* precision radar.

With the appearance of these items of equipment, German radar development reached a position roughly equivalent to that of the western Allies about two and a half years earlier. None of the German centimetric radars could have seen large-scale deployment much before the middle of 1945.

By their nature, centimetric wavelength radars were more difficult to counter with 'Window/Chaff' or electronic jamming than those operating on longer wavelengths. Nevertheless, the Germans had shot down large numbers of Allied aircraft fitted with centimetric radar, and the western Allies had expected to see the introduction of German counterpart systems from the beginning of 1944. Allied scientists had therefore devoted much effort to developing suitable countermeasures. By the beginning of 1945 'Window/Chaff' and electronic jamming systems to counter centimetric radar had

been built and tested, and were ready to go into production as soon as the need arose. That never happened, but it is clear that the *Luftwaffe* could not have secured any long or major advantage from the introduction of these radars.

In Retrospect

Since the war there has been a great deal of speculation regarding what might have happened had the German armed forces prolonged the conflict for a few months longer and enabled the *Luftwaffe* to bring this or that new weapon into large-scale service. In combination, could they have altered the course of the conflict? On the evidence outlined above, that notion does not stand examination.

In truth, the German armed forces had put up a magnificent fight to keep going as long as they did, particularly in view of the overwhelming Allied numerical superiority combined, in many areas, with a considerable degree of technical superiority. Given the desperate position in which Germany found herself from the summer of 1944, only one weapon could have redressed the balance: the atomic bomb. However, when the war in Europe ended in May 1945, German scientists were several years away from producing theirs, while those in the USA were almost ready to explode the first of these devastating weapons. Had the war in Europe continued into the summer of 1945, it is probable that the population of at least one German city would have shared the terrible fate of those living in Hiroshima and Nagasaki.

◄◄ In eastern Germany, the view of the ruins of the city of Dresden offered to the statue on the roof of the city's New Town Hall in May 1945 symbolises perfectly the end of the Third Reich. Many German cities suffered the same fate and there is much photographic evidence of how effective the Allied bombing offensive had been.

▼ The US 6th Armored Division discovered these Fw 190s in the Leina Forest destroyed by retreating German personnel. At least four of the aircraft have completely burned out and although the machine centre right appears to be intact, the rear fuselage has been largely destroyed by flames.

Appendix A   Ranks

Royal Air Force	USAAF	Luftwaffe
Marshal of the RAF	Five Star General	Generalfeldmarschall
Air Chief Marshal	Four Star General	Generaloberst
Air Marshal	Lieutenant General	General der Flieger
Air Vice Marshal	Major General	Generalleutnant
Air Commodore	Brigadier General	Generalmajor
Group Captain	Colonel	Oberst
Wing Commander	Lieutenant Colonel	Oberstleutnant
Squadron Leader	Major	Major
Flight Lieutenant	Captain	Hauptmann
Flying Officer	First Lieutenant	Oberleutnant
Pilot Officer	Lieutenant	Leutnant
(leading cadet)	(leading cadet)	Oberfähnrich
(cadet)	(cadet)	Fähnrich
Warrant Officer	Warrant Officer	Stabsfeldwebel
Flight Sergeant	Master Sergeant	Oberfeldwebel
Sergeant	Technical Sergeant	Feldwebel
	-	Unterfeldwebel
Corporal	Staff Sergeant	Unteroffizier
-	Sergeant	Hauptgefreiter
Leading Aircraftman	Corporal	Obergefreiter
Aircraftman	Private	Gefreiter
First Class	First Class	
Aircraftman	Private	Flieger

In addition, the *Luftwaffe* used the term 'Hauptfeldwebel'. This was not a rank. A Hauptfeldwebel (colloquially called 'Spiess') was the NCO administrative head of a company or corresponding unit (Staffel, battery etc.). His rank could be anything from Unteroffizier to the various Feldwebel.

Appendix B   Combat Flying Units

Establishment of aircraft in the combat units of the Royal Air Force, the United States Army Air Force, and the *Luftwaffe*. Since the establishment varied considerably over the course of the Second World War, the figures given are only approximate.

RAF (Bombers)

Basic unit: the Squadron, comprising 16, later 30 aircraft.
Between 10 and 16 Squadrons comprised a Group.

USAAF (Fighters and Bombers)

Basic unit: the Squadron, comprising some 16 bombers or 25 fighters.
Four Squadrons of bombers, or three Squadrons of fighters, comprised a group.
Three Groups of bombers or five Groups of fighters comprised a Wing.

Luftwaffe (Fighters)

Basic unit: the Gruppe, comprising three or four Staffeln each with nine aircraft, plus a Stab (Staff) unit with three. Three or four Gruppen comprised a Geschwader.

Appendix C   Code-Names

Berlin German airborne interception radar operating on centimetric wavelengths, had just entered service when the war ended.

Chaff US name for metal foil strips used to jam precision radars, known as 'Window' in the RAF.

Egerland German centimetric Flak control radar, on the point of entering service when the war ended. Comprised the Kulmbach surveillance radar and the separate Marbach precision radar.

Fishpond Modification to the H2S bombing radar to enable it to warn of the presence of other aircraft (perhaps enemy) flying at a lower altitude.

Freya German early-warning surveillance radar.

GEE British long-range navigational aid.

GEE-H British radar aid to bombing, which included the GEE system for navigation.

Giant Würzburg German night fighter control radar.

Helle Nachtjagd German system of night fighting using searchlights to illuminate enemy bombers.

Himmelbett German system of night fighting using ground-based radar control.

H2S and H2X British and American systems of ground mapping radar to aid bombing at night or through cloud.

Jagdschloss Advanced German radar with a plan position indicator display for ground-controlled interception. Introduced in 1944.

Jostle High powered communications jammer, carried by some specialised jamming aircraft of No 100 Group.

Lichtenstein The first type of airborne interception radar to be fitted to German night fighters.

Mammut German early warning radar.

Mandrel British jammer to counter Freya and other German early-warning radars.

Monica British tail-warning radar.

Naxos German airborne and ground direction finder, which gave bearings on H2S transmissions.

Oboe British blind bombing aid using ground stations in the England.

Piperack Jammer to counter the German fighters' SN-2 radar, carried in some specialised jamming aircraft of No 100 Group.

Perfectos Device carried in some Mosquito night fighters of No 100 Group which triggered the identification equipment fitted to *Luftwaffe* aircraft, and enabled the crew to home on the reply signals.

Schräge Musik German upward-firing cannon installation for night-fighters.

Serrate British airborne device to enable night fighters to home on the radar signals from their German counterparts. Serrate IV was designed to home on signals from the SN-2 radar.

SN-2 Long wavelength airborne interception radar, with reduced vulnerability to jamming from chaff/window.

Tinsel Scheme for jamming the German night fighter control frequencies, using the bombers' communications transmitters.

Village Inn Fire control radar, designed for installation in the rear turret of bombers, to allow them to engage targets on radar indications alone.

Wassermann German early warning radar.

Wilde Sau 'Wild Boar', German scheme for using single-seat fighters to engage bombers over their targets.

Window British name for bundles of metal foil dropped to confuse enemy radar. Known in the USAAF as Chaff.

Würzburg German precision radar used to control Flak, searchlights and, for a short time, night-fighters.

Zahme Sau 'Tame Boar', German tactic aimed at directing a large number of night-fighters into the enemy bomber stream.

INDEX